Common Whores, Vertuous Women,
and Loveing Wives

Religion in North America

VOLUME 31 IN THE SERIES

Catherine L. Albanese *and* Stephen J. Stein, editors

Common Whores, Vertuous Women, and Loveing Wives

Free Will Christian Women in Colonial Maryland

Debra Meyers

INDIANA
University Press

Bloomington & Indianapolis

This book is a publication of

Indiana University Press

601 North Morton Street

Bloomington, IN 47404-3797 USA

http://iupress.indiana.edu

Telephone orders   800-842-6796

Fax orders   812-855-7931

Orders by e-mail   iuporder@indiana.edu

The paper used in this publication meets the minimum requirements of American National Standard for Information Sciences—Permanence of Paper for Printed Library Materials, ANSI Z39.48-1984.

Manufactured in the United States of America

Library of Congress Cataloging-in-Publication Data

Meyers, Debra, date

  Common whores, vertuous women, and loveing wives : free will Christian women in colonial Maryland / Debra Meyers.

    p.   cm. — (Religion in North America ; v. 31)

Includes bibliographical references and index.

  ISBN 0-253-34193-0 (cloth : alk. paper)

  1. Women—United States—Maryland—History. 2. Women and religion—United States—Maryland—History. 3. Maryland—History. I. Title: Common whores, virtuous women, and loving wives. II. Title. III. Series.

  HQ1438.M3 M49 2003

  305.4'09752—dc21

                                                                                    2002010626

1 2 3 4 5   08 07 06 05 04 03

Contents
ɶ

Foreword
ᐁ

Debra Meyers's book, with its somewhat provocative title, is in fact rather aptly named. In this work, Meyers offers readers an in-depth view of English women in the Maryland colony, mostly in the years from 1634 to 1713. That project may sound overly arcane and archeological at first glance (hence the countervailing title?). To the contrary, however, what Meyers has uncovered in some very close study of 3190 Maryland wills and other personal documents, as well as in an astute reading of material culture, has large implications for our understanding of the social and cultural importance of religion in early America.

In a broadly gauged and yet careful distinction, Meyers situates her study by initially identifying two groups in Maryland in terms of their theological orientation: Predestinarians, who include Particular Baptists, Presbyterians, and a group she calls "Puritans" (generic New England congregationalists with classic Calvinist underpinnings), on the one side; and Free Will Christians, who include Arminian Anglicans (i.e., Anglicans who emphasized human freedom in their religious thinking), Quakers, and Roman Catholics, on the other. This is already an extremely interesting division, since it lumps Catholics together with Anglicans, who have usually been read, for at least a large part of the colonial period, as strongly oppressive of Catholics. The Meyers division likewise, among Protestants, links a left-wing, radical group (the Quakers) to a mainline, establishmentarian group (the Anglicans). What constitutes the great divide between Meyers's two groups, therefore, is whether or not they adhered to a Calvinist theology of salvation—a soteriological typology in which one was arbitrarily predestined as chosen by God to be among the "elect" who would be saved, or relegated by the inscrutable deity to existence among the damned. Free Will believers rejected that understanding and viewed salvation, given the prior work of Jesus Christ, as something left to the individual's "free-will" decision and follow-through in a lifetime of virtue.

Meyers argues that this theological separation between Calvinist predestinarianism and non-Calvinist ideologies of human salvational freedom made an important difference in the social freedom of women in the Maryland colony. While Calvinist Predestinarians tended to be hierarchical and patriarchal in their family structures and very controlling of and among their women, Free Will Christians supported more egalitarian structures and their results in terms of social, political (in the broad sense), and economic equality for women. Thus, Meyers's findings are an essential key to understanding the Maryland colony both in gendered terms and in terms that go well beyond.

Common Whores, Vertuous Women, and Loveing Wives focuses primarily on these Free Will Christians, who, Meyers argues persuasively, had more in common than the religious issues and practices that divided them. She demonstrates convincingly that they intermarried between groups; and—in a brilliant reading of the evidence—she shows that Free Will women, who were "yoke-fellows" with their men, owned land and property, managed it with aplomb, executed wills, and had their day in court.

As Meyers states her own case, her work asks three questions: Was religion a causal factor in history? If so, how was that factor expressed? And if there were shared elements of a worldview among Free Willers, in social terms, how were these religious affinities worked out? Meyers answers these questions superbly for Maryland. And in the process of so doing, she gives us a revisionist reading that corrects the standard Protestantizing reading of early Maryland religious history and also corrects simplistic patriarchal assumptions regarding social practice in early Maryland and America. Indeed, Meyers takes her cue from the Lords Baltimore, George, and Cecil Calvert, men who straddled the medieval and modern worlds as political autocrats, pragmatists, economic aggrandizers, and the like, but were also pious Roman Catholics with Roman Catholic reasons for the religious toleration they extended to Maryland settlers. Like Maryland's founders, her historical subjects bridge older religious understandings and modernizing social arrangements. They live and work in a new world but do so with an abiding sense of the importance of their theological convictions.

Meyers also supplies a welcome study of nonevangelical women in early America, in a gender-studies field in which virtually all of the recent work on colonial America concerns evangelical women. Still more, she scrutinizes the implications for public religiosity of different theological beliefs. As she convincingly demonstrates, Calvinists thought marriage public, while Free Will Christians understood it as a private affair and therefore countenanced a different agenda for women as legal creatures. In making her case, as we have already begun to suggest, she uses material culture astutely—everything from the spatial allocations in church buildings, to their style and location, to ritual representations and gravestones and naming practices for land, exhaustively probing her evidence for its cultural, religious, and theological meaning. Beyond that, Meyers's study is genuinely comparative in its use of English (from England) social practices and mores as a control for understanding Maryland social practice. The importance of the transatlantic dimension of this study is signaled, in fact, by Meyers's introduction, in which from the first she situates her Marylanders as English women and men in a new locale. These comparative concerns permeate the study, as Meyers works deftly from both sides of the Atlantic to situate the Maryland experience more precisely and as she looks past Maryland's Free Willers to give regular attention to what the colony's Predestinarians were doing. Finally, she writes and works with her evidence in ways that provide a strong model of how one can think through material on paper, raise questions about its import, voice objections to the storyline being pursued, sift through the evidence and objections, and come out with an argument that is not only plausible but, even more, persuasive. And although she acknowledges an eighteenth-century season of decline in her conclusion—and gives an impressive survey of ways of thinking about it and explaining it—by pointing to the earlier Maryland pattern of relative equality, she points as well to the social trajectory that would come to characterize the extended saga of women in the United States.

CATHERINE L. ALBANESE
STEPHEN J. STEIN
Series Editors

Acknowledgments
༃

This study would not have been possible without the assistance and support of many institutions and individuals. I would like to thank Routledge for permission to reprint portions of my essay "Gender and Religion in England's Catholic Province," in *Women and Religion in Old and New Worlds,* edited by Susan Dinan and Debra Meyers (New York: Routledge, 2001), 213–230. Early on, the Susan B. Anthony Institute at the University of Rochester helped fund several research trips to Maryland, and the guidance I received at the university from Lynn Gordon, Brenda Meehan, Linda Levy Peck, Jean Pedersen, and the late Christopher Lasch laid the groundwork for my inquiry. On two separate occasions, the Folger Institute's generous financial support allowed me to attend seminars, for which I am grateful. Working closely with eminent scholars both broadened my thinking and sharpened my arguments. And while all of the people at the archives and historic places I visited provided a great deal of assistance, I would like to pay particular respect to Henry Miller at Historic St. Mary's City, Sr. Constance FitzGerald at the Carmelite Monastery in Baltimore, Heather Venters at the Maryland Historical Society, Mary Kavanaugh at St. Anne's Church in Annapolis, and the minister at Old Trinity Church in Dorchester.

Of course, those individuals who agreed to read and comment on the manuscript at various stages of development deserve special thanks. Stanley Engerman, Larry Hudson, Karen Kupperman, Gloria Main, Russell Menard, Philip Morgan, and particularly Lois Carr have all provided thoughtful suggestions. I wish, too, to thank my editors and anonymous reviewers at Indiana University Press. Collectively, their comments have improved this book tremendously.

Finally, I will never be able to adequately express my heartfelt gratitude to my mentor, friend, and occasional father figure John J. Waters, Jr., who always provided words of encouragement and sound advice when I needed them most. This book is dedicated to him as a small token of my appreciation.

*Common Whores, Vertuous Women,
and Loveing Wives*

Introduction

Nineteenth-century historian John Leeds Bozman once wrote that England in the 1630s was the "scene of the most tumultuous contest between three principal sects of the christian religion, the established church of England, the Roman Catholics, and the Puritans." He argued that it was "a contest, not indeed for the *supreme power* merely, but each for its own *existence.*"[1] Bozman's observation points to the importance of understanding religious beliefs and denominational power struggles in order to fully grasp the tumultuous seventeenth century. Religion deeply and powerfully affected the political, economic, and social realities of early modern England, and recent studies have shown the effect religious conflicts had on the lives of women and their families. Early modern English historians Patricia Crawford, David Cressy, and Ralph Houlbrooke have provided us with extensive studies examining how religion affected women's lives and how women, in turn, influenced their religious institutions, their families, and the larger society.[2] As important as these studies have been, our understanding of religion's impact on the family is nevertheless stifled by the early modern English governmental restrictions that prevented many in England from openly expressing their religious beliefs in the post-Reformation years. Fortunately, more can be gleaned about English women, their families, and religion, I would argue, by shifting our focus to the New World. We have known little about English women living in America, particularly in the seventeenth century, due in part to limited sources. Marilyn Westerkamp has opened up this avenue of exploration in her work on the Puritan and

Evangelical traditions in New England, but her narrow focus encompasses only a few of the English religious groups in the New World.[3] This book, using a transatlantic framework, seeks to fill this void in the literature by exploring the social and cultural actions of English women belonging to a variety of religious denominations in Maryland. Gender relations and family formations can be studied in the multiple religious visions of Maryland's English Arminian Anglicans, Particular Baptists, Presbyterians, Puritans, Quakers, and Roman Catholics as they lived and worked together as fellow seventeenth-century settlers, far from the unsettling political and religious climate of chaotic England.[4]

Lord Baltimore, with the help of other English Roman Catholics, established the province of Maryland in 1634 with two equally important goals in mind: the strengthening of English Roman Catholicism and financial gain.[5] Both the recent converts, such as the Calverts, and representatives from many of the old established English Catholic families successfully constructed a dynamic society based on religious toleration and the consolidation of power and wealth, anchored by a feudal manor system of land tenure.[6] Lord Baltimore's ecumenical nature and political savvy enabled Maryland to become a haven for various religious groups in the seventeenth century: Arminian Anglicans (who arrived in 1634), Roman Catholics (also 1634), Labadists (c. 1640), Presbyterians (1649), Puritans (1649), Quakers (1655), and others all sought to seat themselves in the province and conduct their business in relative peace.[7] The uniqueness of Maryland's heterogeneous population, co-existing and prospering—for the most part—has not been studied in depth. Many historians prefer to examine the colonists as a homogeneous group, combining demographics with modernization theory in an effort to understand changes in the province.[8] After a period of neglect in the 1960s, when social historians focused on New England, the 1970s saw a virtual explosion of Maryland colonial history with the demographic work of Lois Green Carr, Gloria Main, Russell Menard, Lorena Walsh, and other scholars using samples from the Prerogative Court wills and other probate materials. The combined efforts of these historians have provided us with invaluable information concerning the aggregate population, leaving us a strong foundation upon which to build a more complete picture of colonial Maryland society. However, their assumption that the Maryland wills were standardized form letters merely indicating a simple distribution of real estate and movable goods prevented them from fully exploiting the information contained in the wills. Rejecting the commonly held notion that the wills began and ended the same, with only the names being changed, I have found that the 3190 wills left by Marylanders between

1634 and 1713 reveal intimate details of the lives of the English settlers at a
time when religion formed the very essence of most individuals and families. Fortunately, Marylanders could express diverse religious positions, for
while the English Crown "vainly endeavour[ed] to arrive at a Uniformity of
Religion at home," it allowed "an Amsterdam of Liberty" in its "Plantations."[9] Thus, the landholding men and women who wrote these wills—and
we believe that they reflected the shared cultural norms of their various religious communities—left us a remarkable abundance of information on
their religious piety, charitable bequests, gender roles (and models), and
hitherto unrecognized historical actors. In addition, court records, letters,
sermons, family genealogies, naming patterns, gravestone verses and iconography, religious architecture, English advice literature, and other probate
records supplement the rich source of last wills and testaments, allowing a
greater understanding of these early modern English folk. Employing these
sources and using religion as a crucial variable of analysis, this work ex-
amines colonial life in general and, more specifically, the various roles for
women in seventeenth-century Maryland. It also emphasizes cultural continuity with the mother country.[10]

The religiously tolerant population in Maryland cries out for examination of its various religious denominations—but not with the traditional
view that renders them in antagonistic terms. The groups mentioned above
lived in communities that were generally interactive; there was, however,
a distinctive division important to my study—that between "Predestinarians" and "Free Will Christians." It is this soteriological divide, I argue, that
helps to explain colonists' behavior in the religious, political, economic, social, and family arenas. Simply put, a believer's notions concerning how
and under what circumstances he or she would gain eternal salvation were
frequently connected to provincial architecture, burial rituals, inheritance
practices, marriage customs, and the role English women were permitted to
play in the public and private spheres during the seventeenth century.

Of course, the religious labels attached to early modern groups as a necessary means of categorization for purposes of analysis are, in fact, anach-
ronistic. Contemporaries often used these terms as pejorative monikers to
vilify others outside their own group. In so doing, rather than accurately
describing another group, they helped to construct their own identities by
drawing attention to behaviors or beliefs that distinguished them from outsiders. Those we call "Roman Catholics" did call themselves by the same
name, but other individuals did not refer to themselves as Arminian Anglicans, Anglicans, Quakers, Particular Baptists, or Puritans. Nor would these
groups have been comfortable being lumped together as Calvinists, "Pre-

destinarians," or "Free Will Christians." Nevertheless, constructing cohorts based on individuals' professions of faith for the purpose of gaining a better understanding of these early modern English people seems justified.

Clearly, differences among Protestants were at least as great as any professed differences between Protestants and Catholics. John Sommerville has also noted the similarity in the piety of the Arminian Anglicans, Catholics, and Quakers. His statistical analysis indicates that the critical theological differences amongst these groups, as posited by some modern historians, were not replicated in their popular contemporary texts. He suggests that Anglicans, Catholics, and Quakers stressed the individual's duty toward social order—the maintenance of tranquility, generosity, and responsibility toward others and the controlling of behavior in the effort to improve one's own moral conduct. Conversely, the Predestinarians believed that they lived in a corrupt and largely unredeemable world. Their underlying patriarchal piety, concerned with spiritual transformation, emphasized one's duty to God as sovereign.[11] These different worldviews, along with their adherence to the doctrine of election or free will, underscore the contrast between Predestinarians and Free Will Christians.

Predestinarians, represented primarily by the Particular Baptists, Presbyterians, and Puritans in the province, adhered to the theology of John Calvin. These Calvinists believed that God had chosen only a select group of saints (long before they were born) to gain eternal salvation, and their theological beliefs contributed to the subservient positions they allowed their females, which were predicated upon an understanding of women as the inherently "weaker vessel"; women were both physically and, more importantly, morally frail. And because females were more likely to fall into the hands of Satan than their male counterparts, they posed a malevolent danger to men. As descendants of Eve, women were wanton, lustful creatures bent on seducing men into committing a multitude of sins. In keeping with this conception of womanhood, these seventeenth-century Predestinarians placed women in subservient, dependent positions in the church, the family, and the larger society, in order to minimize the threat they posed to society, their families, and, of course, themselves. In short, men had a responsibility to maintain social order, at least in part, by controlling and caring for their female kin.

The Free Will Christians, namely the Arminian Anglicans, Quakers, and Roman Catholics, shared a fundamental worldview that tended to unify them more often than their professed differences divided them. These three groups forming my Free Will Christian cohort believed that all human beings could attain eternal salvation if they freely chose to accept God, worked toward their salvation by doing "good works," and asked for God's forgiveness when they sinned. Where Predestinarians believed that living a virtuous life was a sign of election, Free Will Christians decided to lead such lives, doing good deeds for the less fortunate, in order to cleanse their souls, hoping that they would make themselves worthy of eternal salvation. On their deathbeds even the most pious folks had no assurance that their good deeds and godly behavior had secured them a place in heaven. This universal belief that any person could choose to work for eternal salvation tended to place women on a more level playing field with their male kinfolk.

Instead of emphasizing women's evilness as Eve's descendants, English Free Will Christians exalted womanhood. The Arminian Anglicans and Roman Catholics honored the Blessed Virgin as the mother of Christ, while the Quakers believed in a gender-inclusive God—and this belief, among other things, permitted women to play vital roles in their families, society, and churches.[12] Free Will Christian families expected women to act as their husbands' partners, sharing the work, risks, and duties of running the family plantation and raising their children. Consequently, mothers wielded power and authority over their children and other dependents in their homes. This familial authority that Arminian Anglican, Quaker, and Roman Catholic women possessed extended beyond the family into the social realm, and it required a reasonable amount of education. Some girls attended the Jesuit boarding school in Newtown, Maryland, as early as 1667, but many more were educated at home by their mothers from the earliest years of settlement. Land transfer documents testify to the active participation of literate females in early Maryland. Additionally, women acted as lawyers in the courts and they settled complicated estates as executors of wills. Documents also reveal that Free Will Christian women became tavern keepers, ferry operators, and landladies; while the Calvinist businesswoman was an anomaly, the numerous active Free Will Christian women represented the social norm in seventeenth-century Maryland.[13] The liberties Free Will Christian men allowed their women extended into the realm of the church as well. In fact, it was an Arminian Anglican, Mary Taney, who successfully petitioned the king of England and the archbishop of Canterbury for money and a priest to serve the province.[14] Indeed, Arminian Anglicans, Catholics, and Quakers clearly and consistently relied on women, who were expected to be productive, active, and influential in the family, the legal system, the economy, and the church.

The Free Will Christians strengthened themselves as a cohesive group through intermarriage between Arminian Anglicans, Quakers, and Roman Catholics—further proof that their shared values superseded their differences. Arminian Anglican William Digges (1650–97) married a Catholic,[15] while Thomas Gerard (1637–73)—a descendant of one of the leading Roman Catholic families in England—not only married an Arminian Anglican but also built an Anglican church on his property; the Brookes and Carrolls, two of the most prestigious Catholic families to reside in Maryland, intermarried with Arminian Anglicans with some regularity.[16] The Lowes represent a medley of Arminian Anglicans and Roman Catholics, and the Young and Hall families never seemed to favor a particular denomination, as they constantly married landholding Arminian Anglicans, Roman Catholics, and Quakers.[17] Significantly, Free Will Christians almost never crossed the great soteriological divide by marrying Predestinarians.

The study at hand begins with an essential overview of the political and religious context in which Maryland was founded, since this province developed and matured during a period of particular political and religious strife back in England. Specifically, chapter 1 details the Calvert family's reasons for establishing Maryland and the effect religion, in both the Old and New Worlds, had on its early political development, thus correcting the standard "Protestantizing" reading of early Maryland history. Chapter 2 offers an in-depth examination of Marylanders' private lives. The various marriage rituals, family structures, and sibling relationships were determined largely by a religious group's acceptance or rejection of canon law. Further, I submit that the close relationships between Arminian Anglican, Quaker, and Roman Catholic brothers and sisters noted in this chapter contributed to an egalitarian construction of gender relationships in the society.

Chapter 3 essentially justifies my two cohorts—Predestinarians and Free Will Christians—by examining church architecture, burial rituals, religious folks' citation of biblical texts, and their understandings of salvation. Religion informed most Marylanders' behavior and worldview, and consequently their construction of gender roles. Chapter 3's examination of the theology of their Arminian Anglicanism, Catholicism, and Quakerism reveals the remarkable sense of autonomy, intellectualism, gender equity, and familial alliance (both nuclear and extended) that these landholding Marylanders shared. Their vivid professions of faith in the preambles of wills and sermons, their architecture, and their burial practices, as well as a rare collection of colonial Marylanders' books housed at the Carmelite monastery in Baltimore, offer an unusual glimpse into the religious beliefs of landholding English immigrants to Maryland.

Chapter 4 focuses on the impact women had on their religious groups and the influence their religion had on them. Free Will Christian women built houses of worship, maintained sacred communion plate, donated money and land, and were respected by their families and church leaders as influential members of their religious groups. The authority they held in the religious arena spilled over into the private realm of the family.

Convinced that these early modern English people took their religion seriously, we turn to a religious explanation for their inheritance practices. Testing the inheritance patterns of various groups in chapter 5, we find two distinctive formats: Predestinarian testators bequeathed real estate to their sons while Free Will Christians left it to their wives. These two patterns—in conjunction with the literary evidence—suggest Predestinarians conceived of their wives as dependents, not unlike children. A wife's obligation to her family was centered on her ability to procreate, while males maintained a patriarchy similar to that of their Calvinist New England counterparts.[18] A Free Will Christian wife, on the other hand, occupied a position of authority in the family both before and after the death of her husband. We might assume that children submitted to her authority because she possessed the real estate necessary for survival. This chapter corrects simplistic patriarchal assumptions regarding social practice in early modern societies espoused by most historians. Patriarchy, simply put, was not the cultural norm in the early modern period.

Chapter 6 details the way that Free Will Christian women extended their familial authority into the public sphere. Their families and the larger society expected female kin to assume positions as lawyers and executors in court settling complicated financial and legal affairs throughout their adult lives. In particular, an executrix—the legal administrator of the estate—presumably held considerable power as the distributor of goods and land to the testator's heirs. Paradoxically, however, Predestinarian testators named their wives as executrixes of their wills as often as their Free Will Christian counterparts. The evidence suggests that Predestinarian wives, like their Calvinist New England peers and in keeping with their dependent status in the family, frequently relinquished their right to administer their husbands' wills, asking the court to appoint a son or other male relative to assume the responsibility.

The interdependency of Free Will Christian females and males working together to create an ordered society based on spousal partnerships enabled Maryland in the seventeenth century to expand and prosper in an atmosphere of toleration. By closely examining thousands of wills and other personal documents, as well as early Maryland's material culture, this transatlantic study depicts women's place in society and the ways in which religious values and social arrangements shaped their lives. Additionally, this revisionist approach to the study of women and religion in early Maryland has significant implications for our understanding of the social and cultural importance of religion in early America.

1
♻

Maryland's Raison d'être

ór the past two hundred years colonial Maryland historians have
agreed on one thing—George Calvert was the man responsible for
the establishment of the modern religiously tolerant state of Maryland.[1] He was the son of a Yorkshire gentleman, and by all accounts a successful English officeholder. Calvert's statesmanship, honesty, and integrity gained him the respect of Sir Robert Cecil, who served both Queen
Elizabeth and James I as principal secretary of state, and James as Lord
High Treasurer as well. Calvert's acceptance of the position of chief clerk in
Cecil's service formed the foundation of a long and fruitful relationship between the two men. In an indication of this bond, George named his heir
apparent after Cecil and Cecil procured the prominent position of privy
council clerk for George. In 1617 King James knighted George Calvert, and
upon the dismissal of Sir Thomas Lake he appointed Calvert one of the secretaries of state, the most lucrative and prestigious post Calvert could hold
under the king. James I also bestowed other profitable rewards upon George,
such as the 1620 grant of the increased customs on silk for twenty-one years,
and an annual pension of a thousand pounds sterling. Even after George
publicly declared his Roman Catholic faith, the king granted him the title
Lord Baltimore.

While celebrating Calvert's integrity and the self-discipline that made
him the statesman, gentleman, and founding father they generally admired,
historians differed somewhat on why we should honor George as a great
man. Some chose to focus on his pious, altruistic Catholicism that drove

him to embrace religious tolerance—values he inculcated in his son, Cecil, who put them into practice in the New World—with little or no regard for his own aggrandizement. Others paid tribute to George's foresight in establishing a province in the New World, but they welcomed the Protestant ideals of toleration and democracy that came from the majority of Anglican settlers once the province was established. Still others, more recently, applauded Calvert's pragmatism. A man before his time, Calvert made decisions about colonization and settlement based on his own self-interest that allowed a modern state to evolve founded upon the fundamental idea of the separation of church and state. John Krugler said it best when he claimed that a true understanding of the Calvert family's insistence upon religious toleration in Maryland must rest firmly on the fact that the Calverts were "hardnosed pragmatic Catholic entrepreneurs who were attempting to prosper in a world that was predominately [sic] Protestant."[2] In sum, the practical Calverts, as modern Catholics moving toward secularization, expediently seized the political and economic advantages that lay before them, intent upon carving out a significant place for themselves in the modern Protestant world.

None of these characterizations fully capture George Calvert's position in straddling two worlds. Calvert was on the cusp of the "traditional"[3] and modern worlds and his life reflected this tension, as did his son's. He accepted that property, innovation, education, and risk taking, in addition to religious toleration and rational scientific thought, were central to accumulating wealth, and this attitude is often taken to be a hallmark of a modern worldview. Calvert was always interested in increasing the family's wealth by accumulating property, and he and his kin encouraged education as a means to this end. He obtained his bachelor's degree at Trinity College in 1597 and an honorary Master of Arts degree in 1605. Calvert was willing to take substantial financial risks as he invested his wealth in many transatlantic opportunities—innovative means for his time. He was one of the original associates of the Virginia Company, and also served as a provisional council member in England for the temporary government of Virginia in 1624 in order to protect his assets. He also invested capital in the East India and New England Companies, in addition to purchasing a plantation in Newfoundland. His dedication to wealth accumulation, innovation, financial risk taking, education, and the establishment of a religiously tolerant society— carried out by his son—seems to firmly place him in the secularized modern world. And yet his vision for an ordered society in the New World was based upon feudalism—including a traditional land-tenure system. If we are willing to keep in mind Calvert's position, with one foot in the traditional world and the other in the modern, his motivation for settlement in the New World becomes clearer.

Calvert's ties to the Crown, and the wealth and status that they provided, opened the door for his personal adventures in the New World. In 1620 Calvert purchased a patent for a small plantation on the southern tip of Newfoundland from one of his old Oxford chums, Sir William Vaughan. As quickly as he could, Calvert sent Captain Edward Wynne to his new colony in Ferryland with approximately thirty-two laborers to build granaries, storehouses, and a relatively modest residence for the Calvert clan. With a successful province within his grasp, Calvert requested a patent from the king the following year. The unusual patent gave him royal power over the whole southeastern peninsula of Newfoundland, newly christened Avalon. "Avalon" sheds some light on Calvert's future plans and suggests a reason for packing his family up and moving to the New World. He selected the name carefully, just as he had when he named his heir apparent after his mentor and benefactor, Sir Robert Cecil. Calvert's Avalon shared its name with the ancient monastic lands in what is now Glastonbury, in Somersetshire, England. Joseph of Arimathea—honored as the first man to bring the Christian faith to England—established an abbey in ancient Avalon to foster the growth of Christianity in the heathen land. In Calvert's mind, then, the new Avalon must have represented an opportunity in the post-Reformation era to reestablish Roman Catholicism as the true English faith. Not a man to rule by the sword, Calvert would subtly attempt to bring misguided Anglicans back to the fold and strengthen the piety of English Roman Catholics by offering a place to worship in public.

English Roman Catholic literature throughout the Tudor/Stuart period urged Catholics to guide the Anglican lost sheep back into the flock. Taking this directive seriously, George Calvert assisted Sir Tobie Matthew, a childhood friend, in his conversion to the "holie Catholic fayth." Matthew shared George's belief that he could remain a loyal subject of the Crown while also pledging his allegiance to the Roman Catholic Church. English Catholics published an autobiographical account of Matthew's conversion experience to offer misguided Anglicans a model for returning to the true faith. They chose to exploit Tobie Matthew's experience over others because he was the son of the Anglican bishop of Durham.[4] The message was clear; if the son of a high-ranking Anglican cleric could rediscover the true faith, so could other Anglicans. George's larger mission, then, was to provide fertile soil in the New World in which to plant the seeds for the rebirth of English souls far away from anti-Catholic governmental intrusion. There is evidence to suggest that colonists also took it upon themselves to participate in Calvert's endeavor. Calvert's desire to return Anglicans to Catholicism was shared by Jesuits and laymen in the province of Maryland. The Anglican John Grammer testified in court that he had been duped into attending a sermon given by Father Fitzherbert at Mrs. Brooks's house in 1658. The next day Grammer returned to Mrs. Brooks's with his wife, and the Jesuit priest asked him "how he liked his doctrine." Grammer answered that he could accept some of what the priest had said, but certainly not all of it. "Mr. Fitzherbert asked him what he did not like: & walked out together where they had a quarter hours discourse."[5]

In order to succeed in establishing a Catholic missionary settlement in the New World, Calvert needed the support of both the Crown and the Catholic church. Although James I took a decidedly anti-Catholic stance in public—particularly after the Bye Plot of 1603 to kidnap him, and the Gunpowder Plot attempt on his life two years later[6]—his desire to secure the match between his son and the Catholic Spanish infanta and his release of imprisoned recusants (Roman Catholics who refused to attend Church of England services) indicate that this stance was not immutable. In fact, his actions concerning Lord Baltimore suggest that he shared the goal of establishing a Catholic colony (if only to place English Catholics thousands of miles from home, or perhaps to please one of his favorites, George Calvert), for Avalon's charter gave Lord Baltimore royal powers over his new province, as stated in the "Bishop of Durham" clause:

> And furthermore the Patronages and Advowsons of all Churches which as Christian Religion shall increase within the said Region Isles and Limitts shall happen hereafter to be erected, Together with all and singular the like and as ample Right jurisdictions privileges prerogatives Royaltyes, Liberties, Imunityes and Franchises whatsoever as well by Sea as by Land within the Region, Iles and Limitts aforesaid, To have exercise use and enjoy the same, as any Bishop of Durham within the Bishopprick or County Palatine of Durham in our Kingdome of England hath at any time heretofore had, held, used, or enjoyed, or of right ought or might have had, held, used, or enjoyed.[7]

With the blessings of the English Crown and as the *de facto* prince of Avalon, George Calvert set sail for Newfoundland in 1627 with two Roman Catholic priests, Fathers Longvyll and Smith, and at least forty English Catholic settlers.

Tellingly, Calvert secured consequential marriage ties between his family and that of Sir Thomas Arundell (later dubbed Lord Arundell of Wardour), one of the most influential Roman Catholics in England. Arundell himself had attempted to establish an English Catholic colony in 1605 on the shores of Norumbega (later referred to as New England). Arundell's plan had included sending unemployed English Catholic soldiers—who had fought for Spain before James I agreed to peace in 1604—to begin the colonization process. These laborers would be under the direction of a select group of English Roman Catholic noblemen. Arundell's plan was thwarted, however, when resistance to the idea swelled at home.

Fully apprised of the pitfalls that lay before him, Calvert brought his family—save his eldest son Cecil—with him on his second trip to Avalon in the spring of 1628 to begin his own attempt at an English Roman Catholic missionary settlement. His arrival caused the Protestant minister, Rev. Erasmus Sturton, to leave Newfoundland in August of 1628. In England Sturton complained to the authorities that the Roman Catholic Mass was publicly celebrated in Avalon, in violation of English common law. His protests did not, however, deter the king from instructing the Lord High Treasurer to lend six ships to Lord Baltimore so that he could defend the English Catholic colony against the French. Yet even with the support of the Crown and his own sizable financial investment in the settlement, Calvert abandoned his mission. The hostile French fishermen and the cold, harsh climate proved formidable barriers between Calvert and his quest. Perhaps keeping in mind the need to convince other English Catholics to settle across the Atlantic in a Catholic haven, he sought to establish his province in a more suitable environment. His gaze turned southward to the warmer climate of Virginia.

Lord Baltimore sent some of his children back to England and set sail for Jamestown during the fall of 1629 to meet up with his second wife (his first wife having died in childbirth in 1622), who had already journeyed to Virginia several months earlier. Calvert, expecting a hearty welcome from the English settlers that he helped govern at one point, faced a rude and insulting populace when he and his Catholic entourage set foot on the soil. Colonial Virginia records reveal that more than one resident was brought to justice for harassing the English Catholics. Thomas Tindall, for instance, threatened to knock George Calvert to the ground and was publicly punished for his insolence with two hours in the pillory in 1630.[8] Further, Governor Pott and his council demanded that Calvert take the oath of supremacy, knowing that pious Roman Catholics could not swear such an oath without being excommunicated in accordance with the papal bull of 1626.

After being asked to leave the settlement, Calvert returned to England but left his wife and some of their children in Virginia to follow him at a later date. They never made it back to England; their ship was lost at sea in 1631.

His personal losses led George Calvert to write to Sir Thomas Wentworth, "But all things, my Lord, in this world pass away; *statutum est,* wife, children, honor, wealth, friends, and what else is dear to flesh and blood; they are but lent us till God please to call for them back again, that we may not esteem anything our own, or set our hearts upon anything but Him alone, who only remains forever."[9] Despite his loss, Calvert continued his pursuit of a Catholic missionary settlement by petitioning James I for a grant of land east of Virginia. Although George Calvert died before he held the charter in his hands, his eldest son Cecil, the second Lord Baltimore, followed in his father's footsteps when Charles I gave him the charter for Maryland on June 20, 1632. Maryland's charter was based on Avalon's, complete with the Bishop of Durham clause and palatinate status, essentially establishing a hereditary monarchy in Maryland. Thus Charles I also followed his father's lead in his endorsement of a Roman Catholic province where Lord Baltimore would possess powers of near absolute sovereignty. Yet it bears mentioning that Charles I must have been influenced by his Roman Catholic wife, Henrietta Maria, the daughter of one of the most outspoken women of her times, Marie de Médicis. Indeed, Maryland is said to have been named for Queen Henrietta Maria, an apt acknowledgment of her part in establishing Maryland as an English Catholic missionary province. Thomas Vane suggested as much in his published treatise, entitled *A Lost Sheep Returned Home; or, The Motives of the Conversion to the Catholike Faith, of Thomas Vane, Doctor of Divinity, and lately Chaplaine to His Majesty the King of England* (1648). He dedicated this work to his patron "the Most Excellent Majesty of Henriette Marie, Queen of England," who took her duty seriously as "a nursing Mother to the [Roman Catholic] Church" intent on bringing the lost sheep—the English Anglicans—back into the fold.[10]

Others in England saw the value of providing the English Roman Catholics with a safe haven. A pamphlet published in 1646 asked Parliament to be lenient toward the Catholics and allow them "liberty of conscience in England" because they posed no real danger to the state. But "in case the Parliament shall not think fit to do so, they may be pleased to give to so many of them as will accept thereof, free & publick leave to transplant themselves, families, and estates, into Mariland, a Province in America, above 3000 miles distant from England." The author argued that "the more ready way to remove the fears and jealousies which this State hath of the said Roman

Catholicks, is not to keepe them here under the heavie burthen of the penall Laws made against them for their Religion; but either to let them enjoy here the rights, and liberties of other free-born subjects; or else to give them leave to go into another countrey, where they may enjoy them." If the government allowed the Roman Catholics to sell their estates and go to Maryland, then there would be no reason for the English Catholics to enlist the aid of the French or Spanish Roman Catholics and seek revenge. Furthermore, by encouraging English Catholics to settle peaceably in Maryland, Parliament would avoid any further international embarrassment. It was far better to let English Catholics go to Maryland than to watch them flee "into any Forein Princes Dominions; because it will not be for the honour, nor perhaps for the safety of England, to permit another Princes Territories to be supplyed with people, by any considerable number of the Natives of this Kingdome." It would also benefit the English Crown, because "the planting of the said Roman Catholicks in Mariland (wch hath a dependance on the Crown of England) Will conduce much to the honour and profit of this State and Nation, by enlarging the Dominions thereof, by encrease of trade and shipping." This action would certainly form a "strong bond of fidelity" between the English Roman Catholics and "their Native Countrey." In sum, an English Roman Catholic haven in the New World would benefit the entire nation both economically and politically.[11]

One could say that Maryland began with the vision of a Catholic convert and favorite courtier of James I who became the first Lord Baltimore. It had its missionary statement in the irenic prose of the English Jesuit Andrew White's *Declaratio Coloniae Domini Baronis de Baltimore,* and it gained its legal soul in the hieratic Latin of James's son Charles. This triumvirate—the Calverts, the Crown, and the Catholic Church—committed itself to the establishment of an English Catholic colony in the New World as a means of fostering the growth of both Catholicism and the purses of pious families. George Calvert's first attempt to make this a reality at Avalon had left Father Andrew White excited about the prospects of an English Catholic colonization policy, and he formed a permanent bond with the Baltimores (as had the Crown) to achieve such ends. The Stuart kings—married to Roman Catholic queens—supported Baltimore's plans for a new colony with enthusiasm; Charles I bestowed palatinate status upon the Baltimores when the land patent was granted for Maryland. This unusual revival of an antiquated, feudal position that essentially made Baltimore the king of Maryland could only have been an endorsement of such a plan. In fact, Charles declared outright "that Wee [favour] the Pious, and Noble purpose of the said Barons of Baltemore" in Maryland's charter.[12]

Andrew White, Jesuit missionary priest, scholar, linguistic expert, Renaissance man, and world traveler, lived by careful argument and charitable persuasion. Thus he claimed that Maryland was named after "our gratious Queene"—usually understood to be Charles I's wife Henrietta Maria—but could not the "gratious" as likely refer to *Ave Maria gratia plena*? It is certainly a possibility, when we consider that he and the other colonists christened this new land with a host of other saints from the Roman Catholic calendar. The Catholic planters—settling on manors such as St. Clements, St. Gregory, and St. Michael—shared White's vision when they pledged to take "possession of this Countrey for our Saviour, and for our Soveraigne Lord the King of England." White, the scion of an old English gentry family, balanced his religious vow of obedience to the bishop of Rome with his temporal oath of loyalty to his English king. He prayed for the house of Stuart's return to the old faith, he desired peace with Virginia's Puritans, and in Maryland he sermonized Anglicans to return to the ancient Catholic faith.[13] Finally, he argued that with "kind and fair usage" the naturally spiritual natives would become peaceful, friendly, Christian, and English. Obviously White had something of the utopian in his *Relation of Maryland;* and it is in this promotional tract that we see the full extent of his missionary visions.[14]

The second Lord Baltimore made clear his vision for the Catholic province in his instructions to the colonists in 1633. Faced with numerous "adversaries in England, who endeavored to overthrow his voyage" and who continued their hostilities well into the next century, the six-foot-tall, twenty-seven-year-old Cecil demanded that his governor and commissioners be "very carefull to preserve unity and peace amongst all." Because of the limits English society placed upon Roman Catholics, Lord Baltimore's venture had to offer financial gain to Catholic entrepreneurs while ensuring a religiously tolerant society for laborers and gentry alike. Only in such an environment could the Calverts hope to reclaim Anglicans. Maryland's mission statement prioritized the proprietor's agenda, beginning with his duty to God and "the conversion of the savages to Christianity." Baltimore's allegiance to his sovereign appeared next, with "the augmentation of his ma[jesty's] Empire and Dominions . . . by reducing them under the subjection of his Crowne." His profession of assistance and responsibility to the settlers and their material "advancement" was followed with the assurance "that they may reape the fruites of their charges and labors." Baltimore's commitment to wealth accumulation and his loyalty to the king were superseded only by his responsibility to God, for after a fort was built for the adventurers' protection, "a church or a chappel" was to be constructed as soon as possible.[15] For the triumvirate, religion and financial gain were important factors in Maryland's establishment.[16]

In an act illustrative of his religious agenda, Lord Baltimore outfitted two vessels named *Ark* and *Dove*. The *Ark* symbolized a covenant between God and His chosen people in a new world in the same way that Noah's ark had in the Old Testament. The *Dove* represented the Holy Ghost, often referred to as "the Holy comforter" in seventeenth-century Roman Catholic writing. Surely these English Catholics needed a comforter whilst leaving their comfortable homes in England and embarking on a long and dangerous voyage to a strange frontier environment where they would be surrounded by the Calvinist Dutch and radical New England Congregationalists to the north and the heathen Indians and less than friendly Anglicans to the west.

At least 130 emigrants accepted Lord Baltimore's initial invitation to settle in his new Catholic province, and they left England in October of 1633. One of the first settlers, Thomas Cornwaleys, expressed this shared Catholic vision in a letter he wrote to Lord Baltimore in 1638, stating, "Securety of Contiens [conscience] was the first Condition that I expected from this Government."[17] George Alsop recognized that this tolerant government welcomed the misguided Anglicans back into the Catholic fold and provided a safe haven for Roman Catholics as well. Attesting to Maryland's success, he wrote that anyone who "desires to see the real Platform of a quiet and sober Government extant, Superiority with a meek and yet commanding power sitting at the Helme, steering the actions of State quietly, through the multitude and diversity of Opinionous waves that diversely meet, let him look on Mary-Land with eyes admiring." Maryland, for Alsop, was "The Miracle of this Age," where "the Roman Catholick, and the Protestant Episcopal"—referring to Arminian Anglicans rather than Puritans—lived in "friendship, and inseparable love intayled unto one another."[18]

According to Father Andrew White's account, the colonists placed their ships under the protection of God, imploring the intercession of the Blessed Virgin, of St. Ignatius, the founder of the Jesuit order, and of all the guardian angels of Maryland for the success of the mission. Having been at sea for a short time, on November 25 they met with a violent storm that separated the *Ark* and *Dove* for six weeks. The rest of the three-month voyage was relatively uneventful and they finally landed in Virginia, where they were subjected to the same kind of treatment that George Calvert had faced several years before. After purchasing the necessary provisions and livestock from the Virginians they headed for Maryland, where armed natives congregated on the Chesapeake Bay's shoreline, preventing them from landing.[19] At night the apprehensive colonists saw alarm fires in the distance calling other Indians to join the Piscataway warriors.

Finding an uninhabited island on which to land, the English settlers named it St. Clement's Island and stepped onto its shore on the Feast of the Annunciation of the Blessed Virgin—March 25, 1634—and the Jesuits said Mass in the new province for the first time. This traditional rite was followed by a procession led by Governor Leonard Calvert—Cecil's trusted younger brother—and the new council members to a spot where they erected a large wooden cross, dropped to their knees, and recited the Litany of the Holy Cross. This ritual symbolized Christ's carrying the cross upon which He would be crucified, after which His resurrection from the dead would bring new life to all that chose to follow Him. Accordingly, the Marylanders' holy cross represented a new beginning—a new life in a new world—after one hundred years of persecution in England. After giving thanks to the Blessed Virgin, the Holy Trinity, and all the angels and saints in heaven for their safe journey, Leonard Calvert, Father Altham, and a small entourage set off to negotiate with the Piscataway chief from the Algonquin tribe. Seemingly without much trouble, according to White's account, the intercessors convinced the chief of their peaceful intentions and gained his permission to settle within his territory. The Piscataways probably thought that the English might provide some protection against the frequent raids from invading tribes such as the fierce Susquehannocks and Senecas.

Leonard Calvert decided to make his permanent settlement closer to the tip of Maryland's southern peninsula. The scouting party traveled up the St. George's River (later renamed St. Mary's) and anchored at an Indian town named Yaocomaco, where the werowance (a tribal authority) entertained the party and provided a tour of the surrounding area. Finding this location to be suitable for the new settlement, Calvert purchased the town dwellings and lands with the cloth, axes, hoes, and knives brought along for that purpose. Elaborate pacts made between the English and the "proper and tall men" who painted "themselves with colours in oile . . . to keep away the gnats" were intended to guarantee future peaceful relations.[20] Thus on March 27, 1634, the English adventurers took legal possession of Maryland— in the eyes of both the English Crown and the Yaocomacos—and named the new Catholic settlement St. Mary's City after the most revered saint, Christ's mother.

When the rest of their party arrived from St. Clement's Island three days later they settled their livestock and made arrangements for dividing up the new territory according to the proprietor's detailed instructions: on a traditional manorial plan of an English barony. This adaptation of a feudal

system provided a recognizable plan for an English social order. At the out-
set, Lord Baltimore had encouraged Catholics and Anglicans to settle in
Maryland with a headright system, offering two thousand acres of land
for every five persons between the ages of fifteen and sixty who would
come. The settlers paid Lord Baltimore four hundred pounds of wheat per
year for the use of the two thousand acres. When immigrants arrived in
groups smaller than five, Lord Baltimore allowed one hundred acres for
each man or woman and fifty acres for each child or servant. In this case,
the rent amounted to ten pounds of wheat for every fifty acres. These generous terms were pared down somewhat by 1635, when for every five adults
brought to Maryland Baltimore granted one thousand acres at a rent of
twenty shillings. The larger grants—at least one thousand acres—also entitled a colonist to establish him- or herself as the lord of the manor, with
the right to hold courts leet and courts baron, meting out justice as he or
she thought "meet [suitable] and convenient." Remaining convinced of the
importance of his mission to colonize a new Catholic haven, Cecil Calvert
stayed in England to generate interest in emigration and protect the family's
interests from the rising anti-Catholic sentiments at court, an effective tac-
tic that would continue to serve the Calverts until the American Revolution.

Over the course of the seventeenth century approximately sixty manors
were erected, in addition to several six-thousand-acre tracts laid out expressly for the Calvert family, making Maryland's feudal lords wealthy from
rent payments. This traditional system was maintained and encouraged until the end of the seventeenth century, for we see that George Talbot, a
cousin of Lord Baltimore, was granted Susquehanna Manor in Cecil County
—some 32,000 acres—in 1680.[21] The proprietor also enjoyed revenues derived from alienation fees, fines and forfeitures of felons' goods, and the
rights to stray and wild animals and fowl of the region.[22] The proprietor's
right of escheat sometimes drew loud criticism from the colonists, who believed he exercised this right inequitably and even illegally all too often. An-
gry over what he thought were unfair practices, Robert Carvile claimed that
Lord Baltimore was a "ffart" and that "his Lordship appointed fools, knaves
& boys to Office."[23] Edward Erbery concurred with this assessment of Lord
Baltimore's provincial officeholders. Erbery believed that "pitiful rogues
and puppies" occupied seats in the "turdy, shitten assembly" headed by a
"rogue" governor.[24] Robert Carvile's and Edward Erbery's assertions to the
contrary aside, the bulk of evidence seems to suggest that the proprietor and
his feudal lords—despite their character flaws—accepted the responsibility
to maintain social order that came with the material wealth generated by
the province. Although only one manor's court records have survived, those

of St. Clement's, we can assume that most if not all the lords exercised their right and duty to hold courts leet and baron, since vague references in the primary sources do exist. In the proceedings of the Provincial Court, for example, a clerk recorded that "a Court Baron" was held at Mary Brent's manor on March 7, 1656.[25] Lord Baltimore empowered manor lords to sit in judgment on all offences committed within the limits of the manor except for cases involving murder, counterfeiting, or treason. Lord Baltimore reserved for himself the right to execute settlers for high crimes.

Like his feudal lords, Lord Baltimore took his duty to ensure social order seriously. The wealthiest manor lords, along with all other landholders, took an oath of fidelity to the proprietor himself and not to the king of England.[26] This charter right stood in stark opposition to the Crown's *Quia Emptoris* decree of 1290, which stated that in all sales or feoffments of land the holder should bear allegiance to the king and not to the immediate lord or grantor. Maintaining a traditional social order was important to the lords and the proprietor in the Roman Catholic province, and Calvert used his royal powers toward this end. He reiterated this point in a letter to William Stone suggesting that "a small Colony may grow into a great and renowned nation, whereas by experience it is found that by discord and dissention great and glorious kingdoms and commonwealths decline, and come to nothing."[27] Lord Baltimore even went so far as to demand that sheriffs at the local level take an oath that they would "truly and rightfully treat the people of [their] sherifwick, and do right as well to poor as to rich, in all that belongeth to [their] office."[28]

Lord Baltimore, bent on establishing a profitable proprietary province, followed a plan for stability reminiscent of William the Conqueror's feudalism. The intermarriage of the Maryland gentry provided the province with a web of interdependency in which their profits and power were derived from Lord Baltimore, and their blood and marriage relations cemented their allegiance. When Lord Baltimore established his proprietary council, similar to the English House of Lords, more than half of its members were directly related to him. By 1677, nearly the entire membership of the council owed their political careers in the upper chamber to their blood or marriage relationship to his Lordship.

Charles I's charter bestowed upon Lord Baltimore the power to create ports of entry, to erect towns, boroughs, and cities, to pardon felonious offences, to create and command an army, to declare martial law, and to grant lands on such terms and tenure as he thought proper. Baltimore was the ultimate source of justice, having the power of establishing courts, of abolishing them at will, and of determining their jurisdiction and manner of proceeding; and their proceedings ran in his name and not in that of the Crown. Lord Baltimore headed the executive branch of the government, with the power to appoint officers of every description (and thus establish a noble class) and to create and abolish the offices themselves at his pleasure. He was the head of the church, endowed with the power to erect and found churches. Calvert could also promulgate ordinances that had the force of laws, and he claimed as part of his prerogative the power of dispensing with existing laws. In case there was any doubt about Calvert's royal authority in Maryland, the Crown summed up his omnipotent powers in the charter with a sweeping statement that if any clause seemed vague, it was always to be interpreted in Lord Baltimore's favor.

Amid this array of autocratic powers conferred on Lord Baltimore by the Crown, those granted to the English colonists were neither numerous nor explicit. This, however, did not deter the settlers from laying claim to certain rights soon after their arrival. Calvert's charter entitled him to frame all the laws for the province, without having to submit them to the king for his approval. This privilege gave Baltimore a free hand in creating and interpreting laws, so long as they did not directly contradict those of English common law and Baltimore obtained the approbation of the *"Liberi Homines"* and *"Liberi tenentes"* in the province. Yet the freemen in Maryland —conscious of both their duty and the frontier environment in which they found themselves—met as an Assembly in 1635 to draw up law codes and then sent them to England for Lord Baltimore's approval. Calvert summarily dismissed this act of insubordination and drew up a complete system of government for Maryland. When his directive arrived in Maryland, Governor Leonard Calvert presided over the second legislative assembly in 1637. All the freemen—who were not necessarily freeholders—of the province were invited to attend, send delegates in their place, or give their proxies to any individual of their own selection, authorizing him to vote for them.[29] The Assembly rejected Baltimore's law codes and proceeded to pass laws for itself, forty-two in all, which were also rejected by Baltimore. In fact, Baltimore only reluctantly permitted the Assembly to initiate legislation, and he never accepted the Assembly's premise that all the laws of England applied to the colonists.[30] A wholesale adoption of English common law would have interfered with Lord Baltimore's legislative rights according to his charter. Not surprisingly, then, some of the Assembly members were not altogether content with this royal prerogative transplanted to the New World. Inhabitants of Kent Island, led by the Virginian William Claiborne, resisted the establishment of Baltimore's courts in 1637 and his appointed commander of the island, Captain George Evelin. The discontent festered until Leonard Calvert led a military action to bring Kent Islanders under his authority in 1638. But, as we shall see, Claiborne would not capitulate so easily or wholeheartedly.

Most of the men and women who came to Maryland in the seventeenth century were indentured servants, also referred to as "redemptioners." While the majority of white servants served between four and seven years, at the end of which they were rewarded with a few tools and enough dried corn to prevent them from starving for a year, adults with marketable skills negotiated shorter contracts with more advantages. Take, for instance, bricklayer Cornelius Canedy, who bound himself to Thomas Gerrard on St. Clement's Manor for three years. When his term expired, he expected to receive two hundred acres of land, two cows with calves, two sows with piglets, two goats with kids, five barrels of dried corn, a featherbed with a pillow, a rug, and some eating and cooking utensils. In sum, Canedy was promised a life as a freeman equipped to become one of the middling sort with the social mobility rarely realized back in England. Disregarding the seemingly lucrative terms laid out in his contract, Canedy ran away from Gerrard, leaving us to suspect that the working conditions on the manor or possibly the conditions of employment were not ideal.[31] Did Gerrard beat, starve, or otherwise misuse Canedy? Or did Canedy realize that his skills were in such demand that he could readily solicit more profitable work elsewhere? Unfortunately, Canedy's reasons for his behavior were not recorded.

While the nature of most of the surviving documents makes it difficult to recover information about the lives of the laboring poor, the Jesuit records provide us with valuable information about the Native Americans. Jesuits wrote down local Native American words and their English translations, which appears to confirm their own statements that they were interested in saving the peaceful neighbors from eternal damnation.[32] The priests traveled by boat, often accompanied by a lay brother, to various Indian villages, bringing the word of God and baptism (a sacrament needed for salvation) to their newfound brethren. Perhaps grateful for their ministering efforts, the Patuxents gave the Jesuits a large tract of land they called Mettapaunien—renamed St. Mattapany by the Jesuits—on the Patuxent River. In this way the Jesuits had acquired four sizable tracts by 1639.[33] This accumulation of property, illegal under Calvert's charter, enraged Calvert to the point that he appealed to the *Congregatio de Propaganda Fide* at Rome. In his petition he asked that Rome send English priests who did not belong to any order (i.e., secular priests) to replace the Jesuits in his province. Calvert's sister intervened to negotiate a settlement, and ultimately the members of the Society of Jesus remained in Maryland with the land they had acquired.

Baptizing Indians was also important to the governing elites of the province. On July 5, 1640, Governor Leonard Calvert, Secretary Lewger, and other council members witnessed the Catholic baptism and marriage of the Tayac king and queen. These rites served many religious and social purposes, including bridging the differences between the elites of two disparate societies. Partaking in these two holy sacraments meant, among other things, that the English could think of the Indian royal family as near equals. Consequently, after the sacred rituals the king and queen sent their daughter, along with other noble village children, to the Jesuit mission school at St. Mary's City to receive an English Christian education. And to further illustrate this point, the wealthy Giles Brent later married the Tayac princess—newly baptized Mary—just as if she were the scion of an English noble family.[34] Unfortunately, the Native Americans did not record their own perspective on these events, but this evidence does suggest that wealth, status, and religion were defining issues for the early modern English.

Bringing Catholicism to the Indians in an effort to enlarge "his Majesties [Catholic] Empire" did not ensure tranquility between the Indians and the English any more than the initial peace agreements had. The Susquehannock Indians posed a serious threat to the well-being of the province, just as they had to the neighboring friendly Indians when they attacked them in an effort to "get their Women" and establish their "superiority."[35] The Susquehannocks commenced hostilities against the colonists in 1639 and continued to terrorize them sporadically throughout the seventeenth century as the English colonists attempted to maintain peaceful relations with their close neighbors, the Piscataways, Patuxents, and Yaocomacos, all long-time enemies of the Susquehannocks.[36] Writing in 1666 with a mixture of awe and trepidation, George Alsop described the fierce Susquehannock warriors as "seven foot high in latitude, and in magnitude and bulk suitable to so high a pitch; their voyce large and hollow, as ascending out of a Cave, their gate and behavior strait, stately and majestick, tending on the Earth with as much pride, contempt, and disdain." Attesting to their strength and fortitude, the men, women, and even children had "no other Armour to defend them from the nipping frosts of benumbing Winter, or the penetrating and scorching influence of the Sun in a hot Summer, then what Nature gave them when they parted with the dark receptacle of their Mothers womb."

Alsop described their skin as "naturally white, but altered from their originals by the several dyings of Roots and Barks, that they prepare and make useful to metamorphize their hydes into a dark Cinamon brown."[37]

With the English Civil War came rebellion in Maryland, and the fierce "Cinamon brown" Susquehannocks were persuaded to act against the governing Catholics. And as the Puritans' strength increased in England, Governor Leonard Calvert returned home in 1643 to ascertain what course to pursue. In his stead, he appointed Giles Brent lieutenant general, admiral, chief captain, magistrate, and commander. Calvert also appointed Captain Cornwallis to command the militia against the threatening Susquehannock warriors—probably roused by the rebellious William Claiborne and armed by the Swedes and Dutch of Delaware and New York—to the north. The Maryland militia's first attempt, in 1643, to fend off the Susquehannocks was successful, but the following year's expedition was a crushing defeat, with the Indians killing fifteen colonists.

During the governor's absence, the spirit of disaffection amongst the colonists increased and at length broke out in William Claiborne and Richard Ingle's rebellion, also known as the "plundering time." Sailing under a commission from Parliament to assist its colonial supporters in November of 1643, Ingle escaped from custody after his ship was seized by the Catholics upon arriving at St. Mary's City. Quite possibly after conferring with William Claiborne, Ingle returned to St. Mary's on a ship suitably named *Reformation*. Governor Leonard Calvert, after returning to the chaos, was forced to retreat to Virginia and thus could not prevent the plundering that ensued. Ingle and his armed followers destroyed the colonial records and proceeded to pillage and steal (from the Catholics in particular) before he arrested Fathers White and Fisher and left for England to bring the Catholic priests to trial for publicly practicing their religion. Claiborne took advantage of the chaos and claimed the right to Kent Island, a right that he had maintained since Lord Baltimore's charter was first issued. By 1646, Governor Calvert controlled St. Mary's City once again, and within a few months he had also reclaimed Kent Island for Lord Baltimore. But while Baltimore's province survived, the stressful events had taken a toll on Leonard Calvert.

After thirteen years of service, Leonard Calvert died on June 9, 1649, at the age of forty-one. On his deathbed, Leonard named Thomas Green his successor and appointed Margaret Brent his executrix to settle his estate. Margaret, who had arrived with her sister and two brothers in 1638, was lord of her own manor and a relative of the Calvert clan. She was a smart businesswoman well acquainted with the art of persuasion. Leonard's personal accounts were in disarray and she realized that liquidating all of his assets would not satisfy his debts. Leonard had guaranteed payment out of his own estate to the troops enlisted for the recapture of the colony and its subsequent defense, with Lord Baltimore's holdings in the province as additional collateral. Thus Margaret administered Leonard's estate and also acted as Lord Baltimore's provincial attorney.

The mercenary soldiers that Leonard had hired threatened to mutiny when wages were not forthcoming. Margaret Brent met the emergency by paying off the soldiers in cows, heifers, and calves from Leonard's, her own, and Lord Baltimore's private stock. In doing so she saved the province and gained the respect and admiration of the Assembly, but angered Lord Baltimore. When Baltimore criticized Margaret's actions in a letter to the Assembly, members answered him with the following rejoinder:

> As for Mistress Brent's undertaking and medling with your Lordships Estate . . . we do Verily Believe and in Conscience report, that it was better for the collonys safety at that time in her hands then in any mans else in the whole Province after your Brothers death[;] for the Soldiers would never have treated any other with that Civility and respect and though they were even ready at several times to run into mutiny yet she still pacified them till at last things were brought to that strait that she must be admitted and declared your Lordships Attorney by an order of Court . . . or else all must go to ruin Again and then the second mischief had been doubtless far greater than the former[;] so that if there hath not been any sinister use made of your Lordships Estate by her from what it was intended and ingaged for by Mr Calvert before his death as we verily Believe she hath not[;] then we conceive from that time she rather deserved favour and thanks from your Honour for her so much Concurring to the publick safety then to be justly liable to all those bitter invectives you have been pleased to Express against her.[38]

Back in England in June of 1647, the pivotal battle of Nasby was fought, followed within a year by the Puritans' triumph over Parliament. During this crisis Lord Baltimore made choices in order to safeguard the welfare of his province, walking a fine line between appeasing Oliver Cromwell and the exiled heir to the throne, Charles II. By recognizing the Commonwealth's authority after Charles I was beheaded on January 30, 1649, Lord Baltimore secured his rights to Maryland. Though they had little in common in their religious and political beliefs, Oliver Cromwell was willing to deal with a gentleman like Lord Baltimore in order to keep the governmental transition as smooth as possible. In fact, Cromwell worked closely with other Roman Catholic nobles, such as Lords Brudenell and Arundell, in addition to having Sir Kenelm Digby perform diplomatic services for him. Lord Baltimore deemed it important to show Cromwell that Puritans were not intentionally excluded from Maryland, and new acts were drawn up to ensure that the Catholic province could continue to exist. When the Assembly received Lord Baltimore's instructions it enacted laws that restated Baltimore's rights to both land and revenues. Yet the most consequential of the Interregnum laws was the act guaranteeing religious freedom in the province, which was passed on April 21, 1649. It is quite possible that the law was placed on the books in the hope that the Puritans in England would find the Roman Catholic province less repugnant if Puritans were welcome to seat themselves in Maryland. The act reads as follows:

> And whereas the inforcing of the conscience in matters of Religion hath frequently fallen out to be of dangerous Consequence in those commonwealthes where it hath been practised, And for the more [peaceful] government of this Province and the better to [preserve] mutuall Love and [unity] amongst the Inhabitants [here]. Be it Therefore . . . [ordained and] enacted . . . that noe person or [persons] whatsoever within this Province or the Islands, Ports, Harbors, Creekes or havens thereunto belonging professing to [believe] in Jesus Christ, shall from henceforth bee in any waies troubled, Molested or discountenanced for or in respect of his or her religion nor in the free exercise thereof within this Province or the Islands thereunto belonging nor anyway compelled to the [belief] or exercise of any other Religion against his or her consent, soe as they be not unfaithfull to the Lord Proprietary, or molest or conspire against the civill Government.[39]

Penalties were imposed on those using "reproachfull words" against the Blessed Virgin Mary, the apostles, or the evangelists, or calling another person a heretic, schismatic, idolater, Puritan, Independent, Presbyterian, Popish Priest, Jesuit, Jesuited Papist, Lutheran, Calvinist, Anabaptist, Brownist, Antinomian, Barrowist, Roundhead, Separatist, or other demeaning religious label. Still, we can overestimate the impact Cromwell's revolution had on the passing of this act of religious toleration.

This act was, in fact, the legal expression of the fifteen-year-old policy that had been maintained since Lord Baltimore outlined his views on toleration in his instructions to the original colonists. Baltimore gave his brother strict instructions that future governors of the province should take an oath strikingly similar to the act concerning religion. The oath of office declares that a governor will not "directly or indirectly trouble, molest or discountenance any person professing to believe in Jesus Christ for or in respect of religion." Additionally, a governor would not show any favoritism to Roman Catholics when "conferring offices, favors or rewards," but would give the political plums to the most "faithful and well deserving" individuals, according to their "moral virtue and abilities." Above all else, the government's aim was to maintain public unity by preventing the molestation of "any person professing to believe in Jesus Christ on account of his religion."[40]

Lord Baltimore's intention was to convert Anglicans to the true faith without aggressive confrontations. We can see this policy in action even before 1649. On March 23, 1642, David Wickliff, representing a group of Anglicans, complained to the court that Thomas Gerard took the key to the Roman Catholic chapel they shared, along with some Anglican books kept there. The court found Gerard guilty of a misdemeanor, demanded that the books and key be given back to the Protestants, and slapped him with a fine of five hundred pounds of tobacco (which was legal tender), to be used toward the maintenance of an Anglican priest when he arrived.[41] Roman Catholics were also protected by the policy initially meant to encourage the growth of English Roman Catholicism, as shown in the case of Giles Brent. Giles took Edward Commins to court for burning his books, which Commins referred to as "papist devils."[42]

When the Puritans seized control of Maryland in 1655—at the same time that the Puritan Commonwealth gained greater power in England—they immediately repealed the act for religious toleration. It was reinstated when power was restored to Lord Baltimore with his Anglican and Roman Catholic supporters in 1657. Ironically, these rebellious Puritans had been Lord Baltimore's invited guests, in a pragmatic effort to placate rising anti-Catholic and pro-Puritan sentiments in England when Cromwell captured Parliament's authority. These guests, escaping from persecution in Virginia, seated themselves in Somerset County in an area along the Severn River that they called Providence and later renamed Annapolis.[43]

The Puritans of Providence were never enthusiastic, loyal supporters of Lord Baltimore. On June 6, 1654, Governor Stone officially proclaimed Oliver Cromwell Lord Protector, knowing full well that Richard Bennett and William Claiborne were stirring up the Puritans—sometimes referred to by the Roman Catholics as "Round-headed Rogues" and "Dogs"—to a seditious and rebellious fervor against Lord Baltimore.[44] In July, Bennett and Claiborne led a group of Puritans to take control of the government meeting, with little resistance from Stone. Stone's weakness infuriated Lord Baltimore and he vehemently chastised Stone for surrendering to the Puritans so easily. As the proprietor's official, Stone organized an armed military unit in St. Mary's for the purpose of reestablishing the proprietor's control and sent John Hammond to Richard Preston's house on the Patuxent River (which was the temporary seat of Puritan government) to retrieve the stolen provincial records.

Captain William Fuller, the military commander of the Puritan enclave, and his extralegal council members at Providence soon learned of Stone's actions and sent messengers asking Stone to explain himself. Stone issued a proclamation to reassure all Marylanders that he was resuming his duties as governor of the province and, as Lord Baltimore's authorized agent, had every right to seize the illegally obtained records at Preston's house. Then Stone sent an armed party of twenty men under the command of William Eltonhead and Josias Fendel to confiscate the large quantities of arms and ammunition kept at Preston's house, and at the same time he prepared to force the Puritans of Providence to submit to the proprietor's government. On March 20th approximately two hundred armed supporters of Baltimore, along with a dozen small ships, arrived at Herring Creek, where half a dozen Puritan messengers sent by the government at Providence met them. The messengers carried with them a letter remonstrating against Stone's proceedings and desiring to be informed of his authority and power, as well as stating that they—with the help of God—were willing to fight to the death for their cause. Three of the messengers escaped Stone's detainment and made their way back to Providence to warn the Puritans of Stone's imminent attack.

Stone deputized Doctor Luke Barber and Mr. Coursey to lead a small unit to Providence to deliver a message that "in the end of this declaration, the governor did protest, as in the presence of Almighty God, that he came not in a hostile way, to do them any hurt, but sought all meanes possible to reclaime them by faire meanes, and to my knowledge, at the sending out of parties, he gave strict command that, if they met any of the [Puritans], they should not fire the first gun, nor upon paine of death, plunder any."[45] Stone arrived in Providence with his troops the next evening and Captain Fuller called a council of war, at which William Durand, the secretary of the Puritan government, was appointed to board the merchant ship *Golden Lyon*, commanded by Captain Heamans. Captain Fuller and his company of a hundred and twenty men joined Heamans's ship. When the Puritan forces caught up with Stone's, they engaged in a deadly land battle. Baltimore's supporters fared worse, with only four or five of Stone's men escaping to carry news to their confederates. Governor Stone (wounded in the shoulder), Colonel Price, Captain Gerrard, Captain Lewis, Captain Kendall, Captain Guither, Major Chandler, and their army were taken prisoner by the Puritans.

The Puritans executed four of Stone's ten highest-ranking officers. They would have surely killed all ten, including the governor, had it not been for Stone's "popularity with some of their own party, and the intercession of the women!"[46] Back home, the governor's wife, Verlinda Stone, informed Baltimore of the events. She warned Baltimore that Puritan rebels "tried all your councellors by a councell of warre, and sentence was passed upon my husband to be shot to death, but was after saved by the enemy's owne souldiers, and so the rest of the councellors were saved by the petitions of the women, with some other friends which they found there."[47] The Puritans confiscated the prisoners' property, enacted laws to persecute the Roman Catholics, and sacked and plundered the Jesuit plantations at Portobacco and St. Inigoes, causing the inhabitants to seek safety in Virginia.[48] Even after Baltimore's authority was reestablished in the southern part of the province, the Puritans continued to control the north for some time.

The Puritan Levelers in Providence irritated even Oliver Cromwell, who suggested that they not "busy themselves about religion, but . . . settle the civil government." In January of 1654/5,[49] Cromwell restated Baltimore's rights in a letter that chided the Puritans for their zealous and uncivilized behaviors, which "have much disturbed that Colony and people, to the endangering of tumults and much bloodshed there if not timely prevented." Cromwell, Lord Baltimore, and "divers other persons of quality" in England demanded of the Maryland Levelers, "and all others deriving any authority from you, to forbear disturbing the Lord Baltimore, or his officers or people in Maryland; and to permit all things to remain as they were before any disturbance or alteration made by you."[50] After six years of rebellion, Baltimore regained control over his entire province, but his new governor, Fendall, never lived up to Baltimore's expectations. The lower house of the Assembly demanded in 1659 that the governor and council should no longer sit as an upper house and claimed for itself the rights of supreme judicial and legislative power. When Fendall quickly yielded to their demands, the upper house was dissolved and Fendall resigned Lord Baltimore's commission while he simultaneously accepted the Assembly's. Fendall's rebellion was short-lived, as Baltimore's newly appointed governor, Philip Calvert, arrived from England and was met by the general public—desperate to regain peace and tranquility—with enthusiasm.

Apart from the unsuccessful attempt by Baltimore to take Delaware from the Dutch in 1659 (a more aggressive attempt would be made in the early 1670s), relatively uneventful years passed and the colony grew as more

English immigrants arrived. The religiously tolerant society attracted many non-English colonists also. So many, in fact, that the Assembly of May 1666 passed the first naturalization law of any colonial Assembly. Colonists, pleased to finally have an ordered society once again, passed laws in the 1670s demanding that each county erect a courthouse and prison, along with more facetious demands that horse racing and other rowdy activities be prevented at Quaker Meetings.[51]

Since Marylanders were as much a product of their times as the Calverts themselves, they exhibited a modern worldview—accepting the centrality of property, innovation, education, and risk taking as a means to wealth accumulation—while they simultaneously held some traditional notions. Historians have long acknowledged Marylanders' modern desire to become successful commercial planters.[52] In a letter to "his Grace Thomas Lord Arch-Bishop of Canterbury" asking for Anglican "Missionaries" to be sent to Maryland, Thomas Bray warned that prelates must "be of such nice Morals, as to *abstain from all Appearance of Evil* . . . Men of good *Prudence,* and an *exact Conduct,* or otherwise, they will unavoidably fall into Contempt, with a People [Marylanders] so well vers'd in Business, as every the meanest Planter seems to be."[53] The archaeological excavations at Historic St. Mary's City have unearthed evidence suggesting a vibrant commercial society of "well vers'd" businessmen involved in conspicuous consumption. Under the direction of Henry Miller, archaeologists have found Chinese porcelain, Dutch tiles, French glass and stoneware, and German ceramics, in addition to many Italian, Portuguese, and Spanish items.[54] Colonists could procure extremely ornate wine glasses and other exotic imports from a merchant in the center of town. Before the Navigation Acts passed by Parliament during the 1660s, Marylanders purchased international finery and indulged in foodstuffs from around the world, including Spanish olives.[55]

George Alsop, also convinced of Marylanders' commercial orientation, offered this advice to immigrants: "If you send any Adventure to this Province, let me beg to give you this advice in it; That the Factor whom you imploy be a man of a Brain, otherwise the Planter will go near to make a Skimming-dish of his Skull." He added that "The people of this place (whether the saltness of the Ocean gave them any alteration when they went over first, or their continual dwelling under the remote Clyme where they now inhabit, I know not) are a more acute people in general, in matters of Trade and Commerce, then in any other place of the World; and by their crafty and sure bargaining, do often over-reach the raw and unexperienced Merchant." In sum, "he that undertakes Merchants imployment for Mary-Land, must have more of Knave in him then Fool; he must not be a windling piece of Formality, that will lose his Imployers Goods for Conscience sake."[56]

Betty Ring's study of American needlework emphasizes the distinctions between the worldviews found in Puritan New England and Maryland. Samplers from the northeast depicted the alphabet, biblical verse, the family's homestead, genealogical information, grave memorials, heraldry, and poetry. Young girls in eighteenth-century Maryland also made such handiwork. However, young Marylanders sewed the earliest needlepoint maps in America. Girls included counties, cities, rivers, longitudes, latitudes, floral cartouches, and compasses in these intricate scaled reproductions. Commercially motivated parents, interested in a pragmatic education for their daughters, sent them to schools where they learned geography by reproducing recent maps on linen, silk, and wool. Only in Maryland did boarding schools advertise map embroidery when seeking new students.[57]

Profit-motivated Marylanders focused on their international financial pursuits in almost everything they wrote, including their wills. They instructed executors to pay and collect debts while alluding to their international business enterprises. Entrepreneur James Weedon wrote his will when he left Maryland to establish a settlement "near the South Cape of Delaware Bay." Weedon owned a rental property on London Bridge and wanted to advance his holdings in the New World as well. The anticipated benefits must have been great, for the risks entrepreneurs took included premature death from malaria, smallpox, and influenza during their "seasoning" period. Prudent men could do little to minimize this particular risk, but they often wrote wills in an effort to offset the devastating effects of their death. Weedon wrote, "I give unto my Said Wife all such Debts as are due to me by bill bond specialty or accompt or any other wayes whatsoever."[58] Similarly, on his deathbed, George Dundasse went to great pains to remind his wife that the names he had not crossed out in his account books represented unpaid debts to be collected by her.[59] In keeping with this modern commercial mindset, we find many examples of testators demanding an education for their children until they could "read well & write and Cast Accompt ffitt to Doe the business of this Countrey."[60]

The commercially motivated planters in seventeenth-century Maryland rarely forgave debts even to family members. Quaker John Parker listed several merchants who held some of his savings while mentioning his financial ventures in Barbados, England, and Maryland. He also wrote, "I give my Sister Mary Knap the sume of tenn pounds Sterling besides what I do owe her."[61] Only rarely did a testator generously forgive debts, as did Richard Bedworth and John Darnall. Bedworth essentially wiped the slate clean for his stepson Richard Thorbery when he left him "ye summe of 774 lb. of Tob[acco] being soe much hee now oweth mee by acco[un]t."[62] Catholic John Darnall, on the other hand, was a little less generous with his brother Henry when he excused half of the debt "which he oweth to me which I compute to be thirteen thousand pounds of Tobacco or thereabout ye. half p[ar]t not [including] any debts accrueing this year."[63]

Mechal Sobel posits a distinction between modern thinkers and their more communally oriented early modern counterparts. One of the pivotal factors for comparison is their conception of time. Were people conscious of the hours in a day, or did they continue to view the passage of time from an agricultural, seasonal perspective? Clearly the Maryland Assembly—in its outlining of procedures in 1637/8—recognized the importance of time when it insisted on meeting from eight in the morning until noon, resuming at two in the afternoon. Undoubtedly, not everyone had a clock or watch; thus a drumbeat sounded at sunrise and at each passing hour thereafter until eight o'clock. The drum resumed at one to remind Assembly members of their two o'clock appointment to reconvene. At least while the Assembly met, everyone in St. Mary's City knew the time as they passed through their day, and they performed many tasks according to the hour.[64] That Marylanders kept time by the hour seems likely enough, given the fact that clocks and watches in England were very popular amongst the wealthy during the seventeenth century. These popular timepieces were not very precise about marking time, however; most only signaled the hour.[65]

The fact that Marylanders referred, in their wills, to the precise time when their children or livestock were born or when wills were "signed, sealed, and delivered" is evidence that they had a modern sense of time. Witnesses also testified in court as to the precise time events took place. A witness recalled, when asked to testify as to the validity of Thomas Notley's will, that Notley had signed it on the third of April, "on thursday about Six a Clock at night."[66] Additionally, witnesses to the verbal will of carpenter's mate Richard Barry specified exact times. On July 26, nineteen-year-old Thomas Delany testified he had told Barry on the Monday before he died, at "about nine aclock," to move to a better place to get well away from the "Water & out of ye Stench of the marsh."[67]

Unlike many of their contemporaries in Old and New England, Marylanders sought a rational explanation—such as the bad air of the swamp—for events, illness, and death, rather than a metaphysical one according to which God punished the wickedness of humans. Nearly a century before English courts relied on coroners, Maryland judges sought their opinions, based on postmortems, when the cause of death was in question.[68] A court clerk recorded the findings of a postmortem in one case as follows: "[The body was] Cleere of inward bruises, either upon the Diaphrugma or w[i]thin the Ribbs, The lungs were of a livid Blewish Culler full of putrid ulcers, the liver not much putrid although it se[e]med to be disafected by reason of it's pale & wann Couller: the Purse of the Heart was putrid and rotton by w[hi]ch we gather that this person by Course of Nature could not have lived long, Putrifaccion being gott soe neer unto that noble part the h[e]art even att the doore."[69] Midwives and surgeons also served on inquest juries in cases where murder or infanticide was alleged. The reliance on medical evidence and the willingness of licensed practitioners to appear in court reveal a worldview predicated upon contemporary scientific knowledge.

More than one hundred and twenty-five doctors, "Chirurgians," and apothecaries appeared in the last wills and testaments and court records for the period between 1634 and 1713. The extraordinary numbers of medical practitioners in the province did little to prolong the lives of colonists, yet their existence does suggest a modern belief—espoused by both Bacon and Descartes—in the ability of humans to control nature.[70] Clerics in Maryland, like Andrew White, shared this worldview. Discussing the high mortality rates in the province in a letter to Lord Baltimore in 1638, Father White criticized the medical practitioners, but advocated a special diet to cure illness without suggesting that it was caused by sinful behavior. He wrote, "This yeare indeed hath prooved sick and epidemicall and hath taken away 16 of our Colony rather by disorder of eating flesh and drinking hott waters [liquor] and wine by advice of our Chirurgian rather by any great malice of their fevers for they who kept our diett and absteinence generally recovered."[71]

Archaeologist Anne Yentsch suggests that this desire to manipulate one's environment manifested itself in Governor Benedict Leonard Calvert's terraced gardens and his cultivation of oranges. Yentsch posits, "The construction of an orangery and an ornamental garden was an astute move on the part of the Calverts. . . . Its very presence denoted to Annapolis and to Maryland society at large . . . the social rank, wealth, and power of the Calvert household." She adds, "Metaphorically, the Calverts controlled a highly significant social space . . . the Calvert family also controlled nature."[72] This passion for growing citrus fruit in a non-tropical environment probably stems from the fact that early-eighteenth-century American gentry had developed an insatiable taste for "Shrubs," alcoholic citrus drinks. A typical recipe went something like this: "To every Gallon of Rum put one Quart of Juice, and two pounds of best double refined Sugar. Shake the Shrub every day for two Months, and let it settle once more, then draw it off for use.—

The Vessel should be kept close cork'd during the whole process. and to every hundred of Oranges put twenty-five Lemons. To make your Shrub fine all the Materials should be of the best."[73] The cultivation of exotic tropical fruits in Maryland indicates a strong thirst on the part of colonists to master their environment while enhancing their diet.

Marylanders, while adhering to a modern sense of time and focused on capital accumulation, lived in a brutal world that, perhaps, helped foster a premodern worldview. Living on the frontier, where certain levels of brutality were both expected and condoned, and facing the regular occurrence of death, they were desensitized to violence. Yet they did draw a line between acceptable "instruction" and beating someone with malice. Thomas Wynne, for instance, stepped over this line when he kicked his maidservant, Sarah Hall, "on the breech" and then gave her "a box on the ear and threatened to knock her down with a chair." His wife's behavior, however, was much more in line with acceptable social mores, apparently, when she hit Sarah in the head after Sarah refused to answer her.[74] It appears that beating one's servant for two hours straight could be thought of as instructional: although the court documents remain silent on the issue, it seems that Sarah Goulson was never punished for "disciplining" her female servant in this way.[75] When the line was crossed, however, servants either won their freedom or were sold to another master or mistress.

The "extraordinary cures" gained by bathing at "Cool Springs" in St. Mary's County, overseen by Maryland clergy in the late seventeenth century, might also point to a more traditional mindset. The water that produced the cures attracted large numbers of "poor people" who were given religious instruction when they arrived at the popular watering hole. The governor ordered that "Captain James Keech and Mr. Philip Lynes do provide some sober person to read prayers there twice a day, and is pleased to lend the person who reads prayers a book of Homilies, two books of family devotions and a book of reformed devotions by Dr. Theophilus Darrington, out of which books he is to read to them on Sundays." His excellency further ordered that "the said Captain Keech acquaint Captain John Dent, who is the owner of the said house and land, that if he be willing, his excellency will have made a reading desk and some benches to be placed in the new house there for the use of the poor people there gathered together." In addition to their indoctrination, the poor who flocked to John Dent's home were given mutton and corn on Sundays at the taxpayers' expense.[76] It is impossible to say whether these cures were considered divine miracles derived from immersing one's body in holy water or whether the people believed that the water contained natural medicinal ingredients that cured their maladies.

Despite the ambiguity of the water cures, a few colonists in the province relied upon cruentation (the theory that a murdered person's corpse will bleed in the presence of, or when touched by, the murderer) and persecuted witches, suggesting that traditional worldviews were certainly present in this society. In four surviving court cases in the provincial records, a resolution appears to have rested on cruentation tests for identifying murderers.[77] Also in the court records, we find a few references to witches. Grand juries investigated witchcraft charges against Elizabeth Bennett, Hannah Edwards, Virtue Violl, Katherine Prout, John Cowman, and Rebecca Fowler.[78] Either the charges were dropped or the accused was found innocent, with two notable exceptions. Cowman received a reprieve and stay of execution after his conviction, but Rebecca Fowler was not as lucky. A grand jury indicted her in 1685 for "being led by the instigation of the devil" into doing "certain evil and diabolical arts, called witchcrafts, enchantments, charms and sorceries." Her accusers argued that she had maliciously and with "forethought" used her powers against Francis Sandsbury "and several others" from Calvert County. The court found Fowler guilty and ordered that she "be hanged by the neck until she be dead."[79]

Needless to say, not everyone was content with Lord Baltimore's religiously tolerant society that was planted in both the traditional world—with its feudal land-tenure system and autocratic proprietary powers—and the modern—with its reliance on science, capital investments, innovation, and risk taking as a means of accumulating wealth. James Lewis, for instance, stood before a grand jury in October of 1672, accused of "uttering false and slanderous words and Rumours of the Governor, & Chancellors . . . that they were all Roughes and Bastards."[80] But discontent did not reach a fever pitch until Calvinist Marylanders heard about the 1688 Orange Revolution in England, which sparked new hope that the government could be wrested away from the Roman Catholics and their Quaker and Arminian Anglican relatives. The Jesuit chronicler William Treacy wrote that during Maryland's Associators Revolution in 1689 "Puritans took forcible possession of St. Mary's City," adding "that the venerated Catholic settlement was for a time in the hands of the bigotted 'Committee of Safety.'"[81] It had been a generation since the last Puritan *coup d'état,* which also occurred during a steamy, mosquito-plagued July; colonists must have been struck by the similarities.[82] Witnesses to the Associators Revolution supported Treacy's assertion that it was a conflict between the Roman Catholics (supported by their

Quaker and Arminian Anglican comrades) and the radical Puritans. In a letter to Lord Baltimore, Peter Sayer referred to the proprietor's supporters as "men of the best Estates and real professors of the Protestant Religion."[83] Sayer spoke for the majority of Marylanders, who believed Arminian Anglicans and Quakers were the "real professors of the Protestant Religion," not the Calvinists. Puritans and Presbyterians—those who embraced John Calvin's notion of predestination—were seen as radical troublemakers in the province. An excerpt from the Calvinist Associators' declaration underscores the deep-seated hatred these Puritans harbored for the Roman Catholics. The document, dated July 25, 1689, and signed by John Coode, Henry Jowles, Jno. Cambell, Hum. Warren, Kenelm Cheseldyn, Jon Turling, Richard Clouds, and William Blakiston, pointed to both the "private" and "publick outrages and murthers committed and done by Papists upon protestants without redress but rather conived at and tolerated by the chiefe authority." These Calvinists were convinced that Roman Catholic government had been "guided by the councills and instigation of the Jesuits." These dreaded Jesuits influenced the very foundations of the society; they were the "chiefe Judges at the common law in Chancery of the Probat of Wills and the affaires of administration in the upper house of Assembly and chiefe Military Officers and Commanders of our forces."[84]

The successful coup of 1689 followed the Glorious Revolution in England, in which the Catholic King James II was replaced by his Anglican daughter Mary and her husband William. A royal governor was appointed in 1692 and a decidedly anti-Roman Catholic stance permeated the provincial legal system, beginning in 1689 with the exclusion of Catholics from all civil and military offices. The new government also attempted to appropriate most of Lord Baltimore's provincial revenues, but he acted quickly in England to prevent any interruption of his collection of revenues according to his royal charter. Even though his revenue rights were upheld, the province was an official royal colony from 1692 until Lord Baltimore professed his allegiance to the Church of England in 1715.

Ultimately, the center of government was moved (in 1695) from St. Mary's City to its current home in Annapolis. We might assume that the Roman Catholics took as a sign from God the events at the new capital on July 13, 1699. The council clerk recorded that

> It pleasing Allmighty God that a great Clap of Thunder [and] Lightening fell upon the State house the house of Delegates sitting therein which Splintered the flag Staff strook down the Vane burnt the flagg and sett the roof of the house in a flame of fire and Strikeing through the

upper Rooms Shattering the Door posts [and] Window frames, strook down and griveously wounded Severall of the Delegates and more particularly Col Hans Hanson Lt Col [Thomas] Hicks and Mr George Ashman and passing through the upper Room where the Comittee of Laws was sitting, strook dead Mr James Crawford one of the Delegates of Calvert County [and] one of the [said] Comittee to the great Astonishm[en]t of all persons, But it so pleased God by the Active Care and personall [presence] of his [Excellency the Governor, the said] fire was quickly Quenched a show[e]r of rain happening Imediately thereupon And the Records Pr[e]served, as also the house with little or no Considerable Damage And this occasioned the Adjournme[n]t of this Board 'till 8 of the Clock to Morrow Morning.[85]

This event must have confirmed the Roman Catholics' suspicions that God was not pleased with the new Assembly, filled as it was with Calvinists like Hans Hanson. Accordingly, God spared the important provincial records and, significantly, the redeemable Arminian Anglicans, including the governor.

As the new capital grew in importance, St. Mary's City slowly faded; no memorable events took place there after the move to Annapolis, with one notable exception. St. Peter's—perhaps the most extravagant brick mansion with formal gardens built in the English colonies—suddenly exploded in 1695. No one knows who was responsible for the explosion of this Catholic residence, nor do we know why seventeen large barrels of gunpowder were in the mansion's cellar.[86] Were the English Roman Catholics storing the gunpowder in St. Mary's until it could be transported to Annapolis in an attempt to overthrow the Calvinist government? Certainly the Roman Catholics had every reason to believe that they might regain their province from the clutches of the Calvinist usurpers, just as they had done in the past. Or, conversely, had the Calvinists planted the gunpowder in the cellar with the hopes of igniting it when the mansion was full of Roman Catholic gentlemen? By eliminating the most influential Catholics in the province the Calvinists could secure their positions, once and for all, as the true religious and political authorities. Unfortunately the surviving documents remain silent on the issue.

The failure of the English Catholics and their Arminian Anglican and Quaker kin to regain the province does not negate the fact that religion played an important role in its establishment and the conflicts that followed. George Calvert's mission—resolutely supported by the Stuart kings and the Jesuit Order of the Roman Catholic Church—served to inform the government and fostered the generally tolerant attitude that encouraged emigrants (ironically including a substantial number of Puritans) to seat themselves in Maryland. Though Calvinists never made up more than a quarter of the population, Calvinist opposition proved to be an insurmountable barrier to creating and maintaining a profitable Roman Catholic refuge. In the end this barrier also prevented Maryland from achieving its ultimate goal of providing fertile soil upon which Arminian Anglicans could be convinced to return to the true religion.

The wars of religion that began soon after Lord Baltimore invited the Puritans to settle in Maryland continued right into the nineteenth century, although they were fought with very different weapons. Maryland historians engaged in a bloodless war over religion from podiums across the state and in popular history books and novels.[87] With anxiety rising over the increased numbers of Catholic immigrants entering the state in the nineteenth century, Protestants and Roman Catholics each attempted to claim Maryland's founding to justify their own *raison d'être*. The Protestants won this final battle, for school textbooks downplayed Calvert's pious mission to reinstate Roman Catholicism as the true English faith. Instead, these Protestant historians celebrated the coming of a "Protestant" trait—religious toleration—while emphasizing the Anglicans' desire to establish democracy in the New World from Maryland's inception. This desire for democracy was so strong that it propelled the Protestant colonists, who made up the majority of the population, to rise up against the Roman Catholic proprietor and his Catholic kin. This version of the story persisted well into the twentieth century. Since the 1950s, historians—excepting a few Jesuit priests and Quaker Friends—have embraced this nineteenth-century interpretation or have secularized Maryland's past altogether. The secularized version willingly accepts Lord Baltimore's religious toleration as a modern innovation, but strips it of any pious purpose and argues that he acted in this decidedly modern way because of his pragmatism. The practical, self-interested Baltimore saw both the political and economic advantages associated with creating a tolerant modern society based on a separation of church and state. These distorted views of the past fail to consider that the first two Baltimores were neither wholly of the traditional world—interested in merely establishing a safe haven for persecuted Catholics—nor entirely grounded in a pragmatic modern one that emphasized wealth accumulation, religious toleration, and the separation of church and state.

2

Private Lives

*E*aster was a time to commemorate the resurrection of Jesus Christ with joyful celebrations in church followed by the consumption of bountiful portions of wine and good food in the company of family and friends. Yet Easter of 1659 was not so festive for Clove Mace, who lived on St. Clement's Manor. After being beaten to a "bloudy" pulp, he raced to John Shanck's home to seek aid. Clove begged Shanck and John Gee to go to his house and confront his attackers—Clove's wife and Mr. Robin Cox. Shanck and Gee did not act immediately, but when Shanck finally confronted Clove's wife she defended her actions, saying that her husband was to blame for provoking the assault when "hee had abused Robin & her." Shanck persuaded Robin Cox and Clove's wife to agree to end the fight and "bee friends" with Clove. Probably still smarting from his wounds, Clove was reluctant at first, but he capitulated by the next night. This unfortunate event was merely another episode in the unfolding drama that was the Maces' abusive marriage. Clove had threatened "to beate" his wife on previous occasions; his wife, not taking his threats lightly, countered with threats of her own. She confided in Bartholomew Phillipps that if Clove laid a hand on her "shee would cutt his throat or poyson him." If necessary she would get John Hart "to bee revenged on him & beate him." Robin Cox had also confided in Phillipps that he would rearrange Clove's face, vowing that Clove would "never goe with a whole face" again if he abused his wife.[1] Unfortunately we do not know whether Clove's face was permanently disfigured in the beating, whether the Maces continued to live under the same roof, or if the marital violence ended with their pledge to "bee friends." The only thing that can be said with certainty is that Clove and his wife remained legally married until one of them died. Divorce was not an option.

Divorce was not an option for Mrs. Francis Brooke either. Her husband regularly beat her for refusing to give "the dog the pail to lick before she fetched water in it," or when she tried to eat the food that he reserved for himself. Mr. Brooke's weapon of choice was usually made of wood, such as the cane he beat her with until "he [broke] it all to pieces" and the "oaken" board that snapped "in 2 pieces on her." Brooke's violent behavior came to the court's attention after the midwife, Rose Smith, testified that his wife had delivered a dead male fetus prematurely and that "one side of the baby was all bruised." The midwife queried Mrs. Brooke, as was her duty, and she claimed that her husband had caused the baby's death when he assaulted her with a pair of large metal fireplace tongs after she ate one of his stewed "sheeps heads." Armed with this damning statement, Rose Smith demanded an explanation from Mr. Brooke, who told her that his pregnant wife had fallen out of the peach tree. To confirm his innocence, he then turned to his wife and "asked her if She did not fall out of the Peach Tree." Predictably, "She Said yes."[2]

While the Brooke family suffered because of an emotionally unstable and frequently violent husband, other families faced different travails. Robert Robins lived a "pitiful" existence with his wife, who he claimed had been unfaithful to him—so often and openly, in fact, that he frequently referred to her as "a Common whore." Criticized by his friends for tolerating such a demeaning situation, Robert threw up his hands and asked, "what would you have me doe?" Even with a "Good Wittness" to the public spectacle when "William Herde rid her from Stump to Stump," Robert knew he faced few desirable options.[3] He could continue his "pitiful" existence, he could walk away from their home, or he could file for a legal separation in court—a particularly costly and time-consuming option. Pushed beyond his limit when the "Common whore" gave birth to another man's child, Robert chose the latter option. It took two different appeals and the testimony of many witnesses before he received the judgment that he sought. He not only wanted to be rid of the "Common whore," but he desperately wanted to avoid being financially responsible for the maintenance of the child her adulterous affair had produced. After his second appearance (and much testimony), the court finally granted Robert the separation and decided that he did not owe his wife or her child any part of the couple's estate.[4] This unusual legal action, depriving a wife of her third of the estate,[5] freed him from his financial obligations to his wife, but it did not constitute a divorce; neither partner could legally remarry.[6]

Other men, such as Robert Taylor, also banished their unfaithful wives from their homes after they gave birth to another man's child.[7] This drastic action was not new, nor was it without risks. Early modern couples in England separated when partners were unfaithful or their differences proved to be insurmountable, as is demonstrated by the formal contracts of separation in the legal formulary of lawyer John Taylor.[8] In both England and Maryland abandonment or banishment of a spouse may have meant being ostracized from the community (depending on the circumstances of the split), losing control over the use of property, and possibly forfeiting the expected share of the estate after the decease of the other partner. Many times Maryland husbands continued to acknowledge their legal economic obligation to their estranged wives, bequeathing them one-third of the estate in their wills—if they came back to claim it—while others felt betrayed and vengeful and attempted to prevent their wives from claiming what was rightfully theirs. Allexander Chappell bequeathed his entire estate to his good friend Ann Chew, the wife of merchant Samuell Chew, with the exception of one shilling left to his wife, Elizabeth, because "of her unfaithfull Carriage and behaviour to me." As the unfortunate victim who hoped that the courts would not recognize his wife's right to one-third of his estate if she came back to claim it, Chappell explained in his will how his wife had left him and his "familly in ye greatest Streights & Wants" by "keeping Company with a Strange man to her owne great dishonour and my great greife."[9] While Marylanders did not sue for divorce in the seventeenth century, some sought legal ratification of informal separations when marriages failed, particularly when the family had enough property to warrant such action.[10] Historian Mary Beth Norton has noted that unlike Allexander Chappell, who used his will to settle property issues, other estranged couples divided their assets in court. Norton notes that "in October 1656 the Provincial Court confirmed a division of assets worked out by a husband and wife who 'were minded to live a sunder.'"[11]

Edward and Ruth Stevens opted for a non-traditional relationship rather than the more popular alternative of separation when their marriage failed. It is impossible to say whether it failed because Ruth was unable to have children or for other reasons. Still, they stayed together as husband and wife while Edward spent his free time with Florence Tucker. When he died Edward left Ruth more than two hundred and thirty acres of land and one-third of the personal estate in household goods to use for the rest of her life, provided that she "make use of them as to her own propper interest & benefitt." The remainder of the estate—and Ruth's share when she died— went to the "three sonns of Florence Tucker comonly called & known by the names of Edward Stevens William Stevens and John Stevens."[12] Edward had produced heirs outside his marriage while also fulfilling his economic obligations to his legal wife. We can only speculate about the relationship Ruth and Florence shared, for Edward's will may indicate a *ménage à trois*. At the very least, Edward forced the two women into some semblance of cooperation, since he named his mistress his executrix, responsible for collecting the debts and distributing the property outlined in his will.[13]

The difficulties associated with some marriages and the absence of divorce influenced a few colonists when they decided not to enter into a legal marriage. Colonists like St. Mary's County merchant George Yeedon chose to forego marriage but still secured his non-traditional family's welfare. When he died, George left a small token of his affection to his brother in Ireland—three hogsheads of tobacco—and the rest of his sizable estate to his joint executors, the woman he lived with, Elizabeth Shankes, and her son John.[14] George provided for his family without ever having made a traditional spiritual and legal commitment to his life-partner. It is possible that Yeedon and Shankes were unable to marry legally; one or both of them may have been already married to someone else. Others in the province, like Dr. John Wade, found themselves in similar situations. It appears that Wade had a wife and two children in England but set up housekeeping with Anne Smith in Maryland until she deserted him. Maybe as his last peace offering or as a symbol of his undying devotion to Smith, Wade left her a sizable estate in land and personal goods if she and their illegitimate child returned to Maryland to claim it after his death.[15]

By not entering into a formal marriage contract with Katherine St. George, Catholic widower Bryan O'Daly secured his estate for his legitimate son and daughter. Bryan stipulated in his will that Katherine, who claimed to be carrying his child, should continue to care for his legitimate son and daughter after his death. Attentive to his parental duties, he also provided for the basic needs of food and clothing in addition to four years of formal education for his unborn offspring.[16] For Katherine, this pragmatic arrangement assured that she and her baby would continue to have a place to live and food to eat. She also could find comfort in the fact that the education Bryan paid for would provide a modicum of security for her child's future. Surely this was a satisfactory bargain for Bryan as well. He procured a caregiver for his two young children—someone he and his children knew well—and kept nearly all of his estate intact for the use of his legitimate children when they became adults. Unfortunately Bryan did not state his reasons for treating his legitimate and illegitimate offspring differently, but we might venture a guess. It may have been that his deceased wife had provided most (if not all) of the land and household goods he shared with Katherine. If this was so, we could easily understand his refusal to bequeath Katherine's child an equal share of the family's wealth. This might also explain why Bryan never legally married Katherine. Because he had not formalized their union, he took for granted that the courts would not recognize Katherine's right to one-third of his estate after he died and thus his deceased wife's property could be preserved for her children.

Other couples fully intended to solemnize their unions, but sudden death prevented them from completing their plans. When Rice Williams fell ill at Colonel William Digges's house at Notley Hall, he drew up a will on February 6, 1684, revealing his unfinished marriage plans. Rose Pinner had moved in with Rice after she buried her husband and they looked forward to formalizing their union when the itinerant clergyman passed their way.[17] Rice expected to recover from his illness, and he optimistically instructed Rose "to looke after his house in his absence." Still, he recognized the very real possibility of his demise and he wanted to protect his new partner's belongings if his estate was inventoried and then liquidated to pay off his debts. Thus he declared that Rose had "brought into his house one Feather bed & boulster one Rugg and two blanketts and pewter dishes" in addition to the highly prized "Iron Kettle." These items and "all the wearing cloathes" that had once belonged to Rice's dead wife were Rose's property, separate from Rice's estate.[18] Rose and Rice chose this unconventional, albeit temporary, living arrangement because they knew how short life could be in colonial Maryland; each had buried at least one spouse already.

Rose and Rice delayed their marriage because of the frontier conditions in the new province. While Rose and Rice chose to live together without the benefit of clergy, other partners sought to have their unions publicly recognized in "irregular" ceremonies—without the sacramental blessing of a priest. After having given birth, Elesabeth Lockett testified in court that she and Thomas Bright had followed the English espousal rite—breaking "a peace of munye [a gold or silver coin] . . . betwext" them, in front of witnesses.[19] To be sure, Elesabeth must have hoped that the couple would, at the very least, rejoin the two coin halves in a clandestine ceremony sometime after the initial rite and then live together as husband and wife before her baby was born.[20] The court would have recognized this traditional coin-breaking ritual as a legal and binding contract had Thomas not already been legally married to another woman. Of course we cannot determine whether or not Thomas really was married at the time. In England the ecclesiastical courts were sometimes tricked into voiding legal marriages through jactitation, in which a third party falsely alleged that the spouse petitioning for a separation had already been married to him or her. When ecclesiastical courts pronounced a marriage null and void for ignoring accepted legal requirements, any offspring produced by the couple were then recognized as illegitimate (which prohibited them from claiming any inheritance) and the couple had no property rights stemming from the relationship.

Other examples of irregular marriages proved by citing the traditional espousal rite of breaking a gold or silver coin exist. Yet it is difficult to uncover how extensive irregular marriages were in the province, since we gain a glimpse into these unions only when they appear in the legal records, as in the case of Mary Cole and Joseph Edlow's contested marriage.[21] A layman named Thomas Seamor "read the prayer and the matrimony" from the Arminian Anglican Book of Common Prayer, as a priest would have done, to join Joseph and Mary as husband and wife before they "did lie together." Attempting to establish the legitimacy of the proceedings, Samuell Gosey testified that "he heard Seamor say that he read more than the minister used to read." This particular example was preserved in the official provincial documents because Mary, an indentured servant, had failed to get the approval of her master, Henry Coursey, before committing herself to Joseph. Mary further complicated the matter by already being married to Thomas Breamstead.[22]

Certainly other couples allowed laymen to join them together in irregular marriages, and they may have lived as common-law husbands and wives for their entire lives without incident, just as couples did back in England. In Maryland (as in England) irregular marriages were recognized as legitimate, indissoluble unions even though no licensing or solemnization took place. As long as they had exchanged words signifying a verbal contract (preferably in front of at least two witnesses) and lived in the community as a married couple, men and women considered themselves married for life. Their communities recognized these unions as legally binding as long as the partners were consenting free adults and their unions did not violate the incest taboos outlined in the "Table of Kindred and Affinity" (figure 1). Couples joined in irregular marriage thought of their offspring as legitimate and they distributed family property in much the same way that "regularly" married folks did. Such marriages must have been fairly common in the province, for in 1702, while Maryland was under the temporary control of the Crown, the Crown passed "An Act for the establishment of religious worship in this Province," insisting "That Marriages forbidden by the Table of Marriages of the Church of England be not performed," and "that no marriage be performed by a layman in any Parish where a Minister or Incumbent shall reside."[23]

These intriguing examples of dysfunctional and irregular marriages indicate a wide range of means by which men and women shared their lives and property in the early modern province of Maryland. However, an examination of the "regular" marriages and the kinship networks they formed will underscore the larger thesis of this book about diverse religious customs in early modern Maryland. English society had long promoted legal marriages for the maintenance of an orderly society which, in turn, encouraged property ownership and capital accumulation. When enough property was involved, couples (then as well as now) recognized the need for legally and religiously sanctioned marriages to ensure that their estates would be preserved for their children and future generations, rather than wasted in funding legal disputes. Additionally, by participating in traditional religious marriage rites, new families established themselves as conforming church members, confirming and securing their status and position in the larger community. No less important to many of these families was the religious significance of marriage as a holy sacrament that symbolized their spiritual unity with God.

Most landholding men and women in Maryland chose their life-long partners with care and did so largely free from overt parental coercion. Governor Calvert's letter to Lord Baltimore in 1672 expressed this limited freedom: "I am sorry my [cousin] Lukner thinkes not of Marryinge yett, because that Match would have Brought a great deale of Honnour besid[e]s the Advantages of a Plentifull fortune."[24] Mothers and fathers—presumably confident that their successful parenting strategies meant they could rely on their children's judgments—allowed their children a great deal of personal choice when it came to selecting marriage partners.[25] This custom indicates that many early Marylanders accepted the dictates of (Catholic) canon law in this regard. As long as two consenting adults were not breaking any incest taboos, a priest would marry them without parental confirmation. Priests were not under any obligation to even inform parents of the marriage.

Following this tradition, which was based on the ubiquitous belief in free will, less than five percent of the 3190 testators leaving wills between 1634 and 1713 in Maryland sought to limit their children's selection of a mate. These few cases included testators who had serious misgivings concerning a particular candidate. Jane Long, for instance, left her daughter Tabitha twenty thousand pounds of tobacco, a bed, and some livestock, but only if she did not marry George Chaney. Another testator, John Phillips,

A MAN MAY NOT MARRY HIS	A WOMAN MAY NOT MARRY HER
1. Grandmother	1. Grandfather
2. Grandfather's wife	2. Grandmother's husband
3. Wife's grandmother	3. Husband's grandfather
4. Father's sister	4. Father's brother
5. Mother's sister	5. Mother's brother
6. Father's brother's wife	6. Father's sister's husband
7. Mother's brother's wife	7. Mother's sister's husband
8. Wife's father's sister	8. Husband's father's brother
9. Wife's mother's sister	9. Husband's mother's brother
10. Mother	10. Father
11. Step-mother	11. Step-father
12. Wife's mother	12. Husband's father
13. Daughter	13. Son
14. Wife's daughter	14. Husband's son
15. Son's wife	15. Daughter's husband
16. Sister	16. Brother
17. Wife's sister	17. Husband's brother
18. Brother's wife	18. Sister's husband
19. Son's daughter	19. Son's son
20. Daughter's daughter	20. Daughter's son
21. Son's son's wife	21. Son's daughter's husband
22. Wife's son's daughter	22. Daughter's daughter's husband
23. Daughter's son's wife	23. Husband's son's son
24. Wife's daughter's daughter	24. Husband's daughter's son
25. Brother's daughter	25. Brother's son
26. Sister's daughter	26. Sister's son
27. Brother's son's wife	27. Brother's daughter's husband
28. Sister's son's wife	28. Sister's daughter's husband
29. Wife's brother's daughter	29. Husband's brother's son
30. Wife's sister's daughter	30. Husband's sister's son

1. Table of Kindred and Affinity

stipulated that his sons Thomas and Bennony "shall not Marry w[i]th any of [John] Robsons daughters" or the boys would not collect their inheritance.[26] These examples might represent parental efforts to discourage a child from shackling him- or herself to a mate with a serious character flaw, or the interference might be motivated by a family feud over disputed property. In either case, these limited numbers of parental restrictions found in the testamentary evidence usually focused on a single individual or clan and suggest to us that if parents influenced their children's decisions, the interference was normally much more subtle than in these examples.

Less intrusive were the parental stipulations that children must choose partners who professed the same faith or obtain the consent of a guardian or the surviving parent to wed. Mareen Duvall left his ten children portions of a huge estate when he died, cautioning that if his unmarried offspring "shall inter Marry with any particular person without the knowledge and advice or Consent of [my wife] that then it shall be left to the Discretion of my [wife] wether to assisst them with the aforesaid moneys that is bequeathed and granted to them."[27] Most Marylanders who sought to influence their children's marriage decisions, however, expressed the less constraining sentiments of Widower George Allumby, who simply asked his daughter Dorothy to take on the responsibility and ownership of the family estate when she was seventeen or when she married, "provided she marry not und[e]r Sixteene yeares of age."[28] Marylanders generally adhered, like most English people, to a central Catholic tenet—marriage could only take place when the couple entered into it of their own free will. Any evidence of compulsion would be grounds for an annulment.

Joan Scott and Louise Tilly, in their classic work *Women, Work, and the Family,* suggest that while parents allowed their children to choose their spouses without overt pressure, they limited their children's choices by restricting the pool of potential partners. These parents sought to preserve social status and wealth by allying their children with a limited group of similarly wealthy families. Thus, "parental consent functioned as a verification of the couple's resources." Yet Patricia Seed in her study of colonial Mexico argues persuasively that religious beliefs determined whether or not parental consent was sought when couples wanted to marry. Calvinists, with their "emphasis on . . . fathers . . . and the patriarchal family," stressed obedience "even if a marriage were contrary to what the child wanted or needed." On the other hand, Arminian Anglicans and Roman Catholics, in keeping with their free-will theology, granted their children the "right to marry of their own free will." This fundamental difference suggests that Calvinists "granted civil authorities the right to regulate all aspects of marriage" while the Free Will Christians thought that marriage was a private affair.[29] This framework, as we shall see, seems to fit the Maryland situation.

We gain a rare glimpse into the colonists' courtship rituals through George Alsop's observations in 1666, intended to promote immigration to the new colony. He described the young men as "confident, reservedly subtle, quick in apprehending, but slow in resolving." He, and others, could not help but notice how practical and acquisitive these men were, who could "spy profit sailing towards them" quicker than men could back home. Maryland women were very similar in this respect. This pragmatic and entrepreneurial society extended its practicality to courtship rites. When approached by a potential marriage partner women were "bashful at the first view, but after a continuance of time hath brought them acquainted, there they become discreetly familiar, and are much more talkative then men." Marylanders had jettisoned the very formal rites of courtship found in wealthy circles back in England. Here women preferred "plain wit" and not "the Tautologies of a long-winded speech" that traditionally turned women's heads. Without such straightforward discourse a man would "fall under the contempt of her frown, and his own windy Oration."[30] Alsop's observations suggest that couples had a good deal of freedom in selecting an appropriate mate of "plain wit."

An unsuccessful courtship preserved in the provincial court records reveals colonial expectations regarding this rite of passage. Robert Harwood, evidently physically attracted to young Elizabeth Gary, followed her around, softening her heart with his "plain wit" and declarations of his love for her. After a year of this, Robert went with Elizabeth to collect vegetables from her mother's garden and there he persuaded her to "lie with him." Her family did not appear to have been concerned when the couple failed to return in a timely fashion. During the previous year, Robert and Elizabeth had probably engaged in love play, fondling, or other public displays of affection that would have suggested to the community and Elizabeth's family that they intended to marry.[31] English culture, generally speaking, accepted sexual relations between betrothed couples. Elizabeth, however, did not want to marry Robert, which is why this case came to the court's attention. Following sexual intercourse, Robert told her that she neither should "nor could have any other man but him," yet Elizabeth had not been interested in marrying him before the "filthy act he committed with [her]" and had no intention of marrying him after the "filthy act." Robert believed that their physical union would impel his beloved to marry him when his "plain wit" apparently was not doing the trick. Elizabeth's refusal to marry Robert after their "filthy act" presented a problem for Elizabeth's family. Anxious to have the matter settled, her stepfather, Peter Sharpe, drew up a contract with Robert stipulating that he would have six weeks to convince Elizabeth to marry him, and if she still refused, Robert would have to leave her alone. Their meetings would be chaperoned to ensure that Elizabeth's decision was based not on hormonal desires or unfair coercion but on "plain wit."[32] This unusual courtship underscores a landholding family's insistence upon marriage relationships based on love and companionship.

The lack of compulsion in Maryland encouraged most young women entering marriage as landholders to cultivate partnerships based on love and companionship—as in the Smith and Lytfoot cases.[33] In 1678 Arminian Anglican priest John Yeo described a woman who deeply loved her husband. Probably because Mrs. Smith could not write, Yeo wrote to Henry Smith, who was attending to business in New York, that "Mrs Smith presents her Affections to you, she is mightily troubled at your absence."[34] Others thought so much of their life-long companions that they used sacred terms when referring to them. Completely devoted to his wife, Rebecca, Catholic Thomas Lytfoot referred to her as his "most loving & affectionat comforter on this Earth," equating her, his earthly comforter, with the Holy Ghost, his "Holy Comforter."[35] Thus, for his survival on earth and his eternal salvation after his death, Thomas Lytfoot depended upon the love of both his wife and the Holy Ghost.

The devotional literature in the library of the Neales, a leading Catholic family, contains many references to the religious marriage of souls with Christ, and in these we can uncover the prescriptive views of Maryland Roman Catholics on marriage. The author of *A Memorial of a Christian Life* (1688) described the ideals that formed the foundation of an English Roman Catholic marriage, stating, "Behold, the Bridegroom [Christ] cometh, go forth to meet him. For in effect, there is no Sacrament, in which our Lord so openly declares himself to be the Bridegroom of our Souls, as in the Sacrament of the Eucharist; its proper Effect is to unite to him the Soul of the Communicant, and to make of two but one thing; which is indeed a spiritual Alliance. That you may then go forth to meet this Bridegroom . . . He comes to you, full of Charity, Goodness, Sweetness, and Mercy."[36] In addition to contributing to our understanding of English Catholic theology, this text, and others like it, intimates the spiritual ideal behind marriage and the expectation that marriage would be a gratifying partnership and an "Alliance." Katherine Digby, in her manuscript of spiritual exercises, described a true believer's marriage with God as a sensual, mutually satisfying relationship between lovers.[37] Catholic sermons given in Maryland also insisted on marital partnership. Jesuit priest Peter Attwood portrayed fathers and mothers as tender partners when he preached in the province. Attwood insisted that children recognize both their parents as co-authorities to be reckoned with, though they possessed the patience and forgiveness of Jesus, the Blessed Virgin Mary, the Holy Ghost, and God. And if the admonitions in these sermons accurately reflected social behavior, these marriage partners engaged in pleasurable and sensual "delights" as well.[38]

Jesuits, strategically stationed throughout the province, officiated at the marriages of white English Catholics and any Arminian Anglicans who sought their sacral rites. These Jesuits also encouraged Native Americans to convert and then blessed their unions by marrying them according to the sacramental rites of the church. Moreover, Jesuits insisted that their black slaves be formally married, even if they had to purchase a slave's mate from another owner in order to accomplish this. Marriage was one of the seven holy sacraments for these Catholics and the ceremony emphasized the participants' renewal and ratification of their special relationship to God as an outward and visible sign of the partners' internal grace. Because it was a sacrament, the Catholic Church considered marriage indissoluble. Catholics were also forbidden to marry during certain times of the year. An old verse outlines the seasonal restrictions: "When Advent comes do thou refraine / Till Hillary set thee free again/ Next Septuagesima saith thee nay / But when Low Sunday comes thou may/ Yet at Rogation thou must tarrie / Till Trinitie shall bid thee marry." A fifteenth-century English lawyer suggested that marriage contracts could be drawn up during these periods, but matrimony was not to be solemnized "from the first Sunday in Advent until the octave of Epiphany exclusive; and from Septuagesima Sunday to the first Sunday after Easter inclusive; and from the first Rogation day until the 7th day after Pentecost inclusive."[39] Accordingly, most Roman Catholics married immediately after Easter, in June, or in December.[40] Ceremonies often took place on Sunday mornings so that most of the community could witness the rite in a reasonably sober state. It is no coincidence, therefore, that Calvinist Puritans avoided Sunday weddings and had no restrictions on the time of day of a wedding in their never-ending efforts to distance themselves from "popish" practices.

According to English custom, after a couple agreed to marry, the man gave the woman a betrothal ring to wear on her right hand. This ring was often inscribed with a loving phrase that stated the partners' commitment to each other. Marylanders followed this custom, for numerous examples of such rings have been unearthed at Historic St. Mary's City. Traditionally, the signing of the dowry contract in front of witnesses followed the ring-giving ritual; in Maryland, a will could serve as the written confirmation of an oral dowry contract. Wealthy Catholic Henry Darnell employed his will to confirm the many marriage contracts he had made for his daughters. Promises had been made to potential in-laws and his will outlined them. He wrote, "Itt is my will that whereas I have marryed unto the land Mr Clement

Hill my Daughter Ann Darnall and upon the Said marriage have entered with him & Mr Clement Hill Senr. into certain articles it is I say my will & I doe hereby appoint order and Empower my Exec[u]t[or] [his son] hereafter Named fully to performe all the Said articles to all Intents and Purposes."[41]

On the day of the sacramental ceremony, the officiating priest celebrated Mass and, after the consecration of the Eucharist, gave a nuptial benediction while the couple stood under a cloth or veil (called a pallium). The betrothal ring was blessed by the priest and transferred from the woman's right to her left hand. As the newlyweds left the church they were crowned and a wedding breakfast of blessed wine, cake, biscuits, or bread was served at the church. Back in England these festive celebrations often got so out of hand that a publication advised people not to allow children to attend weddings, "for nowadays one can learn nothing there but ribaldry and foul words."[42]

The vast majority of Arminian Anglican men and women who owned or stood to inherit real estate sought a religiously sanctioned legal union that closely mirrored the Roman Catholic one. Arminian Anglican Robert Ridgly acknowledged this in his will when he wrote, "my Dear and well beloved wife Martha Ridgly with whom I joined myself in the face of God refusing all other women in the blessed Estate of Honable wedlock by whom also by the blessing of God I have now 3 sons and one Daughter living."[43] The candlelight wedding of the young William Dent and his bride Elizabeth Fowke sheds some light on colonists' wishes to recreate the solemn ritual and festive celebrations of marriage they had enjoyed in England. Arminian Anglican priest John Turlinge—fully licensed by "the Hon'ble Wm Diggs Esq." to perform marriages in the province—officiated at the ceremony in Elizabeth's mother's home on February 8, 1684/5. If this couple followed English tradition, William transferred Elizabeth's espousal ring from her right hand to her left thumb, then to her second, third, and fourth fingers (thought to contain the vein that led directly to her heart), while reciting "In the name of the Father, Son, and Holy Ghost, Amen."[44] This particular young couple shared their happiness with family and friends by inviting "Mrs. Anne Fowke, Coll. William Chandler Mad'm Mary Chandler Mr. Gerard Fowke Mrs Mary Fowke Owen Newen & Divers others" to attend both the ceremony and the subsequent feast.[45] These relatives and friends may have donned the traditional rosemary or bay leaves meant to ensure the couple's happiness.

The Arminian Anglican Book of Common Prayer used in the wedding ceremony followed the Catholic Sarum Missal's nuptial rites quite closely, with a few minor adaptations. Like the Catholics, Arminian Anglicans were subject to the requirement, first promulgated by Pope Nicholas in 866, to make four public announcements, called banns, of the couple's intention to marry. These banns allowed any member of the community to object to the union if the couple were known to be related to each other or if one of the betrothed had already promised him- or herself to another partner. For the Roman Catholics these announcements were made during the regular church services preceding the wedding. The Arminian Anglicans followed this procedure, but allowed the fourth to be made during the marriage ceremony itself. In Maryland, these banns also played an essential economic role. Before solemnization, the public posting of banns was a way to ensure that no minors, couples "within the forbidden degrees of consanguinity" (i.e., related to each other), or "precontracted" people (indentured servants or those already promised to another) would marry. An indentured servant's "unfree" status would make a marriage illegal unless the master had consented to the union. After 1658 a couple had to post banns three weeks prior to solemnization, allowing for any objections to be made public, and then they obtained a certificate declaring their free status that entitled them to marry.[46]

The Arminian Anglicans also strayed from tradition when the priest said a prayer for the couple as the betrothal ring was transferred to the left hand during the (pallium-less) ceremony rather than blessing the ring with holy water, as a Catholic priest would have done. Influenced by the Lutherans, Anglican authorities had also added the phrase "those whom God hath joined, let no man put asunder" to the traditional rite in the Book of Common Prayer. Finally, the Arminian Anglican priest delivered a sermon on married life and the newlyweds left the church without being crowned. Despite these minor alterations, the rites were similar enough that an Arminian Anglican couple might seek the sanctification of their union by a Roman Catholic priest—since both groups believed that marriage was a holy sacrament—if the short supply of Arminian Anglican priests meant a long delay in completing their marriage plans.

The English Puritans, on the other hand, embraced a very different set of rituals, and their conception of marriage was radically different from that of the Arminian Anglicans and Roman Catholics. This difference stands out most clearly in the Puritans' refusal to use the Book of Common Prayer because of its "popish" origins. In fact, when they came to power in England the Puritans eliminated the book's use in religious services in 1645 and replaced it with *The Directory of Public Worship*, which cleansed religious worship of all the Roman Catholic–derived ceremonies and rites. This leads us to believe that the Puritans (and other Calvinists) in Maryland did not follow the Book of Common Prayer during a formal wedding ceremony. And since the Calvinists reduced the number of sacraments from seven (baptism, confirmation, the Eucharist, penance, extreme unction, ordination, and matrimony) to two (baptism and the Lord's Supper), they stripped the wedding ceremony of its religious significance by making it merely a secular, legal union. Because they refused to recognize "popish" canon law, it was the Puritans who initiated the first *civil* directive in England (1645) making three banns mandatory before a valid marriage could take place.[47] Taking the secularization of marriage to its ultimate conclusion, partners in incestuous marriages were guilty of a felony in England by 1650. An incestuous marriage and the children it produced were not recognized by the state, and the couple could face death sentences if brought to court for their illegal act. And while no one in Maryland was executed for marrying his or her relative, we can assume that Calvinists in early Maryland supported the secularization of marriage, since they detested anything that smacked of "popery" and they supported the Interregnum regime. We might also assume that Calvinists in early Maryland adopted Oliver Cromwell's 1653 decision that marriages would be civil ceremonies performed by a magistrate—not a minister or priest—in the presence of two witnesses.[48] Not surprisingly, the use of a ring was forbidden.[49]

Whether a Puritan couple sought a civil magistrate or engaged Arminian Anglicans or Catholics chose a priest to officiate at their wedding— at the cost of one hundred and twenty pounds of tobacco—the Maryland Assembly decided that the traditional vows should be recited. The Assembly required that each and every couple wishing to be legally married hold hands before at least two witnesses and repeat the following words: "I [name] doe take thee [spouse's name] to my wedded [wife or husband] To have and to hould from this day forward for better or worse for Rich or for Poore in Sickness & in health till death us do part and thereto I plight thee my troth." After this the priest or magistrate declared, "I being hereunto by law authorised doe pronounce you lawful man and wife."[50]

Quakers in the province, like the Arminian Anglicans and Roman Catholics and unlike the Puritans, sought religiously sanctioned marriages. Quaker Meeting records reveal that when two people decided to marry they first approached the Men's and Women's Meetings to ask for permission. This had to be done in person and repeated the following month, and then the couple submitted a formal written request to marry. This procedure, similar to the English banns, allowed the entire adult community to pass judgment on the proposed union while it also gave the young couple time to think about their important decision. The Quakers focused on other issues as well as incestuous relationships and prior commitments to other people. Were the two candidates well suited to each other? Did they realize the magnitude of the commitment they were undertaking or were they merely acting impulsively, out of physical attraction? An English Quaker marriage manual suggested that God's answers to these questions would be revealed during the three-month waiting period. The author cautioned men and women to "be watchful that you run not forth in a hasty eager mind among your selves, but waite that ye may have clearnesse in the counsel of the Lord."[51] Presumably the three-month-long process assured the community that the couple took their commitment seriously and that God had confirmed the union. Convinced of their sincerity and the desirability of the match, the community gathered to witness the formal wedding ceremony, as it did for William Southbee and Eliza Read in 1668. At Isaac Abrahms's house William "solemnly in the fear of God, took Elizabeth Read . . . spinster, to be his wife; and she, the said Elizabeth Read, did then and there, in the like manner, take the said William Southbee to be her husband, each of them promising to be faithful to each other."[52] Those attending the ceremony dutifully signed their names as witnesses in the Meeting's record book.

The Quakers' requirement of a three-month-long process—approximately three times the minimum waiting period for Arminian Anglicans and Catholics—underlines their disdain of the notions of love at first sight, overwhelming passion between two people, and sex with non-Quakers. Influential Quakers on both sides of the Atlantic stressed, in both speeches and writings, the importance of marrying within the faith. William Smith presented a blissful picture of marriage between two Quakers in his advice manual when he wrote that "The Honourable Marriage is in the Seed of God, Male and Female in the seed are one, and lies down together in the bed undefiled, where God blesseth them and their Seeds Seed for ever." He warned his readers to beware "lest the Sons and daughters of strangers [non-Quakers] entice any of your minds to join with them, and so you goe into the defiled bed and loose the honour."[53] This message did not fall on deaf ears, yet not every young couple followed this advice, either. Quaker Rachel Hall, for instance, married Arminian Anglican Walter Smith in 1686 and they lived happily together for twenty-five years before Walter died. Rachel and Walter's "disorderly" union was not as unusual as the Maryland Quaker leaders would have liked. Cleaving to the canon law requirement that couples must enter into unions of their own free will, Quaker Meeting record books exhorted young people not to "go disorderly together in

Marriage" or "go to the Priest or Magistrate to be Married."[54] More than a few young Quakers, whether wishing to marry a "stranger" or simply eager to marry before the waiting period had ended, sought out priests like Arminian Anglican James Clayland, who gladly performed the sacred ritual for a fee.

These prohibitions highlight the Quaker belief that sexual purity and a marriage partnership between two devoted Quakers were necessary for the indwelling of the Holy Spirit. Quaker prescriptive literature also admonished couples for "Hunt[ing] after one another and then Leave[ing] one another [to] goe to Others."[55] English Quaker William Smith agreed when he suggested that the "Covenant of Marriage is to be preserved by not allowing your eyes to wander." Remaining faithful to a partner might ensure that "you will die a satisfied, content person." Quaker marriage partners need not be equals in "outward substance" (wealth) or close in age, but they would be happy if they were "thus joined together of the Lord, & abides faithful with him, his blessing rests upon them every way, & he preserves them."[56]

Non-Quaker English marriage manuals came to the same conclusions about the importance of love. Love at first sight, marrying for money, and marrying to please one's parents were not recipes for happy unions. One author adamantly warned parents not to arrange marriages for their children. If they dealt "with their Childrens Marriages, as they do with their Fruit Trees," parents would "soon find, that the Minister can only joyn their hands, but 'tis the free-will offering of the heart, that can only unite and Graft their affections together." Moreover, "this free-will offering is to be led by Love, not drawn by the Cords of Wedlock, for the Will is a free faculty, and consequently cannot be forcibly determined to any act, but yet is capable of admitting perswasions, and inducements, and so may be by them inclin'd but without them cannot be forced."[57] Once a proper mate was selected, the couple ought to be "as two oxen that draw together in one yoke." Manuals also argued that because "two eyes see more than one [and] two hands despatch more business than one," a wife should be an economic partner as well.[58]

Unlike the Quaker literature, other English manuals condemned the marriage of an older woman to a younger man and the equally "unnatural" union between an old man and a young woman. One author described both of these "unnatural" conditions as "Match[es] fitter to make sport for others, than to raise joy to themselves," for only partners with similar sexual appetites and physical abilities could find true happiness here on earth.[59] Thus it was important for partners to be reasonably close in age. In practice,

English men and women tended to select mates that were similar in age, and they married for the first time when they were in their mid- to late twenties, unless they were from the very wealthiest families. However, in Maryland, where high mortality rates throughout the seventeenth century disrupted the normal English marriage patterns, sixteen-year-old girls occasionally married considerably older men, sometimes with foreseeable results.[60] Perhaps more than a few of these young Maryland brides found sexual fulfillment in extramarital affairs, if we can rely on the examples discussed at the beginning of this chapter found in the court records and the land-naming practices in the province that provide clues about female behavior. An inordinate number of land parcels with names like "Cuckold Maker's Palace," "Cuckold's Delight," "Cuckold's Desire," "Cuckold's Hope," "Cuckold's Mess," "Cuckold's Point," and "Cuckold's Rest" suggests a significant level of frustration with female infidelity amongst some Maryland husbands.[61]

This frustration with female infidelity did not, however, afflict the entire society. Although Maryland was not a matrilineal society, Marylanders did value the contributions of females in the formation of new families. After all, fathers often left their young daughters real estate that would become theirs when they reached sixteen or when they married. When the wealthy colonist Ignatius Causine gave his daughter Jane, Jr., one hundred and fifty acres of land if she chose to marry a propertyless man, he allowed Jane to enter marriage from a position of authority.[62] A daughter combined her wealth with that of a chosen mate's and the new couple worked to increase the estate in order to provide legacies for their children. Owning land at marriage entitled women to exert power within the family, as we see in the will of Arminian Anglican Henry Hyde, who gave his "Loving wife Frances" total control of their estate "for the Childrens use during her life *with as much freedom as it were I my self in my lifetime* [emphasis added]."[63] When a husband died, he left his wife at least one-third of the estate—and in many cases much more than that—"to be absolutely att the disposall and discression of my Said wife . . . to doe with the Same what shall seeme good unto her."[64] A widow normally remarried soon after her husband's decease to form a new partnership and household as well as to augment the original family's coffers.

With the death of a second husband a widow ideally had accumulated a substantial estate—including wealth from her father and husbands—which she, in turn, passed down to her children.[65] Men allowed women this option, for we see their testamentary patterns supporting it. Accordingly, Katharine Wright's husband, Arthur, acquiesced to her demand that he revise his will to ensure her ability to accumulate wealth. Lawyer Michael Miller testified that when Katharine asked him if her husband's will protected her rights "to hold the Land" and he replied that it was not foolproof, she then "desired this Deponent [Miller] to aske him [Arthur] if he would make another will" to ensure Katharine's complete control over their estate.[66] Arthur, accepting his wife's objections, agreed to a new will. Arthur and Katharine's story seems to confirm the seventeenth-century statement made by Sir Charles Cornwallis: "From the time of Adam (whoe had the firste taste of the force of a womans perswasions) untill this daye, many more wilbe found perswaded by their wives, then wives by their Husbands."[67]

The vast majority of legally married partners stayed together for the duration of their lives and began producing children soon after their nuptials.[68] Pregnancy held out the hope of creating healthy, sensible heirs that could continue the family name and provide valuable labor during the farm-building stage of colonial development.[69] Puritans in England seem to have placed a particularly strong emphasis on having children. Many prominent early modern English Puritan ministers, such as Robert Cleaver, Henry Smith, William Perkins, Alexander Nicholes, and William Gouge, stressed procreation as the primary purpose of marriage.[70] The women and men in Maryland who wrote about pregnancy chose gender-inclusive terms—couched in biblical phrases—when referring to their unborn offspring, speaking of a woman being "with child" or of having a "child in my wives womb."[71] Colonists occasionally mentioned the possibility of having twins, as did John Carrington when he wrote, "the Child or Children that my wife now goeth with."[72] Maryland will writers—particularly Arminian Anglicans, Quakers, and Roman Catholics—hoped for healthy children without articulating a strong preference for male heirs. Testators expressing a desire for male children in New England wills did so when they adhered to a patriarchal hierarchy in which male children were more valued for their ability to continue a family name or provide for their parents in their old age. English historian Amy Louise Erickson has noted an English pattern similar to Maryland's, in that "An overt preference for boy children in early modern England [was] relatively rare."[73]

Marylanders thought of their offspring as children from the time of quickening—when a mother first felt fetal movement—until they became adults.[74] Quakers and Roman Catholics seemed to mention pregnancy more frequently than other testators did, though only a small number of wills referred to the possibility at all. This is peculiar, considering the large number of children women bore during their lifetime. High mortality rates probably kept many parents from placing too much emphasis on the prospect of another pregnancy, as we see in the will of Quaker John Hance.[75] In a codicil to his will, John added,

> And whereas my wife soposes her self to be with Child my will is that if She be now with Child & that it Shall Live to attain its full age to Receive a portion according to Law. . . . In Case my Daughter Elizabeth Shall happen to dye before She attain her full age and without Lawfull Issue of her body that then her part & portion of my Estate as above shall be to the Child my wife Expects She Goes with but if my wife be not now w[i]th Child or if She be & the Child dye before itt Shall attain its full age according to Law then my son Benjamin & his heirs to have all the Right.[76]

Quaker Thomas Everendon aptly summed up the process of child-rearing as "a pilgrimage of Tears" in this era when nearly one-third of the infants born did not live to see their first birthday.[77]

This stark reality, however, did not prevent parents from bonding with their children. Early modern English literature abounds with examples of warm and affectionate relationships between children and their parents. In England Anne Dormer, for instance, wrote to her son in 1691, calling him her "first love" that she valued "above her own flesh."[78] This was replicated in the Catholic province, where Marylanders also expressed their love for their children above most others.[79] Widow Elizabeth Harper felt the same about her granddaughters and grandsons, as she left each one some livestock "in Consideration of the naturall Love I beare unto" them.[80] Children returned parental love as well, despite the great separation colonists often endured; this was true of Catholic Robert Lee, who sent his tobacco profits to England for his "dear Father Michall Lee and my dear Mother Christian."[81]

Mothers and fathers afforded their children love, but they also felt obligated to give their children an education, clothing, and food during their minority in addition to part of the family legacy when both parents died.[82] When Sarah Corkee, mother of nine, wrote her will, unlimited financial assistance was not part of the bargain. Her son Thomas had borrowed money from her and she had expected him to pay her back in full. Sarah felt no obligation to pay her son's way in life indefinitely.[83]

Occasionally, parents did not fulfill the responsibility implied by parenthood, and a grandparent stepped in. Arminian Anglican grandmother Eleanor Howard was distraught over the living conditions of her grandchildren after the death of their father. Her grown children probably expected to receive equal shares of both Eleanor's land and her personal effects after her death, but Eleanor had another plan in mind. She made up a will several years before her death, after taking into consideration "the frailty & uncertainty of Life, & desireous that the small worldly substance wherenwith God has blest one beyond my Deserts may not after my decease be the Least occasion of Discord amongst my Children."[84] She tried to justify her desire to leave her entire estate to her grandchildren by reminding her grown children that she had already given them "such part of my worldly substance . . . as could in Reason be spared from my owne Support." She blamed her inept deceased son-in-law for the change in plan. As Orlando, Sophia, Charles, and William's grandmother, she felt that she had to step in after their father failed to provide for them, leaving them in a deplorable "Low Destitute condition." We might safely assume that Eleanor's disgust with her deceased son-in-law, preserved for all time in her will, was not a feeling that she kept to herself. This fact serves to underscore the cultural belief that parents had a moral responsibility to provide the children they brought into this world with basic necessities and the means to become independent when they were allowed to strike out on their own.

Much to the dismay of Eleanor and her grown children, Orlando, Sophia, Charles, and William became a financial burden to the extended family because of their father's inadequacies. But for most families children represented an important economic investment in this early modern world. Marriage was largely centered on the procreation of children because children secured the continuation of the family and provided essential labor in an agricultural economy. To ensure that they would profit from their investment in their children's welfare parents customarily tied their children to the family until boys reached twenty-one and girls sixteen. Parents expressed their children's familial responsibilities in terms of enslavement and ownership that may seem morally questionable to today's readers but that accurately described the realities of the seventeenth century. James Anderson of Dorchester County instructed "that my Children maybe Sett free at the age of Eighteen,"[85] but Catholic Sarah Syms O'Neal was not willing to wait until her son John turned eighteen. Sarah wanted him to "be from the very moment of my death free and at his own disposal to act in all things as [owner of] his Estate but with my obligations on him as he does me."[86] This "freeing" of children did, in fact, imply ownership by the parent, but the larger issue was control of the child's labor rather than his or her person.[87] The parent-child relationship revolved around a mutual and reciprocal set of obligations binding one individual to another unequivocally, particularly during a child's nonage.

Parents expected their children to provide a great deal of labor and to feel a considerable sense of obligation to the family until they left this world. In Maryland Widower Allexander Williams wished to preserve the family's legacy for future generations and his instructions to his son Charles reflected children's obligation to fulfill a parent's wishes. Williams stipulated in his will, "I give and bequeath unto my s[ai]d sonn charles all wholly and singularly such debts as are now due or owe unto me from any p[er]son or p[er]sons willing and requiring him my said son as a dying father that dearly loves him to take and follow the advice of my Executors at all times as occation shall require & nott prodigally or Extravagantly to make away the Estate left and bestowed upon him."[88] And John Porter's last wishes typify a pattern of allowing a wife to decide whether or not the children had fulfilled their family obligations. If Porter's children worked hard enough, his wife could reward them accordingly. He wrote, "I Do Give & bequeath all the remaining part of my Estate that it be Equally Devided between my af[oresai]d Loveing wife and my Children born of her body Each an Equall Proportion and it is my will & Desire that my Sons continue with their Mother while they attaine to the age of twenty one years & ye Girles untill they attaine unto the age of Sixteene." He further stipulated, "if my Said wife Shall think fitt to Sett Either of my Children at their Liberty as She Shall think Meet paying them their Proportion of my Estate at their Going off from her."[89]

Likewise, Roman Catholic John Parsons expressed similar sentiments when he gave his wife the "care and tuition and government of my said children till they attain the said age of one and twenty years and I doe hereby will and require my said Children to be dutifull and obedient to their said mother and to stay and live with her and assist her with their labour till they shall come to their said age of one and twenty years unless she my said wife shall otherwise for the good of any my said children shall permit them to leave her or consent to their departure leaveing them in that case to her discretion and prudence."[90] Many times, children continued to fulfill their mother's labor requirements until she died. This parental entitlement to offspring's labor often extended to all the dependents residing in the household, including nieces and nephews.[91]

Children's obligations to their families only ended when they died. Children, regardless of age, were a reflection of their family and therefore they were expected to behave accordingly. These colonists brought this notion with them from England.[92] When Englishman George Alsop left for Maryland he reminded his brother of his duty to their parents. He instructed him to always show "Respect and Reverence to your aged Parents, that while they live they may have comfort of you, and when that God shall sound a retreat to their lives, that there they may with their gray hairs in joy go down to their Graves."[93] This duty to one's family applied to the extended family as well. Governor Charles Calvert wrote to his father, Lord Baltimore, "I am heartily sorry to heare that my Cozen [Sir William] Talbot hath so behaved himself both towards yo[u]r Lo[rdshi]pp and his mother, and truly I must Confesse that in this he hath much Deceived me in my thoughts of him, for I alwayes supposed him to be a person of that honor and worth, that unkindnes to a mother, and ingratitude to a Relac[io]n that had so much oblidged him as yo[u]r Lo[rdshi]pp had beene much below the Generosity of his Temper."[94] As punishment for this bad behavior, Lord Baltimore revoked Talbot's commission and told him not to return to Maryland. Sir William Talbot's story reveals the close scrutiny family members fell under despite their age and status in the society.

When children failed to live up to their end of the reciprocal arrangement mandated by the customary parent/child relationship, parents might exclude them from inheriting. Thomas Pattison's son received a mere "Two Shillings and six pence Sterling" because "he hath suffred and upheld his wife [father, mother, and siblings] to abuse . . . at a most prodigious rate."[95] Only Thomas, Jr.—out of eight natural children and one adopted child— warranted such treatment. With her widow's share of the estate, including "houses and fences Gardens and Orchards Timber Woods and underwoods and my part of Cattle and Hogs there on runing," Ann Pattison continued to exert authority over her dependents, for she controlled the disposal of the family's property. Thomas stipulated that Ann continue to have "full power and Authority to dispose of all or any of my said Lands and personall Estate by her Deeds according to Law or by her will after my decease as she shall think fitt and convenient for the payment of my Just debts and her maintenance dureing her naturall life and to give what of the premisses she shall think fitt to all or any of my Children or Grand Children before or after her decease any law or Custome to the contrary notwithstanding."[96] With the force of two parental authorities to contend with and the hopes of inheriting a portion of the family legacy, few children moved outside the boundaries established by the parent/child relationship.

One of the most persuasive examples of joint parental authority used to extract the cooperation of children lies in the will of Quaker William Stockwell of Talbot County. The Stockwells' eldest son, Thomas, received a mere five shillings because of "his disobedience to God and to his parents." William's wife, Mary, held the estate during her life "and she [was] to dispose of it at her death to Our Children that best deserves it." The parental partnership in this family worked toward the common goal of securing the family's estate. The parents formed a practical strategy, realizing that over the course of time people and circumstances tended to change and that Mary had to have the liberty to manage the family's wealth as the needs of the family shifted. William warned his son John to "live a Godly life" and heed the advice of his mother and "the people of God called Quakers but if he should become a [lewd] man and not take his mothers advise and the afores[ai]d people of God called Quakers then I doe by these presents Impower my wife to dispose of it [their home plantation] as she shall See good and to disinherit him."[97] Offspring recognized this sense of family obligation in their wills as well. Thomas Bale wrote about his "duty" to his mother and sister after leaving his mother sixty pounds sterling and his "Great Silver tankard" as his "Last tender of my Duty."[98]

When four hundred pounds of tobacco was roughly equivalent to one pound sterling and with the cost of food, clothing, and education factored in over the course of their productive years at home, children probably cost a family half as much as day laborers, who might earn approximately twenty pounds of tobacco per day. Hence, children furnished parents with relatively cheap labor. Yet progeny served another fundamental purpose in this early modern province too. Children provided their mothers and fathers with a sense of immortality at a time when death lurked in the dark corners of every household. Naming a child after a parent indicated that the child was not only a reflection but also an extension of the parent, almost as if the parent said, "you are I."[99] Repeatedly in the wills that Marylanders left behind one finds an unbroken chain of actions after individuals died, as if their lives continued through their progeny. Debts were to be settled, land transactions were to be completed, and large tracts of property—endowed with the family name—were to remain intact for generations to come. The unbroken chain of actions included everything from selling and buying land—as exhibited in Thomas Newbold's will—to the general maintenance of the family's plantation—as was true of Richard Kendall's. Newbold asked his "two Eldest Sons Thomas Newbold & William Newbold, by and with the help and assistance of my Loveing wife Jane Newbold to take care to pay for the aforesaid three hundred acres of Land also to assist in building a fiveteen foot Dwelling house on Each part of the Said Land for my two youngest Sons."[100] Other instructions indicated interest in the maintenance of the land for generations to come, as when Richard Kendall requested that his grandson, Daniel Foxwell, "plant an Orchard of one hundred apple Trees upon the" land he bequeathed him and "secure it with a good ffence."[101] Accordingly, fathers entailed the property to ensure that it would remain in the family for generations.[102] Daughters as well as sons were enjoined to preserve the family estate. Humphrey Tilton divided three hundred acres amongst his daughters, "freely to them & their heires of their body forever but if any of my three Daughters should sell morgage or Lease for any Longer Term or Space then seven yeares then such Lands to fall to the other Sister yt shall not so morgage Sell or Lease."[103]

Certainly not every child was named after a mother or father. Naming additional children after other relatives often implied some kind of financial agreement—explicitly stated in some wills, such as those of James Collier and John Willoughby. James Collier left his daughter four hundred acres of land: "my father Robt colliers Dwelling Planta[ti]on Provided yt of my father in Law *George Betts* Doth Give & Confirm unto my Son *George Betts* Collier this Plantation I now Live one upon [emphasis added]."[104] Collier assumed that his son, named for his father-in-law, would become his father-in-law's primary heir. John Willoughby could not have been clearer when he gave his wife Sarah full power to sell or mortgage his estate and stated that it was to pass to her grown son Robert Franklin, Jr., when she died, as long as he "shall hereafter att any time or times happen to have one or more son or sons Lawfully begotten or to be begotten *shall name one of them Willoughby and use utmost Endeavour allways to continue one of that name soe long as he and his heirs Shall Enjoy any part of my Estate* [emphasis added]."[105]

Children's hopes of inheriting family land carried with them the burden of providing labor for the family's welfare, but in this era of high mortality rates children often avoided the added responsibility of caring for elderly parents who were no longer able to care for themselves. When aging parents realized that they might outlive their ability to provide for themselves they negotiated their maintenance with their children and used their will as a contract to confirm the agreement they reached. Aging Catholic John Fossee, in an effort to secure care for himself when he was no longer self-sufficient, wrote his will while still in "good health of body & of sound p[er]fect mind & memory," giving his daughters their expected shares of land and stipulating the particulars of the agreement reached between himself and his son. Fossee stated, "I do make my son Harbart Thomas my Ex[e]c[utor] in full after my deceas[e] . . . [and] unto my Son Herbart do give all my Rents [and] Creditts to him for my life time for to maintaine me w[i]th: good sufficient meate drink & cloathing during my life."[106] The child that bore the burden of caring for an elderly parent often was substantially compensated for doing so. Certainly, this unequal distribution of property between brothers and sisters could have caused a great deal of unrest in any family. Laying out the details of such an arrangement in a will, in a way that pointed out the reasons for the unequal disbursal of wealth, allowed testators an opportunity to mitigate (as much as was humanly possible) sibling discord after their deaths.

We have looked at marriage and at children, the natural product of such unions, in order to understand the personal lives of early Marylanders and the significance of familial relationships. Still, not everyone married in Maryland. The early years found many bachelors in the province—roughly one-third of the male population—because of the large numbers of young male indentured servants that ended up there. Many men simply could not find women to marry in the colony. Yet as extraordinary as it may seem— considering that women made up only about a third of the population— some young women chose not to marry for some of the same reasons that their counterparts did in England. In England during the seventeenth century women who never married made up between 10 and 20 percent of the female population.[107]

Of course, females in Maryland could choose not to marry because their fathers had bequeathed them a tract of land. Quaker William Chapline provides a glimpse into the partial autonomy he was willing to grant his daughter Elizabeth along with her share of the family's land and personal estate: "my will and pleasure is that my Daughter Elizabeth Chpline have her [seat] and her cloathing every way Convenient with washing & lodging here att my now Dwelling house at Patuxent in ffishing Creekes from the time above Said, untill the time of her Marriage or her going away of her own accord."[108] Catholic Joshua Doyne shared Chapline's sentiments, leaving his daughter, Jane, Jr., more than three hundred acres in addition to "one Mallattoe boy called Lewis and a Negroe called Mary Provided she Marieth a Roman Catholick *if* she betake her selfe to ye Seate of Mattrimoney [emphasis added]."[109]

While we have no definitive means for ascertaining whether or not women remained single throughout their lives, the names of women who presumably never married show up in the wills, such as the "spinsters" Urath Bale, Elizabeth Baker, Elizabeth Berry, Anne Chapman, Elizabeth Darby, Jane Halfhead, and Hannah Prosser. Not all of these women had the option of marriage, as did Elizabeth Chapline, Jane Doyne, and Sarah Goddard. Some spinsters were indentured servants who signed a contract limiting their ability to marry while in the service of their masters. Surely, some indentured females experienced virtual enslavement if they became pregnant too often while under contract with a master who added years to their servitude for the inconvenience. Still others had grown too old to seek partners when their contracts expired. Yet it seems highly likely that a few landed spinsters, such as Patience Burkett as well as Mary and Margaret Brent of

St. Mary's County, had quite consciously decided that the risk of childbirth and the possible loss of autonomy were not attractive options.[110] When landed families had more than one heir, they could afford to offer the option of spinsterhood to daughters. This strategy helped to alleviate the inevitable shortage of land that resulted from generations' repeatedly parceling out tracts to their progeny. Widower Richard Marston of Charles County hoped his daughter would choose this option in order to preserve the meager fifty-acre estate for his eldest son. Richard wrote, "if my Eldest Daughter Mary Marston whilest she keepes herselfe Single and is Willing to live With her Said brother and to keep his house then it is my Will and desire that my Sonn Robt. Shall Allow her Maintenance as long as She shall remaine With him."[111]

This customary family strategy did not preclude spinsters from exerting authority in the family. Sisters demanded their fair share of the partnerships they entered, as is revealed in the testimony regarding the nuncupative (verbal) will of Benjamin Brasseur. The court clerk recorded the testimony of Anthony Kingsland, a fifty-four-year-old laborer, in which he related how he had heard Martha, Benjamin's sister and housekeeper, "tell the Said Benja. that now her time was out . . . and demanded what he would give her for the time that she had been with him." Benjamin agreed to give her his entire estate (and name her his executrix) if he died a bachelor. Another witness related a somewhat different scenario. A thirty-six-year-old laborer, William Howard, stated that he heard "Martha Brasseur demand of her brother Benja. Brasseur what he would give her for the time that she had been with him where upon the said Benja. told her that if he dyed a batchellor he would leave all to her the said Martha Brasseur. Where upon the said Martha told him that he would not." To put to rest his sister's serious doubts about his sincerity, Benjamin felt compelled to call Anthony Kingsland and William Howard into the house to bear witness to their contract.[112]

Martha and Benjamin Brasseur must have gotten along fairly well, since they lived and worked together for some time before this showdown occurred. Most siblings shared at least this measure of intimacy with each other, and quite often there proved to be a deep and lasting affection between brothers and sisters. Seaborn Battie laid bare his strong attachment to his sister on his deathbed when he wrote, "I give and bequeath unto my loveing sister Dinah the wife of Mr. Thomas Knighton Eight pounds Sterling to be layed out in a peice of plate and markt S.B. in remembrance of my true love & affection I bear to her."[113] And as an expression of his love, Anglican Arminian gentleman John Contee, after taking care of his wife and three stepchildren, gave "unto my Dear and Loving mother Mrs. Grace

Contee and to my Loving Sister Agness Berry . . . all my two parceles of Land in Charles County."[114]

English Roman Catholic siblings on the other side of the Atlantic also expressed strong bonds of love and affection in their writing. In a letter to his father, Lord Baltimore, Governor Charles Calvert expressed his sincere love for his sister when he received "the sad news of my Sister Blackstones death which has been a great Affliction to mee ever since, I hope shee is happy our prayers shall not bee wantinge, It is a great Comfort to mee that shee was soe well prepared and Resigned as I understand shee was, I Caused all the Good Men [priests] here to say Masses for her soule."[115] Dame Barbara Constable (a Benedictine nun) wrote with great affection to her brother on June 16, 1663: "To my most deare brother Sir Marmaduke Constable, I wish all health and happiness. My dearest brother since my affection and good will for you is not lesse then for the rest of my friends to whom according to my poor capacity I have indeavoured to contribute a little of the expence of the idle time my condition affords towards the good and sancifying of their soules according to the varietie of their conditions and necessities." In this letter Barbara strongly urged her brother, for the good of his soul, to be a better Christian and live a godly life. Barbara worried that her brother was too interested in giving himself "to an idle & vain life, taking pleasure and seeking after the riches and honours of the world."[116] Both Charles Calvert and Barbara Constable deeply loved their sister and brother and continued to show a keen interest in the salvation of their eternal souls.

Anthropologists Sherry Ortner and Harriet Whitehead, in *Sexual Meanings: The Cultural Construction of Gender and Sexuality,* shed some light on the significance of these strong sibling associations. Given a culture that values loving, respectful relationships between brothers and sisters, the society, in turn, predicates its definition of "womanhood" on these same relationships. People in such a culture tend to characterize women as friends, companions, confidantes, and partners, not evil, wanton, lustful creatures bent on seducing men into committing sins. This understanding of womanhood based on loving sibling relationships, they claim, produces a society that is "more sex-egalitarian and less sex-antagonistic."[117] Ortner and Whitehead's observation may speak directly to the situation in seventeenth-century Maryland (and England), where strong female-male sibling relationships abound and we also find a distinctive female authority present in most personal relationships. Therefore, we might assume Marylanders—especially Arminian Anglicans, Quakers, and Roman Catholics—tended to be more egalitarian in gendered intercourse and that gender roles were predicated on sibling associations of parity.

These brother-sister relationships that fostered a "more sex-egalitarian" society also extended beyond the immediate family to the spiritual family of friendship. Fitz William Lawrence, for example, bequeathed his "Deare and Loveing friend," the widow Judith Stanley, his entire estate.[118] Spinster Phoebe Loftus benefited when her loving friend Timothy Goodridge left his estate to her, his "trusty and well beloved friend for the love and affection which I beare."[119] Men and women such as Nathaniel Smith and his "Loveing friend Margaret Holland" shared a special relationship of sincere, mutual affection for each other. These friendships were sometimes part of an expansive network of spiritual family members, such as that of Philip Cary, William and Susanna Thomas, Samuel Barrot, Susanna Dunn, and Thomas Polton. This closely knit group of married, single, and widowed adults was a network of intimate friends dependent upon each other for day-to-day support. When faced with death, they bequeathed property to each other and witnessed the signing of each other's wills.[120]

Contemporary English advice literature praised the sanctity of true friendship between men and women. Anglican minister Jeremy Taylor, for instance, found scriptural evidence to support his notion that the "greatest love, and greatest usefulness, and the most open communication, and the noblest sufferings, and the most exemplar faithfulness, and severest truth, and the heartiest counsel and the greatest union of minds" existed between male and female friends. The Bible endorsed these intense friendships, Taylor assured his readers, saying that "the more we love, the better we are, and the greater our friendships are, the dearer we are to God." These relationships were often closer than the intimate friendships between brothers and sisters. Taylor explained that "A Brother does not always make a friend, but a friend ever makes a Brother and more."[121]

These spiritual families made up of close friends provided more than just emotional support; they also served a very practical need as well—as guardians for children. English men and women had long considered spiritual kinship to exist between themselves and the close friends they named as godparents to their children at their baptism. Such friends were called "gossips" (god-sibs), a word that indicated spiritual affinity and kinship.[122] As spiritual siblings, gossips were expected to treat each other's children as if they were their natural nieces or nephews. This extended family of gossips acted as surrogate parents when circumstances mandated. Many youngsters were orphaned during these years of high mortality rates—in both England

and Maryland—and gossips could step in to care for children when their natural kinfolk could not. For William Anderas, a gossip could act in his stead after his death to rectify any injustice done to his child, even if his wife was still alive. William optimistically bequeathed his entire estate to his wife, Ann, during her life, after which it was to pass to his daughter Elizabeth. However, William stipulated that "the tuition of my Said Daughter Elizabeth anderas unto the tenderness of my said wife to be provided for during her minority Provided that she the said Ann Anderas do not suffer the said Child to be any ways abused by a father in Law [stepfather] if she the Said Ann Anderas should Chance to be [re]married." If a stepfather treated his daughter badly, then William's spiritual sibling, "Elizabeth Parsons wife of Thomas Parsons," was to "have the Tuition of my Said Daughter during her Said minority."[123]

Marylanders valued their spiritual families so highly that we are not at all surprised to find men like Nathaniel Smith with several male "Loving friend[s]."[124] John Bayne said it best when he wrote of "the Especiall Trust true Love and pure affection I have and bear to my before [mentioned] Trustees Coll. John Courts Major James Smallwood coll. John Addison Major William Dent and Mr. Benjamine Hall." To show these loving friends just how much he cared for them, he gave "Each and every one of them ten pounds Sterl[ing] to buy each a mourning Ring Suit and Gold Rings," even if the cloth for the suits had to be sent from England at an additional cost to his estate.[125] Men tended to use the same affectionate terms for their male friends as they did for natural family members or female friends. These spiritual kinships, which often crossed gender lines, frequently traversed religious barriers as well, for we see that Catholic Thomas Diniard found solace with male Catholics, Quakers, and Protestants.[126]

Occasionally, a same-sex friendship became a partnership more closely resembling a marriage. For example, Roman Catholic Edward Cotton used his last will and testament to reiterate the oral commitments he had made to his "Mate," Barnaby Jackson. Wanting to ensure that justice was served after his death, Cotton confirmed his agreement with Jackson about the disbursement of his personal estate although "there was never anything concluded on nor the hands of neither party over Sett to any absolute bargain or agreem[en]t." Cotton added that he had "often Desired" to formally ratify their informal contract, noting that "Once for Instance I desired him to goe with me to the Secretarys to Conclude our agreem[en]t which he put off." Jackson apparently wanted to avoid this formal confirmation of their agreement by giving Cotton a flimsy excuse that Cotton refuted in his will. According to Cotton, Jackson had promised to come for him when he was at "Richd Williams Work" so that they could "goe [together] to Mr. Hattons" to put down on paper their economic commitments to one another. But Cotton lamented that "he never did." Perhaps this same-sex partnership (and others like it), with both its implicit and explicit responsibilities, developed out of necessity in a society with so many surplus males.[127]

Women also shared intimate same-sex relationships. Women who had the luxury of having natural kin in Maryland tended to form female networks within their families, as did Elizabeth Gouldesborough of Talbot County. Elizabeth left her two daughters, Mary and Elizabeth, her entire estate and named her sister, Priscilla Bruen, executrix.[128] Elizabeth's mother, Mary Sargeant of Queen Anne's County, also left a will that further illustrates this female network.[129] As a remembrance of her love for her granddaughters, Mary and Elizabeth, Mary left them each a gold ring. She named her daughter Priscilla and another daughter, Katharine Bowdell, administrators and residuary legatees. These females constructed a support network of other female family members whom they could depend upon when tragic events—such as death and illness—visited the family. Thus, women tended to gain emotional support from female relatives and extended this network to include many male friends.

As we have seen, intimate familial relationships extended far beyond the nuclear family in seventeenth-century Maryland. Mirroring family structures in England, families often spilled over the boundaries of the nuclear family, consisting of a father, a mother, and their natural offspring. Pragmatic constructions may have included a single parent raising a deceased spouse's children, godchildren, or cousins, since this was a time when men and women rarely lived to see their grandchildren come of age.[130] These families tended to scatter across the province as adult children sought their fortunes on land that parents increasingly purchased outside their immediate communities.[131] Grown children took their seats in other counties or moved to Carolina, Pennsylvania, and Virginia, or as far away as Barbados and England, as did the family of Arminian Anglican Henry Jowles. Henry had one son living in England, a daughter in Prince George's County, and a son in Calvert County, where he himself lived.[132] It is unclear how often family members (both natural and spiritual) saw one another once they had moved away, but we can be sure that most continued to serve their families in any way that they could despite the great distances.

With the magnitude of overseas trade undertaken by Marylanders, it would be safe to assume these literate colonists exchanged letters with great frequency, although only a few have survived. We know also that Marylanders had a regular intra- and intercolony postal service by 1695. The few letters that have managed to survive emphasize Marylanders' strong desire to maintain communications with kin. For example, Abraham Tilghman apologized profusely for not having written before his 1697 letter to his cousin Richard in England. Having received three letters from his cousin, Abraham explained that the war "hindered Relations and ffriends thus distant from conversing & exchanging affections in a desirable way."[133] Whether natural or spiritual family members were separated because of marriage or business, female and male colonists continued to cultivate and nurture family relationships both for the sake of emotional support and for the economic benefits kinship networks provided in their burgeoning staple economy.

Seventeenth-century Marylanders predicated their intimate relationships on a set of complex mutual responsibilities that continued to bind individuals to their extended families—both natural and spiritual—for the duration of their lives. While love and emotional support certainly formed the foundation for these relationships, economic concerns also had an important role to play. Property concerns sometimes shaped solutions to interpersonal problems and passions in a society in which the household was the basis of the family's economy. The variety of solutions speaks to both religious differences—in the definition of marriage and the religious group's role in it—and the frontier conditions of early modern Maryland. Because of the colonists' cultural and religious traditions, which they brought with them to the Catholic province, the patterns of partner selection, child/parent relations, marriage, and separation found here in Maryland closely resembled those of England.

This chapter also exposes a persistent and pervasive adherence to canon law in Maryland with regard to partner selection, marriage, and separation. Canon law's strongest adherents were the three largest English religious groups present in the province—Arminian Anglicans, Quakers, and Roman Catholics. Conversely, Puritanism—in Maryland and England—literally defined itself as the antithesis of all things Catholic. Thus the Puritans (and other Calvinists) summarily rejected the conception of marriage as a holy sacrament, and in so doing they stripped it of its religious significance. Additionally, females and males shared commitments—implying a sense of mutuality—within the society, as expressed in joint parental authority and patterns of child-naming. If we accept the argument put forth by anthropologists Sherry Ortner and Harriet Whitehead—namely, that societal understandings of gender based on sibling relationships lead to a "more sex-egalitarian" society—then we must delve deeper into the lives of these early modern people to find out just how "egalitarian" their society was while simultaneously examining the degree to which religion affected this society.

3

∾

Religion in the New World

In the wake of the Reformation, Protestants in parts of England found
themselves saddled with ancient Roman Catholic stone cathedrals,
churches, and chapels. Some English congregations began stripping
church interiors of idolatrous statues, stained glass, elaborate stone altars,
and monstrous roods, yet the church structure reminded congregants of
the dreaded "popish" ways of the past.[1] Although congregations dutifully
painted over sacred symbols and hid or sold silver chalices, altar stones, and
roods, some drew the line at destroying the churches' elaborate and expen-
sive stained glass, merely knocking out the small faces of saints from the
pictures; this reservation leaves us wondering how committed to the ideas
of the Reformation they truly were.[2] Fortunately, English architecture in
the New World offers a clearer picture of congregational commitment to
Calvinist theology in the post-Reformation era. Largely unhampered by
fears of shifting political and religious ground or substantial fines for non-
compliance, English colonists in the New World erected religious buildings,
buried their dead, and left us deathbed statements that reflected their particular theological understandings, free from overt governmental coercion.
In order to make clear religion's impact on the lives of English settlers in
the New World it is important to lay out their theology, not only to underscore the fact that doctrine mattered to these people, but also to delineate
distinctive differences and similarities amongst religious groups. The various groups that settled in Maryland held theological beliefs that separated
or joined them in ways that are significant for understanding their approach

to property ownership, gendered access to power, and the allocation and inheritance of land in the New World.

The deeply religious Puritans in seventeenth-century New England, and
most likely in Maryland, chose to construct for their churches unpretentious
clapboard structures resembling houses that did not in any way approxi-
mate Roman Catholic churches.[3] These buildings were not placed on consecrated ground and Puritans decided not to bury the dead in or around a
meetinghouse during the early years of settlement.[4] When congregants entered a simple rectangular Puritan meetinghouse they passed through a
door much like any other door in the community. In fact, Puritans consciously chose not to create sacred consecrated space, because they found no
scriptural directive to do so. When they passed through the meetinghouse
door, congregants merely moved from external space to an internal space
whose scant architectural embellishment was intended to avoid any sym-
bolic transition into the space. The meetinghouse, for Puritans, was not a
place to personally meet and interact with God. Instead, it was an edifice to
contain the entire community of God's new Israelites. This meetinghouse,
then, served both civic and religious functions by helping to define who the
new Israelites were and providing them with a place to worship together as
God's chosen community. Centrally located within the community, the
meetinghouse also hosted political and other public meetings, in addition
to public school. Puritans chose this multi-functional configuration because it reflected their central tenet that religion and government were in-
tertwining pillars of their commonwealth. A separation of church and state
functions was not desirable in the hearts, minds, or architecture of early
modern English Puritans.

Since the Bible was central in Puritan theology, the pulpit—where the
Bible was read and explained—stood as the focal point of the interior space.
As communities matured and had more time and money to invest in these
buildings, monumental multi-tiered pulpits were added which seemed to
be suspended in midair between heaven and earth, just above the heads of
congregants. The position of the Bible in the meetinghouse indicated its position in Puritan thought. Strategically centered between the ceiling and
floor, it reminded the new Israelites of its ability to bridge the gap between
the temporal and spiritual worlds. Because Puritans insisted that reading
and understanding God's message to His chosen people was crucial, seats
were provided for the comfort of the men, women, and children who would
listen to several hours of sermons and readings every Sunday morning and
afternoon. The unadorned interior walls were often painted white and the
plain window-glass allowed the unadulterated sunshine to brighten the

large room. This insistence on austere simplicity reflected the Puritans' desire to purify the church, and it encouraged congregants to focus their attention upon God's word rather than temporal aesthetics. For Puritans, religious meetings were stimulating intellectual exercises meant to improve congregants' understandings of God's word as preserved in the Bible. The Bible alone determined the form their religious service would take, particularly in regard to sermons and communion. Having stripped Christ's Last Supper of its un-scriptural Catholic ceremony, Puritans remembered it several times during the year (in some cases once a month) by bringing a small portable table near the pulpit, around which full church members assembled to partake of both bread and wine.[5] Sitting around this simple table to remember the Lord's Supper served to confirm their faith in Christ. Puritans also stripped other religious rites of any un-scriptural "popish" ceremony; the new Israelites refused to use the ring in a wedding ceremony, stand while reciting the creed, wear the surplice when officiating at a service, or make the sign of the cross in baptism.

Puritans constructed meetinghouses shortly after their arrival in Anne Arundel County, Maryland, probably beginning with the one on Magothy River.[6] Unfortunately, Maryland Puritans failed to preserve their meetinghouses, so a direct comparison with those of New England cannot be made. But we can compare the New England Puritans' gravestone iconography—indicative of their theology and worldview—with that of Marylanders. As the culture in New England matured, the markers used to signify the final resting place of the deceased changed from simple wood to engraved stone and the cemeteries moved from outside the town to the center of town. Typically headstones were topped with either a winged death's-head or a skull-and-crossbones motif functioning as "an emblem of mortality" that served to remind the living to prepare for their own deaths.[7] Historian John Brooke argues that these headstones and their proximity to the community reveal much about the theology and worldview of New England Calvinists. During the early years of settlement, the deceased were buried without ceremony in a cemetery outside the boundaries of the community and impermanent markers were erected over the graves. Calvinists believed that souls would either gain eternal salvation in heaven or endure damnation in hell, but no worldly act could change a soul's fate. As Predestinarians, these Puritans believed that God had decided the soul's destiny long before the individual was born; therefore prayers for the dead, in a meetinghouse or at the gravesite, were neither necessary nor desirable. Communities moved cemeteries to the center of the town and marked the dead's final resting place with stone markers in response to the unsettling diaspora that oc-

2. Calvinist Associator Nicholas Greenberry at St. Anne's Church in Annapolis

curred as mature communities outgrew the confines of their villages and their members scattered across the countryside. Deceased saints, represented as winged death's-heads or skulls and crossbones, could cast their steady gaze upon the Congregationalists as "icons of cultural memory intended to keep the faithful bound to covenant theology" when they gathered for funerals.[8] Thus funerals helped to reconstitute dispersed communities and Puritan gravestone iconography served to remind Calvinists of their duties as God's chosen people.

Significantly, Calvinist iconography does not show up in seventeenth-century Maryland, with the exception of one location, Annapolis. When Lord Baltimore invited the persecuted Puritans from Virginia to settle in Maryland, they tended to congregate in the area now known as Annapolis. Maryland Puritans must have embraced the New England Calvinists' worldview and theology, or their gravestone iconography would be unlikely to appear in this particular location. It seems plausible to assume that the Puritans in Maryland—since they shared a common theology and a common gravestone iconography with New Englanders—constructed similar austere, house-like buildings for worship in which the Bible and pulpit remained the focal point of the interior space. These buildings would help define the new

Israelite community in Maryland and offer a place for both worship and civic meetings.

To underscore the separation of the temporal and spiritual worlds, St. Mary's Roman Catholic chapel never functioned as a public meeting space used to discuss politics or other worldly affairs. Nor was it a space for educating children in order to prepare them to face a competitive economic world. Unlike the Puritan meetinghouse, the Catholic chapel's function was to transcend the temporal world and provide congregants with a taste of the spiritual world that awaited them if they chose—of their own free will—to work toward their salvation by doing good works. Consequently, when these Free Will Christians passed through the massive front doors to enter the monumental brick structure, they found themselves transported to another world. The burning incense, a vivid painting of clouds and fire, colored-glass windows, and spiritual hymns sung in the mystical ancient tongue would have encouraged an uplifting feeling of ecstasy.[9] Here the community's living and dead (for the elite were customarily interred in crypts beneath churches) were reunited in a heaven-like environment where God, Christ, the Holy Ghost, the Blessed Virgin, and all the saints gathered to celebrate God's commitment to all human beings who freely chose to follow Him.

The chapel's interior focal point was the massive stone altar, draped with a colorful embroidered cloth and flanked by enormous candles. In addition to a large chandelier, a silver pyx—for the reserved Eucharist that was always available for the sick—typically hung over an English Catholic altar.[10] The altar's centrality was further enhanced by its position on a raised platform and its separation from the congregation by either a rood screen or a railing.[11] This elaborate altar stood beneath an imposing rood symbolizing Christ's willingness to sacrifice Himself for the salvation of humanity. This sacred space was where the miracle of transubstantiation took place. Witnessing the changing of bread and wine into Christ's body and blood was the primary reason for attending Mass. In Catholic Europe, parishioners often drifted from altar to altar in a cathedral to witness repeatedly the raising of the Eucharist over the priest's head in recognition of the miraculous transformation of bread into Christ's body. Congregants rarely consumed the holy Eucharist, believing that they had to truly repent their sins before physically taking Christ into their body. While European Catholics took communion at various times during the year, Easter—after forty days of fasting, abstinence, and penance—was by far the most popular day to do so.[12] Marylanders seem to have set custom aside and chosen to take communion more often. In 1639 one of the priests observed that "the attendance on the Sacraments here is so large, that it is not greater among the faithful in Europe, in proportion to their numbers."[13] Regardless of how many times a year Catholics consumed the holy Eucharist, they flocked to this sacred space at least once a week to witness the miracle of transubstantiation and Christ's omnipotent presence (housed in the silver pyx) in the sacred space.

In this highly charged atmosphere where believers came in close contact with God, Catholics would alternately stand or kneel in God's holy presence and therefore benches or pews were rarely provided. Nor were they particularly necessary, since Mass typically lasted about ninety minutes; Catholic sermons, largely a response to Protestant inclusion of sermons in services, were relatively new additions to the Mass and tended to be short in comparison to Puritan ones.[14] If the Catholic chapel in St. Mary's followed English tradition, there was another reason seating was not provided in it. The chapel's traditional cross-shaped floor plan provided additional sacred space for two smaller altars. Here, two other priests, in keeping with the medieval Roman Catholic custom, could say prayers and celebrate Masses for the dead to assist their entrance into heaven. Pews or benches would have hindered worshipers moving between these altars. For these early modern Catholics, Mass provided an opportunity to directly experience God's holy presence here on earth while it also paved the way toward personal salvation for both the living and the dead.

Faced with high mortality rates, the Catholic priests struggled to keep up with the demands of their flock. One of them reported back to Rome that "The most ignorant have been catechized, and catechetical lectures have been delivered to the more advanced every Sunday; on feast days they have been very rarely left without a sermon. The sick and the dying, who were numerous this year and dwelt far apart, have been assisted in every way, so that not a single person has died without the Sacraments. We have buried very many, but we have baptized a greater number."[15] In the minds of these Catholics, the dead buried beneath the chapel probably had a better chance of gaining eternal salvation. Those wealthy enough to afford crypt space also left substantial bequests to priests in their last wills and testaments, which ensured a continuous stream of prayers and Masses for their departed souls. In 1799, a group of curious Marylanders examined some coffins that had been found in a vault under the ruins of St. Mary's Chapel. One of the explorers left us a detailed account that bears repeating at length. After opening a wood coffin that hid a lead coffin that opened to another wooden coffin, the chronicler recorded,

When the face of the corpse was uncovered it was ghastly indeed, it was the woman. Her face was perfect, as was the rest of the body but was black as the blackest negro. Her eyes were sunk deep in her head, every other part retained its perfect shape. The loss of three or four of her upper fore teeth was supplied with a piece of wood between. Her hair was short, platted and trimmed on the top of her head. Her dress was a white muslin gown, with an apron which was loose in the body, and drawn at the bosom nearly as is now the fashion only not so low, with short sleeves and high gloves but much destroyed by time. Her stockings were cotton and coarse, much darned at the feet, the clocks [stocking decorations] of which were large and figured with half diamonds worked. Her gown was short before and gave us a view of all her ankle. Her cap was with long ears and pinned under the chin. A piece of muslin two inches broad which extended across the top of her head as low as her breast, the end was squared and trimmed with half inch lace as was the cap. The body was opened and the entrails removed and filled with gums and spice, and the coffin filled with the same. She was a small woman, and appeared delicate. In the coffin of the man was only the bones which were long and large. His head was sawed through the brain removed, and filled with embalmment, but he was not so well done as the other, or had been there much longer as he was much more gone. The winding sheet of the body was marked in such letter as these [three crosses with the letters A and L].[16]

Recent archaeological digs have revealed additional information about the chapel vault's occupants. A third coffin—only eight inches wide and thirty inches long—contained the remains of a six-month-old baby girl who suffered from malnutrition, which caused rickets, and a serious cranial infection. The three coffins held the remains of Philip Calvert (d. 1682), his first wife, Anne Wolsey Calvert (d. 1680), and Philip's daughter by his second wife, Jane Sewall Calvert. Philip, the youngest brother of Cecil Calvert (the second Lord Baltimore), served Maryland as governor between 1660 and 1661 and as chancellor from 1661 until his death.[17]

Although the wealthy buried in chapel vaults appear to have had some advantages, the deceased who could not afford to be buried in such a way were not destined to rot in hell. Baptized Catholics who had not fully redeemed themselves by doing sufficient good works here on earth waited patiently in Purgatory until family members, friends, and parish priests helped them enter into heaven with their prayers.[18] This kept priests very busy saying Mass and prayers for the dead. The English Catholic Sarum Missal dictated that the "Bidding Prayer"—said in English—always include a list of all who were to be prayed for during the celebration of every Mass.[19] Possibly with the idea that their proximity to sacred space helped their cause, Catholics chose to be buried in the consecrated ground surrounding the sacred building whenever feasible. The dead—wrapped in linen with sprigs of rosemary resting on their chests—were placed in wooden coffins and buried with their heads to the west. This configuration would allow them to rise up and face God in the east on Judgment Day. Commoners in the churchyard were not embalmed like the wealthy Roman Catholics under the chapel, nor were their wooden coffins sealed in lead. They might have expected the wealthy elites to gain entrance into heaven before them, but they knew that their chances of getting to heaven were still better than those of the reprobate or unbaptized. Few colonists were thought to be damned reprobate, but the church reserved a segregated place for the damned just in case. Archaeologists uncovered the body of such a person in the unconsecrated ground on the north side of St. Mary's Chapel. This person—who would face the west with his back toward God on Judgment Day—was probably a mortal sinner who had not made any attempt to humbly ask for forgiveness of his sins before his death.

Grave markers for the true believers around the chapel tended to be simple wooden planks listing the name and possibly the date of death or the age of the deceased. Catholics did not need elaborate headstones, as they were remembered at the weekly Mass in the prayers for the dead. Catholics who were buried on their plantations frequently had large flat stones placed over their final resting place. The occasional stone slab that included an engraved image almost always touted the family's coat of arms. In a few cases, small plantation chapels were erected over the dead.[20]

Significantly, Anglicans, after years of sharing sacred space with their Roman Catholic masters, friends, and kin, eventually built churches that resembled traditional pre-Reformation English churches rather than Calvinist Puritan structures. Old Trinity Church (c. 1675) typified the Maryland Anglicans' architectural representations of their Free Will Christian beliefs.[21] When congregants entered the large brick building they passed through a massive door reminiscent of that of St. Mary's Chapel. Following a Roman Catholic floor plan, the front door was on the west side of the church and the altar in the east. Similarly, the focal point for this sacred space was the raised altar, draped with embroidered cloth and flanked by candles, standing directly opposite the front door. At Trinity, the partially railed altar was secured in a separate sacred space made more prominent by a semi-circular

architectural appendage meant to create a barrier between the altar and parishioners.[22] This semi-circular chancel—not common in England until the
following century—was also found in other Maryland Arminian Anglican
churches, such as St. Paul's of Kent County (c. 1693).[23] Rather than the massive rood hanging over the altar in a Roman Catholic church, however, the
Arminian Anglicans at Trinity allowed the sun to provide this important
reminder of Christ's willingness to die on the cross for humanity. A large
rood-like shadow from the cross-shaped window frame graced the altar
during Sunday morning gatherings as the sun rose in the east. Celebrating
the Lord's Supper in this sacred space certainly might have suggested to believers that a miracle was taking place in front of them. Most accepted the
Roman Catholic idea that this rite was a holy sacrament and their behavior
implies that they had not moved very far from the Catholic ideals. A contemporary observer noted that common folk took the communion ritual
very seriously; they donned "their best clothes, and behaved in a more moral
way for several days after."[24] Many Catholics took communion only on Easter (a medieval church custom) and Arminian Anglicans tended to follow
this custom. Although official Arminian Anglican doctrine did not declare
the miracle of transubstantiation, it is hard to say exactly what the parishioners thought about this sacrament. Despite the ambiguity of Holy Communion in the minds of the Maryland Arminian Anglicans, Old Trinity
Church stands as a concrete example of continuity with St. Mary's Roman
Catholic chapel, with its sacred space.

While Old Trinity Church supports the assertion that Maryland Arminian Anglicans were similar to their Roman Catholic brethren, the structure also reveals its congregation's adherence to some mild Protestant reforms. For instance, an elaborate pulpit stands solidly against the north side
of the church to emphasize the importance of scripture and congregants
probably listened to fairly lengthy sermons, as seating was provided in the
original layout. Still, it is important to note that this massive pulpit was not
the focal point of the interior space and it was not hovering in space between heaven and earth. Moreover, it appears that the Bible was not read
from the elevated pulpit. The Bible was located just below the priest, at parishioners' eye level, indicating its importance in relation to the sacred altar. For these Anglicans scripture and the sacral ceremony celebrating the
Lord's Supper were of equal importance. Additionally, reflecting their Protestant reliance on the written word, Arminian Anglicans prominently posted
within the semi-circular sacred space—in English rather than in the Catholics' Latin—the Apostles' Creed, the Ten Commandments, and the Lord's
Prayer. Roman Catholics would recite the Apostles' Creed and the Lord's

3. Partially Railed Altar in the Semi-circular Chancel at Old Trinity Church

Prayer silently in English when the priest signaled them to do so during Mass, but the Catholic church did not fill its sacred space with the written word—especially when that word was written in English.

Consecrated burial space also offers evidence of some Protestant influence. Since the ground on the north side of Trinity Church holds many graves, it seems doubtful that these Arminian Anglicans followed the Roman Catholic propensity for reserving the north side as unconsecrated space for the reprobate or unbaptized. Nor is there evidence that the dead were placed in crypts beneath this particular church as the Arminian Anglicans did in Williamsburg, Virginia. Yet the gravestones and the positions of the bodies around the Arminian Anglican churches in Maryland suggest similarities with the Roman Catholics. In 1886, parishioners of Trinity Church found a forgotten large slab gravestone belonging to Rev. Francis Sourton that had been buried several inches below ground. Engraved under the Sourton coat of arms was a Latin inscription: "Francis Sourtin Anglican of Devonshire, son of Francis minister of evangelic truth. He was sedulous in a life often afflicted, and was buried in 1679. And thou reader living in the Lord Jesus Christ, keep the faith, and thou also, though dead, shall live."[25] The iconography and Latin text reflect a strong Roman Catholic influence.

Arminian Anglican John Lawson's final request in his last will also suggests that these Anglicans shared a great deal with their Roman Catholic brethren. Lawson wrote, "I give to the Earth my Mother to be buryed in a Civill and Christion like mannor and if possible at my burial to have read the buryall form according to the Canon of the Church of England but not a gun to be Shott by reason I was never exorcised in Military affairs and my body to be laid by or with my dear and well beloved wife my only and true beloved Wife Dorcas Lawson."[26] Arminian Anglicans often used the metaphor of "mother earth," but more importantly, this Anglican attempted to procure the rites of the Book of Common Prayer—which were largely based on the Roman Catholic Sarum rite and the Greek Orthodox missal.

Given the Roman Catholic burial rites, gravestone iconography, church floor plan, interior focal point, and concerted effort to create sacred spaces, these Arminian Anglicans seem to have been more closely related to their Roman Catholic brethren than to the Calvinist Puritans. The Arminian Anglicans at Old Trinity, while similar to the Maryland Roman Catholics, were also closely aligned with their counterparts back in England. When James I came to the throne he ordered his Anglican bishops to adopt the Five Articles of Perth, which can be read as far more Catholic than Puritan. Under these articles Anglicans were required to kneel when they received communion, they were to keep the Roman Catholic calendar of saints, private communion and baptism were allowed in certain cases, and members had to submit to an episcopal confirmation of their faith.[27] While reinstating the kneeling posture for receiving communion, James also allowed the communion table (that had replaced the stone altars) to remain in its traditional location in the east end of the church (the chancel), thus confirming what Elizabeth I had ordered years earlier.[28] James's son, Charles I, also published his thoughts on church services, and they too suggest a greater affinity to Roman Catholic ideals than Calvinist Puritan ones. Charles declared himself a "Catholique-Christian as believeth the three Creeds" while also accepting the Roman Catholic calendar of saints. Additionally, he claimed to embrace the teachings of the first five hundred years of the Christian church, the Roman Catholic church fathers, and the first four Roman Catholic councils.[29]

Like the earliest Arminian Anglicans, Quakers, when they arrived in the province after 1655, did not immediately construct separate edifices for religious devotion, opting instead to meet in the homes of other Friends or in schoolhouses until their numbers increased.[30] Quakers often congregated in the homes of gifted Quaker ministers, such as Howell Powell, John Edmondson, Will Stevens, Wenlock Christison, and Anne Ayres Chew. When Quakers finally built separate meetinghouses, the buildings reflected their

4. Third Haven Quaker Meetinghouse

theological understandings. Third Haven Meetinghouse (c. 1682)—the old-est Friends meetinghouse still in use in America—illustrates how Quaker beliefs were represented in architecture. After many years of use as a gen-eral meetinghouse in which several Quaker Societies met four times a year, Third Haven was taken over by the faithful from Betty's Cove in 1693 for their weekly meetings.[31] There have been some structural modifications to the building, but the intentions of the seventeenth-century members can still be deciphered. The original single front door was perched at the top of a set of stairs signifying a transition from the ordinary temporal world into the higher elevation of the spiritual world. The door opened into a large room filled with benches where the "convinced" Quakers sat, who had accepted—of their own free will—the Holy Spirit into their bodies. The Holy Spirit, which they often referred to as the Light, coaxed them to serve God and diligently work toward their salvation by doing good works in much the same way that the Arminian Anglican and Roman Catholic Free Will Christians did.

One such good work was to share God's inspirational message—deliv-ered directly to them through the Spirit within—with others during the regular meeting. The room full of male and female ministers, radiating with the love of the Holy Spirit inside them, waited patiently for the Spirit to reveal God's message for the day. The Spirit could speak through any one of them, but more often than not, the message probably came from one of the more gifted ministers in the Society. As they waited for the Spirit to move someone to speak, the congregation sat facing a long, narrow, raised platform that ran almost the entire length of the right side of the meetinghouse, where the most gifted ministers faced the gathering of worshipers. It is important to note that these ministers were not ordained or in any way qualitatively spiritually different from the other members of the congregation. Placing them above and facing the rest was a way of showing deference to the Holy Spirit, which seemed to be more active or perhaps more apparent inside these elevated Friends. Correspondingly, the railing along the raised platform served to distance the most sacred space from the mass of Friends gathered to worship and listen to God's message.[32]

There was no hovering pulpit, no rood, and no sacred altar. Immediately upon entering the meetinghouse the participant was confronted with the focal point of this religious space, the Holy Spirit residing inside each of the congregants. Although the outside façade of this simple wooden structure appears to mirror the Calvinist Puritans' insistence upon shunning any and all things that reminded them of Roman Catholic ceremony, theology, or iconography, these Quakers should not be grouped with the radical nonconformist Puritans, as many previous historians have suggested. Generally speaking, Quaker worship, with its emphasis on spirit rather than scripture, was closer to the Arminian Anglican and Roman Catholic experiential religious gatherings in a sacred space than to the Calvinist Puritans' intellectual meetings in an academic, civic space. Unlike the Calvinist Puritans, the Arminian Anglicans, Quakers, and Roman Catholics gathered weekly to personally experience God's benevolent presence in a sacred space.

While the evidence is decidedly sparse, what little remains suggests that early Quaker burial practices were similar to the Arminian Anglican and Roman Catholic rites. Professed Quaker Abraham Naylor's inscribed gravestone, dated 1683—found near the Herring Creek meetinghouse in Anne Arundel County—makes it clear that some Quakers inscribed stones with both names and dates, although later Friends abandoned this practice.[33] Nevertheless, Naylor's last request looks very much like an Arminian Anglican one. He insisted that his corpse be buried in a coffin and a minister, specifically Mr. Thomas Dayefeild, be given four thousand pounds of tobacco "for preaching my funerall Sermin & decently burying of my Corps . . . & doe ord[e]r that my corps may bee pailed [fenced] in when buryed & 2 grave stones to bee sent for & sett up one att my head ye other att my feete with my name engraved in them & the time of my death."[34] It is quite possible that Naylor was unwilling to forego the burial rites of his previous Anglican faith. Yet it is also possible that Naylor's request is an example of Quaker burial practices in the New World that mirrored those of the Roman Catholics and Arminian Anglicans. The evidence provided by Bryan Omelia's, William Parrott's, and Walter Powell's wills suggests that during the same time period—at least in Somerset and Talbot Counties—an unusual Quaker practice existed that was similar to the Arminian Anglican and Roman Catholic rites.[35]

Burial practices, gravestone iconography, and architectural evidence indicate that the Free Will Christians—the Arminian Anglicans, Quakers, and Roman Catholics—shared similar notions about salvation, God's presence on earth, and the centrality of spiritual experiential worship. The practices and material culture of these Free Will Christian groups stand in stark contrast to those of the Predestinarian Puritans. Nevertheless, the practices and material culture of a religious group may or may not reflect the beliefs and practices of individual members. Unfortunately, the personal letters and diaries that might shed some light on this issue do not exist for early modern Maryland. Abraham Naylor's will, however, suggests that last wills and testaments might be used to discover individual religious beliefs and practices. Fortunately, 3190 last wills and testaments have survived. But how can we be sure that these wills are not just standardized legal documents that will tell us nothing about their authors?

A witness would later recount the last hours of Joseph Horsley's life as he languished on his deathbed in February of 1670 at Richard Bayley's inn. The court clerk dutifully recorded the witness's testimony that Horsley "perused [the will] Severall times" before signing it, and did so only after he had discussed the contents with those present. This narrative, and numerous others like it, suggests that testators selected their last words with the utmost of care. We can only assume that early Marylanders would not have signed a will that misrepresented their spirituality, since a will acted as a testator's final effort to comfort him- or herself. Unhampered by clerical and governmental regulations that constrained testators back in England, Marylanders were free to use their wills as testaments to God, revealing both religious beliefs and practices.[36] And indeed they did so, self-consciously crafting a highly diverse collection of preambles that often point to a particular religious affiliation or at least to a testator's soteriology, based on a belief in either predestination or the power of free will.[37]

Many would agree that the Arminian Anglicans and Roman Catholics in England had much in common, including their church architecture, gravestone iconography, and burial practices. After Henry VIII's break with the pope in 1534 the Church of England retained a Catholic liturgy in its Book of Common Prayer, closely following the Roman Catholic Sarum Missal. Thus it is not at all surprising that Arminian Anglican and Roman Catholic testators expressed similar theological views in their liturgical quotations, since in effect they used variations of the same sources.[38] Furthermore, Arminian Anglicans continued to identify and describe themselves as "Catholic" in both the Old and New Worlds.[39] As previously pointed out, Charles I declared himself to be a "Catholique," and the Arminian Anglicans in Maryland claimed this identity over and over again, referring to themselves as Christians who subscribed to "the Catholick faith . . . [of] the Church of England."[40] Other Catholics specified their Roman allegiance when asking to have prayers for their salvation said in the "Holy Catholicke Church" in testimony that they "dye a Roman Catholicke."[41]

Architectural evidence and burial practices open the possibility that the Free Will Christian groups had more in common with each other than they did with the Calvinist Puritans. Yet, at the same time, the Quakers' austere meetinghouse and resistance to formal ceremony imply some ambiguity. Here the wills are particularly helpful in grouping the Quakers with the other Free Will Christians. The elaborate statements of faith made in Quaker wills easily reconcile themselves with the sentiments expressed in Arminian Anglican and Roman Catholic testaments, all of which emphasized a belief in free will as opposed to predestination. Sharing an awareness of death, testators of every religious persuasion included in their wills a statement of personal comfort that indicated a familiarity with the New Testament. Although Catholicism—Arminian Anglicanism and Roman Catholicism—are traditionally thought of as liturgically rather than biblically based faiths, adherents of both, surprisingly, included biblical references in their wills.[42] Because of this, both groups can be convincingly linked to the Quakers. The portions of the Bible that groups chose to emphasize indicate their distinctiveness; the similarities in the choices of biblical text among Arminian Anglicans, Quakers, and Roman Catholics shows the logic of grouping them as a Free Will Christian cohort.

Arminian Anglican testators shared with the Roman Catholic and Quaker Free Will Christians a sense of uncertainty about whether they could ensure their salvation. Arminian Anglican wills portray a strong belief in God's clemency tied closely to penance and humble petitioning for forgiveness. An Arminian Anglican priest, Hugh Jones, wrote—partially paraphrasing the Book of Common Prayer's oblation—"I Comit my soul into the hands of almighty God hopeing by the merits death and passion of my blessed Saviour Jesus christ to Inheritt Eternall life."[43] In addition to a good dose of humility and regret for past transgressions, Arminian Anglicans such as Philip Lyne believed that an intercessor was necessary to gain entrance into heaven. Lyne wrote, "Trusting in ye Mercy of God and powerfull Intercession of His Son Jesus Christ my blessed Saviour and redeemer I humbly & heartily recommend and offer up my Soule to its Creator hopeing to Enjoy his peace & presence Everlasting."[44]

Innovative Free Will Christian Arminian Anglicans of Maryland constructed for themselves a religious life, despite the lack of formal spiritual guidance in the early years of the province. They read devotional literature, taught their children the Bible, and continued to observe the holy days with prayers, fasting, and feasting. We might also assume that like-minded neighbors, servants, friends, and relatives gathered together regularly to worship God without the assistance of a priest. Arminian Anglican priest John Yeo, in a 1676 letter to the Archbishop of Canterbury, lamented this "deplorable estate and condition of the Province of Maryland, for want of an established ministry." He went on to describe how laypeople filled this void in Maryland although they "never had a legall call or ordination to such an holy office." Yeo could not contain his displeasure with the fact that these people not only acted as "dispensers of the Word" but also took it upon themselves to "administer ye sacrament of Baptism."[45] It appears that Arminian Anglicans in the province sought out people at least marginally conversant in the creed, such as Joseph Tilley of All Hallows' Parish and Thomas Tench at Herring Creeke, to fill the void when they lacked ordained priests.[46]

The will of William Hopkins of Anne Arundel County reveals some of the theological underpinnings of the Maryland Arminian Anglicans. He wrote, "I give my Soul to the almighty God that gave it and my body to the Earth from whence it came . . . to rest in Certaine hope to be raised again att the day of ressurreccon and through the merits of my Redeemer Jesus Christ I doe believe being heartily Sorry from the bottom of my heart for my sins Comitted that thro his Sufferings I shall be redeemed from my Sins and both my Soul and body be reunited together and received into Glory what that Comfortable Expressions of my Redeemer which Says unto his Elect Come ye blessed into a Kingdom prepared for you before the foundation of the world."[47] Evidently, Hopkins believed the Bible stood out as the ultimate authority on how to gain salvation. His words were taken from Matthew 25:34, which reads in part, "Come, you that are blessed by my Father, inherit the kingdom prepared for you from the foundation of the world." It is important to note that the term "elect" is not used in the Calvinist sense of "God's Elect and Chosen"—meaning those predestined, through God's grace alone, for salvation. Here the term refers to those who fulfill the sanctification process. The sanctification process was one in which an individual worked toward salvation, as opposed to the Calvinist predestinarian theology of passive reception of saving grace from God. Initially, Jesus had to die on the cross as Hopkins's redeemer. Next, as a human being and thus destined to sin, Hopkins had to acknowledge, reveal, and repent of his sinful behavior in order to purify his soul with the help of his intercessor, Jesus Christ. This process required sinners to use their free will and have faith in Jesus Christ in order to be saved. Finally, on Judgment Day, if Hopkins had efficaciously fulfilled the above criteria—for he had every hope, but could never be sure—he would gain everlasting life in heaven.

While Arminian Anglicans probably made up the most significant portion of the population in Maryland, the Society of Friends certainly drew many new converts during the second half of the seventeenth century. Elizabeth Harris brought the new faith—commonly called Quakerism—to Maryland as early as 1655.[48] Quaker converts in Maryland tended to accommodate their new beliefs to their previous piety, creating a peculiar Quakerism in the seventeenth century. They swore oaths when taking office and testified under oath in court; they served in the military; and they often adhered to a more hierarchical structure in their fledgling institution than they did in the eighteenth century. All of these had expressly been prohibited by George Fox in England. This unique branch of the Society of Friends can best be analyzed if we first examine the behavior of the believers in Maryland and then turn to their English counterparts.

While sharing the Arminian Anglican (and Roman Catholic) uncertainty concerning their salvation, Quakers used coded terms that readily identified their devotionalism. Quakers used the word "Spirit" to identify the Holy Spirit (or Ghost) present within their earthly bodies. The inclusion of the Holy Ghost or "Spirit" in the Arminian Anglican, Quaker, and Roman Catholic wills indicates their emphasis upon biblical passages on which Predestinarians chose not to focus.[49] While Quakers overwhelmingly referred to the "Spirit," they also fondly cited Jesus as the "Light of ye world" (John 8:12, 9:5), and this term also appears in the Sarum Missal and in the Book of Common Prayer, in both its Latin and English editions.[50] Henry Willcocks of Talbot County typifies the elaborate theological statements found in Quaker preambles. As he prepared to die, Henry baldly revealed his understanding of his chosen religion by writing,

being whole in mind & of p[er]fect memory but weak of body I my body soul and spirit have given up unto ye Lord w[i]th w[hi]ch I have glorified God: w[hi]ch: all are ye: Lords and I have beene long given

unto him And now I do comend my body soul and spirit into my
Sav[io]r and Creat[o]rs hands for all is his; I dye in ye Lord in whom I
have lived and moved and had my being a true and Loyall Protestant
Christian & a memb[e]r of ye true reformed Church in Christ Jesus
w[hi]ch was in ye Apostles dayes befor ye Apostacy was; of w[hi]ch
Church Christ Jesus was and is ye whole head husband Mediat[o]r Redeemer and Sav[io]r and no mortal man nor false Christian by whom
I have been a great sufferr for bearing a true testimony to ye Lord's
blessed holy name in whom I rest.[51]

The phrase "Mediator, Redeemer and Savior"—found in all versions of the
Book of Common Prayer and in Arminian Anglican and Roman Catholic
wills—indicates a shared notion of Christ as intercessor.[52] The rest of the
language used, though similar in perspective to that of the Catholics, reveals
a distinctly Quaker worldview. This is especially true of Willcocks's last two
lines, acknowledging the Quaker belief that salvation can only be obtained
through the recognition of Jesus Christ.

From Abraham Naylor's and other wills, it is evident that Maryland
Quakers adhered to a hierarchical structure of religious ritual. Quakers believed everyone could receive the "Light" of the Holy Spirit, so that any male
or female could be transformed into a "minister" who would be expected
to evangelize with the hope of converting others. Several wills, however,
mention particularly outstanding ministers with the kind of reverential regard accorded to priests in the Arminian Anglican and Roman Catholic
churches. Men like Thomas Dayefeild, Richard Johns, Ambrose Landerson,
and William Richardson were clearly revered Quaker ministers. Both the
English and Maryland members of the Society of Friends encouraged elite
families to convert with the hope that they would take an active role as leaders. Yet the Marylanders' adoption of the Arminian Anglican and Roman
Catholic institution of a hierarchical episcopacy appears to be a colonial
innovation based on their particular circumstances and the influence of
their previous beliefs before conversion.

Colonists often detailed some of the philosophical underpinnings of
their faith in their wills, as did Quaker John Ellet of Talbot County, who
proclaimed that he had seen the "truth and the Tender Dealings of the Lord
w[i]th me: Doe believe the people called Quakers are Gods people with
whom I walked th[ese] many years: & that all are faithful: to the requireings
of Gods holly Spirit in them to the end of theire days shall assuredly be
Saved when time shall be noe more heare with them in and through the
Merritts of our Lord Jesus Christ togeather with his grace workeing our

good workes in us and for us which gifts are plane in his sight: and peace upon A sick bed blessed be God for his Mercy."[53] By stressing his belief in God's benevolence, John provides a glimpse into the world of Maryland Quakers. In particular, he points to the importance of accepting the Holy Spirit into one's body and therefore having faith in one's ability to gain salvation through one's free will, and God's continued intercession on behalf of sinners during their lives. For Ellet, God had not predestined his soul to be among either the damned or the saved. John had to repent his sins, accept the Holy Spirit, and work toward his salvation by doing good works.

Historian Kenneth Carroll stresses Maryland Quakers' Free Will Christian theology. He suggests that Quakers believed everyone had "the capacity to perceive God and to respond to his truth and his will. . . . This belief in the universality of the Spirit probably angered the English Protestants more than any other belief, for it denied Calvin's doctrine of man's 'inability' following the Fall and also struck at the religious pride and arrogance of the 'Elect.' Fox and his followers also believed that the Spirit [could] overcome and eliminate sin. The same Spirit that was in Christ was also in them." Especially because Fox was not a theologian and his educational background did not provide him with the philosophical rhetoric necessary for such endeavors, Quakers placed little emphasis on doctrine, creed, or indeed book-learning. Thus Carroll affirms that for Quakers "salvation came through union with the Spirit. Salvation really meant following the Spirit," requiring individual believers to aggressively work toward purification of their souls through good works.[54]

Lest this sound too much like Arminian Anglican theology, we might emphasize some of the distinctive characteristics of Maryland Quakerism that Carroll's research has revealed. Quakerism centered on the "four main facets of community, peace, equality, and simplicity." Thus leading members of the Quaker community would reprimand any who "goe From the truth and is not faithful in their Testimony in Every particular," "follow Drenkeness, pleasures or Gameing," or were "not faithful in their callings and Dealings nor honest and just." Quakers also kept good records and read devotional literature to deepen their faith; they were "to Buy Convenient Books for Registering Births, Burials, Marriages and all other things appertaining to the Order of Truth." Underscoring the Maryland Quakers' interest in education—albeit for religious purposes—the Talbot County meeting hired Isaac Smith as "school master" in 1683. Admonitions like "All Friends to take Notice of the Poore to Ease one another" emphasized the need to do good works in caring for the poor and underprivileged. Eastern Shore Quakers set down these rules regulating behavior in 1676, indicating their desire for structure, a modern understanding of time (in their publication of meeting schedules), and also their right to decide for themselves what kinds of organization and laws they would attempt to live by.[55]

George Fox's soteriology, according to Douglas Gwyn, rested on his belief in experiential knowledge. In other words, Fox emphasized an individual's personal experience of God. God made His will known to humans when they allowed the "Light" (or Holy Spirit) to enter their bodies. Fox's principal statement of faith, "Christ is come to teach his people himself," exemplifies this notion. Gwyn tells us that Fox "denied scripture to be the Word of God and touchstone of doctrine, but instead affirmed it to be the words which God inspired the prophets and apostles to write, the record of the Lord's dealing in the world."[56] Thus the Bible was important—primarily for evangelizing—but not essential. Even illiterates with no knowledge of the Bible—such as the Native Americans—could be saved by the word of God emanating from the "Light" within. Gwyn quotes Fox as saying, "My desires after the Lord grew stronger, and zeal in the pure knowledge of God and of Christ, without the help of any man, book, or writing. For though I read the scriptures that spoke of Christ and God, yet I knew him not but by revelation [Gal. 1:12, 16], as he who hath the key did open, and as the Father of life drew me to his Son by his Spirit."[57] For Quakers, then, reading the Bible served to help sinners recognize Christ, but did not preclude the need to receive the Holy Spirit into their bodies in order to fully know Christ. The certain knowledge received after one accepted the Light demanded that one preach to the unconverted. Once a "minister" convinced new followers to admit the Light, as the apostles had done, the minister's job was done, for the new converts would know Christ through the help of the Light.[58] Thus authority rested within the Holy Spirit and was freely given to any male or female who chose to acquiesce.

Gwyn also assures us that Fox completely rejected Calvinist predestinarian theology, as it placed the "fault for sin upon God." Moreover, Calvinist Puritans and Free Will Christian Quakers differed fundamentally over the nature of man. For Calvinists, humans—whether elect or reprobate — would forever be evil. Quakers, on the other hand, knew men and women were wicked, but with God's presence manifest in the Light they could be free of sin. The purification process started with a human's free choice to admit the Light and thus gain faith, predicated upon God's grace in giving humans the opportunity to be saved. Once individuals were counted among the faithful, they faced the onerous task of purifying their souls through continuous good works made known to them through the Holy Spirit.[59]

While sharing many similar Arminian Anglican and Roman Catholic

tenets, English Quakers advanced their own unique ideas with regard to social conventions. In keeping with their emphasis on humility, meekness, and
spiritual (if not social) equality, they refused to show respect to their social
betters by bowing or removing their hats. They also denounced "house
creeping"—worshiping in secret—something Roman Catholics (and others)
had done to survive when persecuted. Additionally, Quakers concluded that
the Light's entrance into one's body constituted baptism, making the conventional water ritual unnecessary. And Fox took an apostolic view of communion. The apostles—true to their Jewish heritage—had taken communion in the form of feasting in the home; so too did the Quakers. Finally,
no single minister or priest led a Quaker meeting or followed a prescribed
ritual: anyone compelled by the Spirit—whether male or female—could
speak up and share the revealed word of God with all Friends present at the
meeting.

 Roman Catholics expressed many of the same sentiments as the Arminian Anglicans and Quakers—humbly imploring Jesus Christ to intercede on their behalf—thus underscoring shared theological tenets. Much
like their pre-Reformation predecessors, Roman Catholic testators continued to bequeath their souls to God, the Blessed Virgin, and all the saints in
heaven, and they also exposed their devotion to the cult of the dead with
money left for clerics to say prayers for them or their loved ones.[60] John
Wynne asked that his body be laid to "rest untill ye joyfull day of Resurrection when soul & body shall be reunited & made [partakers] of ye Joyes
of ev[e]rlasting glorie which Christ Jesus hath purchased for all such as
truly & unfeignedly repent & believe by his meritorious death & passion &
p[er]fect obedience."[61] Wynne paraphrased a passage from the Catholic
Sarum Missal that was translated in the Arminian Anglican prayer book as
"He pardoneth and absolveth all them that truly repent and unfeignedly believe his holy Gospel."[62] The desire to repent and the fundamental belief
in the testator's lack of worthiness permeate all the Free Will Christian preambles.[63] Some Roman Catholics added the "Glorious Virgin Mary" and the
"Holy Companyes of the S[ain]ts and Angells in Heaven" as mediators in
their effort to gain admittance into heaven.[64]

 In an act indicating their piety which was unique in all the colonies, the
Roman Catholics of Maryland named their first city after the most revered
female, St. Mary—the mother of Christ. Father Andrew White placed the
Ark and *Dove* under "the protection of God especially, and of His most Holy
Mother, and St. Ignatius" before setting sail for Maryland.[65] Many early
manors were named after saints, such as St. Thomas's, owned by the treasurer Giles Brent; St. Gabriel's, owned by Mary Brent; St. Elizabeth's, owned

by Thomas Cornwaleys; St. Peter's, the 1679 home of Commissioner Jerome Hawley; St. John's, the 1638 home of John Lewger, the first provincial secretary; and St. Barbara's, where another of Governor Leonard Calvert's councilors lived. Moreover, Captain Cornwaleys, chief councilor of the governor, commanded two armed boats called the *St. Helen* and the *St. Margaret* in an altercation with Virginia in 1635. Parents named their children after major saints; the Boarmans, for instance, named their children John Baptist, Francis (for either St. Francis of Assisi, founder of the Franciscan order, or St. Francis Xavier, a Jesuit), Ignatius (for St. Ignatius Loyola, founder of the Jesuit order), Benedict (for the founder of the Benedictine order), Mary (for the mother of Christ), Elizabeth (for the mother of St. John the Baptist), and Clare (for the founder of the Poor Clares).[66]

Wills provide more specific details of Catholic piety, as we see in the preamble to that of Thomas Gibson of Charles County, who bequeathed his "soule to ye Almighty God my maker & Jesus Christ my redeemer & to ye Holy Gost my Sanctifier & my body to ye Earth from whence it came to be buried in such decent & christian like manner as to my Executors shall be thought meet & convenient there to rest untill my soule & body shall meet againe & be joined together at ye Joyfull resurrection to be partakers of ye never fadeing joyes of Imortality w[hi]ch God of his mercy has promised & prepared for all those yt. truly repent & unfainedly[?] believe in him."[67] This passage illustrates several fundamental tenets of Gibson's faith, but its most noticeable theme is its eschatology. Maryland Catholics often referred to the end of the world, when the final judgment would take place. At this time, their souls would reunite with their bodies and "be joined together at ye Joyfull resurrection." The ultimate goal they worked to attain was the "never fadeing joyes of Imortality." While God offered salvation to all who "truly repent[ed]" and had faith, salvation could not be guaranteed. If an individual performed good works and followed the teachings of the church, he or she could hope to gain entrance into heaven.

William Jeffry's description of the Holy Ghost helps us to discern what Gibson meant by the term "Sanctifier." Jeffry relied on the Holy Ghost to assist him in gaining salvation when he "humbly beseech[ed] the holy Ghoest to Enlighten my minde and Understanding to Guide me to the Eternall Reward of an incorruptible and Blessed Immortallity in the Life to Come."[68] Explaining the Jesuit view of the Holy Ghost, Father William Hunter—who served Maryland from 1692 to 1723—gave a sermon on *"Repleti sunt omnes Spiritu Sancto"* ("They were all filled with the Holy Ghost," Acts 2:4, 4:31) on Pentecost Day, the seventh Sunday after Easter, the day on which the Holy Spirit descended on Jesus' disciples. Hunter told his congregation it was

the Holy Ghost and the manifestation of His power and glory that transformed congregants from sinners into penitent believers of God; the Holy
Ghost in his description is much like the Quaker Light.[69]

English Roman Catholics were accustomed to personalizing their spirituality in order to preserve their faith. In the province they had to accommodate Jesuit clerics' peculiar slant on doctrine. More accustomed to Dominican and Franciscan priests in England, the gentry perhaps listened to
the words and teachings of the Jesuits and then continued to follow their
families' traditional para-liturgical practices.[70] Newly converted Catholics
acted as their Quaker counterparts did—they melded the old and new beliefs to construct a customized religious experience. While some Catholic
priests found this adaptation process problematic, the church itself had a
long tradition of encouraging such behavior. Thus Maryland Roman Catholic spirituality was a hybrid. In order to fully understand this peculiar group,
we must consider the intriguing mix of militant Jesuits and gentry English
Catholics.[71]

Lord Baltimore, trying to temper the Jesuits' influence because of their
interest in land accumulation and their differing rituals, promoted the immigration of other Catholic orders. He sent three secular priests and two
Franciscans to the province, presumably to dilute the Jesuits' power.[72] Colonists navigated the waters of religious conformity intertwined with innovation, as Father Ferdinand Pulton noted in 1640, when he reported to the
Pope, "The Catholic settlers are not inferior in piety to those in other countries; in urbanity of manners, according to the judgment of those who have
visited other colonies, they are considered far superior to them."[73] The colonists themselves attempted to fit the Jesuit institution to their needs by
sending sons back to Europe to become Jesuits or by surrounding themselves with like-minded Jesuit uncles or nephews. In their own way, they too
had become Maryland Catholics.

The collection of rare seventeenth-century books housed at the Baltimore Carmelite monastery offers a glimpse into the unique theology of elite
English Catholics in early Maryland. Words of rationality and practicality
prevail in de Granada's preface to *A Memorial of a Christian Life*. He wrote,
"For as good Work—men take care to furnish themselves with all Instruments, necessary for their Trade, and as those, who apply themselves to any
Art or Science, do all, they can, to have some book, in which they may find,
whatever concerns the knowledge, they would acquire, that they may ease
their Memory by inclosing it (as it were) in one only place: for it seems to
me very expedient to do the like in the Science of Christianity, which is the
Art of Arts and Science of Sciences."[74] English Catholic theology called it-

self "scientific," indicating a valuing of systematic rhetoric and thought. Similarly, the *Journal of Meditations for everyday of the year* (1687) delineates the "order and method" of proper meditation. The preface explains, "Meditation is nothing else but an exercise of the Interiour Powers of our Soul, viz. Memory, Understanding, and Will; whereby we consider God, and the Mysteries of our Faith, entertaining our selves in affectuous discourses with his Divine Majesty; begging of him his gifts, and negotiating with him the main affair of our salvation and perfection."[75] English Catholics, both females and males, conversed and negotiated with God. This discourse, and the contemplation of beliefs, presupposed a rational, educated, autonomous religionist working toward salvation. The *Journal* also cites numerous ways to ruminate on biblical text; almost twenty percent of these involve positive female roles, the most persuasive of which are Marian in nature—which is to say, relating to the Virgin Mary. The book asks the reader to consider "what Reverence, Confidence and Love you ought hence to have towards this Sacred Virgin: Reverence, for the Excellency of her Dignity; Confidence, for the greatness of her Goodness; Love, for the tender bowels of her charity towards us; For she vouchsafeth to be a Mother she is of us: What might you not hope for, if you had a Mother that were Empress of the whole World? Love therefore, that you may deserve to be loved, and protected by so powerful a Lady."[76] Granted, the Catholics did not deem the Virgin Mary an ordinary woman. Yet the centrality of this female presence of maternity and power—along with many other less powerful but no less pertinent female saints—can be detected in the familial, economic, and civil lives of Maryland Catholics.[77] William Neale, a wealthy gentleman and descendant of the early colonial gentry, exemplified how these values influenced personal relationships when he augmented the Carmelite library with many books from the Neale family library. For example, William gave *A Liturgical Discourse of the Holy Sacrifice of the Masse By way of Dialogue* (1669) to Ann Brook, a Carmelite nun, in 1731.[78] This work referred to the Catholic church as "our Holy Mother" and posed dialectic discourse in the tradition of St. Thomas Aquinas's *Summa Theologica*. Of course, Ann and William were related, but more importantly, William assumed Ann to be a rational, contemplative intellectual.[79]

While Maryland Roman Catholics enjoyed a certain amount of liberty to shape their faith, we must consider the English experience—for surely their Catholicism was grounded in the English tradition. After Parliament had passed the Protestant Acts of Supremacy and Uniformity in January of 1559, reestablishing the state church, English men and women had to shift their religious allegiance once again.[80] This time, in a break with their earlier behavior, many English clerics refused to convert and were subsequently forced out of office. While banished and waiting for the demise of this new Protestantism, men like Thomas Stapleton produced massive amounts of literature systematically articulating English Catholic theology.[81] Stapleton argued that religious *illuminati*, such as St. Augustine, St. Thomas Aquinas, and the participants in the Council of Trent (which first met in 1545), had to interpret the Bible for general consumption, because the text itself was ambiguous and contradictory.[82] In direct opposition to the Calvinists, Stapleton specified that the Bible in and of itself was not the ultimate authority on the word of God for the Catholics.

The Council of Trent, in particular, provided a solid foundation for Catholic theologians defending their faith against the Calvinists by defining "justification" for Catholics. The Council restated the traditional theology that sinners had to choose—of their own free will—to cooperate with Christ, whose grace was essential to salvation. Catholics were "justified" through the remission of sin and the "sanctification and renewal of the whole" person, achieved by following the Ten Commandments and performing good works. Thus, in contrast to the Calvinist position, abiding by the Ten Commandments was a duty and an intrinsic component in the process of purification, not merely a reflection of one's justified state. Catholics reiterated their traditional view, arguing that good works, faith, and grace were essential to one's salvation. The church itself played an intrinsic role, then, as it brought sinners into the fold. The Catholic church welcomed reprobate and pious persons, as did the Arminian Anglican and Quaker denominations; they were allowed to participate in the Mass, since all persons could work toward their salvation if they chose to accept Christ, perform good works, and humbly ask God's forgiveness for sins committed.

Significantly, Stapleton recognized only two religious sects in England —Calvinism and Catholicism. Elizabethan English Catholic theologians like Stapleton primarily focused their attacks on Calvinism and its predestinarian theology, because the largely unsystematic doctrine of Lutheranism, centering on the tenet of "justification by faith alone," posed less of a threat to the English Catholics. After all, " 'Calvin had vomited out more blasphemies' than the whole school of Wittenberg combined." Stapleton's treatise on Martin Luther, Philip Melanchthon, and John Calvin was almost exclusively devoted to a refutation of the "Contradictions of Calvin," rather than to debating Luther's or Melanchthon's ideas. In fact, in "England the Calvinists had become so numerous and powerful that they had driven underground all the other sects, and they preached that Luther was virtually a papist."[83] For Stapleton then, only two religious ideologies divided

Englishmen—Calvinism and Catholicism—and their mutually exclusive soteriology and views on sanctification rendered them irreconcilable.[84]

Parliament passed several acts against recusancy—the crime of refusing to attend Church of England services—between 1558 and 1627, forcing families to devise ways to avoid the stiff penalties while continuing to practice their Catholicism; they would later transport this adaptability with them to Maryland.[85] Patrick Malloy suggests that because English Catholics were often deprived of clerical guidance in England, recusant devotional books in general and manuals in particular helped inform Catholics about theology, soteriology, and epistemology through a daily ritual of prayer. Even before the English Reformations, this traditional ritual had played an integral role in the lives of Roman Catholics, since the mystical language of the Mass and the separation of clergy and congregation by a rood screen necessitated a method of catechizing men, women, and children through daily prayer and devotions.

John Bossy has argued that after the Stuarts lost the throne and Parliament passed the Toleration Act in 1688, English Roman Catholics were largely free from molestation. Bossy makes the point that the Toleration Act effectively abolished the offence of recusancy by making church attendance unenforceable. English mobs still attacked Catholic chapels, but government authorities did not prevent priests from saying Mass in them. Largely uncensored, Catholic theologians also continued to print their views in England. Bossy suggests that "the English Catholics . . . were not on any reasonable judgement an oppressed minority. . . . [The Catholic Church's] membership increased; it kept its children by careful catechizing and pastoral care, and acquired converts, mainly by marriage. It kept up its morale through a fairly intense religious practice, and through the relatively generous prospects of employment and betterment which existed for the majority of its members." English Catholics were nothing if not adaptable. "[I]t was frequently impossible for a priest to get a decent chapel built without [the help of local Anglicans]. There grew up in such chapels, and probably in others, a quite vigorous tradition of vernacular congregational prayers which put the formal liturgy into a relatively participatory frame." Catholics, historically accustomed to para-liturgical behavior in church and wishing to customize their individual religious experience, "preferred to spend their time at Mass in meditative and personal communication with their Saviour present in the sacrament of the altar."[86] In effect, this was also the Maryland way.

The common threads of shared language and biblical emphasis, humility in asking for forgiveness of their sins, the uncertainty of salvation, and a dependence on intercessors cemented the Arminian Anglicans, Quakers, and Roman Catholics as a cohort and helped to mark a large group of Free Will Christians. Free Will Christian wills contained distinctively phrased preambles expressing similar sentiments; testators wrote that they were "heartily Sorry" for their sins and hoped "to have forgiveness for ye same by ye Merritts of Jesus Christ."[87] The spiritual similarities within this cohort allow us to identify hundreds of individuals as Free Will Christians whose specific religious denomination remains elusive.

The Predestinarians' certainty regarding their eternal salvation contrasts sharply with the hopeful yearnings of the Free Will Christians and their humble begging of God's forgiveness as a means of gaining entrance into heaven. Predestinarians most often referred to themselves as among "God's Elect and Chosen," while pronouncing that they "believe[d] assuredly to be Saved." Thus Bartholomew Ennalls wrote confidently, "I give and bequeath my soule unto almighty god who gave it with a full & absolute assurance of the pardon and remission of all my sinns in and through the merritts and Suffrings of my Lord and Saviour Jesus Christ."[88] Bartholomew's faith in Jesus Christ provided the means to salvation, but Jesus was not a mediator between Bartholomew and God. Bartholomew believed Christ's death on the cross entitled him to salvation. Additionally, the notion of justification by faith—a central tenet of predestinarian theology—is also present. Teague Riggin, Sr., of Somerset County wrote, "I freely Committ my Soule to god Who gave it by whose mercy and free grace I Expect alone to be pardoned and to his Son Jesus Christ by whose Death and Bloud I Expect Sallvation and by the Impution of whose Righteousness I belive to be Justified."[89] Predestinarians had no need for intercessors and did not beseech God to overlook their transgressions. They believed themselves saved through justification by faith alone, with the grace of God, independent of any worldly good works, thus making them easy to identify by the terms used in their preambles. Although most testators' particular denomination (e.g., Particular Baptist, Presbyterian, or Puritan) remains shadowy at best, the ability to identify Predestinarians by their bald soteriological statements provides us with a useful category of analysis.

Like the Calvinists in New England and England, Maryland Calvinists appear to have believed in five basic tenets, often simplified by religious historians as "TULIP." The T stands for total depravity, U for unconditional election, L for limited atonement, I for irresistible grace, and P for perseverance of the saints. Total depravity meant that since Adam's fall from grace, humans did not have the capacity to seek either God or goodness. Humans' thoughts and desires were corrupted by sin even when they attempted to seek God or abide by the Ten Commandments. Unconditional election meant that God had selected certain individuals to be saved by his grace and the rest of humanity was destined to eternal damnation. Humans could do nothing to alter their condition. In the minds of the Calvinists, limited atonement was reserved for the elect, meaning that Christ died on the cross to pay for the sins of God's chosen, not the damned. Irresistible grace meant that even if one of the elect wanted to live a sinful life and hate God, when the Holy Spirit called him or her to God, he or she would be converted. The elect could not resist God's grace. Conversely, no matter how godly a life a reprobate led, God would still hate the eternally condemned. And since the elect had no control over God's grace, they were unable to fall out of His grace. Thus the perseverance of the saints meant that the elect were eternally secure in their election.

Since the Puritans immigrating into Maryland tended to come from other American colonies, an examination of the Massachusetts Calvinists seems appropriate.[90] Puritans in New England relied solely on the Bible as the foundation for doctrine, ritual, and church structure. The information in the Bible had come directly from God and thus if an action or concept appeared in the Bible, it was justifiable. The soteriology of the Arminian Anglicans and Roman Catholics had taken a less literal form, with a reliance on interpretive theology expressed in terms of liturgy rather than based strictly on the Bible. Edmund Morgan suggests the Calvinists of New England concentrated their efforts on constructing a "visible church" resembling St. Augustine's "invisible" one. In other words, the New England Calvinists insisted on a church made up solely of "visible saints"—those who had already passively received saving faith. This conception of faith—and of the absence of human free will—deviates substantively from the Arminian Anglicans'. Moreover, the Calvinist minister's duty to his congregation was not to evangelize in order to save sinners, as the Arminian Anglicans, Catholics, and Quakers did, but rather to remind the saints of their inherent evils and the covenant of grace that God had mercifully bestowed upon them. Sanctification, then, was a gift from God, not a process relying on free will. Humans—inherently and unredeemably evil—gained salvation only if God elected to accept them into heaven regardless of their sin.[91]

The colonists' adaptability, which was due in part to the scarcity of the comforts of home, helped them to replicate their old world by means of some ingenious innovations, the most important of which were religious practices. By evaluating each religious group, we have analyzed the continuity between Arminian Anglican, Quaker, and Roman Catholic architecture, burial practices, and doctrine. Granted, these three groups did not readily acknowledge their shared religiosity—their doctrines varied enough to distinguish each from the others. After all, Arminian Anglicans refused to accept the Roman Catholic pope as their spiritual leader and put a temporal prince in his place. Quakers in England and Maryland shared a unique apostolic vision that included a firm belief in the efficacy of women ministers. And while Arminian Anglicans and Roman Catholics retained the medieval episcopacy, celebrating Mass at the sacred altars on Sundays in their ornate vestments, Quakers maintained a fluid yet austere gathering in which any male or female might illuminate converts with God's words. Still, the similarities amongst these groups seem all the more remarkable, as Roman Catholic devotional literature referred to their Arminian Anglican brethren as "fallen" Catholics, with the sincere belief they would eventually see the error of their ways and return to the fold. As late as 1855 in Maryland, the Arminian Anglicans were called by historians "Protestants of the Anglo-Catholic type" to differentiate them from the Calvinists.[92] And the significant rate of intermarriage amongst these three groups in Maryland substantiates their fundamental affinity. We are not surprised to find that Calvinists found these three Free Will Christian groups similar enough to use the pejorative term "papist" to describe them all.

The conceptual constructs of each group permit an analysis cementing the Arminian Anglicans, Quakers, and Roman Catholics as a Free Will Christian cohort. These Marylanders—who often paraphrased scripture in their wills—had an intimate knowledge of the Bible. Yet the Bible was not the ultimate authority relating God's word to His people, as the Calvinists had argued. The Arminian Anglicans and Roman Catholics relied on prelate interpreters to devise rituals for church services and home routines of feasting, fasting, and daily prayer founded on theological premises. These liturgical and para-liturgical experiences served to inform both reprobate and saintly parishioners alike. Moreover, Roman Catholics and Arminian Anglicans shared the same religious calendar and equivalent liturgy, in either the Roman Missal or the Anglican Book of Common Prayer. Quakers also adhered to scripture less literally than did the Calvinists. They armed themselves with biblical passages in order to convince others of the truth. Yet—like Arminian Anglicans and Roman Catholics and in stark contrast to Calvinists—they held that salvation could be obtained without ever having read the Bible. All three Free Will Christian groups in Maryland constructed church hierarchies in which religious authority primarily rested within a small group of supreme priests or ministers. And while colonists observed the sanctity of religious offices, they were inclined to construct their personal lives according to their own needs and desires.

Innovation proved essential to the vitality of all of the English religious denominations in the early years of the province, yet colonists adhered to some basic creedal understandings derived from English sources as well. All three groups recognized every sinner's capacity to work toward salvation. The salvation of an individual's soul depended largely on the decision— allowed by free will—to accept God's grace and thus have faith. This marked merely the commencement of a process of purification intended to rid the soul of sin. With God's assistance, sinners toiled diligently (some more energetically than others) toward salvation by performing good works, though they could never be quite sure they had been successful in their struggles. This basic belief in the ability of human beings to redeem themselves through faith and good works was antithetical to the Calvinist understanding of depraved sinners' election and justification.

A pattern emerged that closely ties the Quakers in early Maryland to their Roman Catholic and Arminian Anglican brethren. This pattern also serves to distance these believers in free will from the Calvinists of both New England and Maryland. Gerard Croese summed it up quite nicely when he wrote in 1697 that "The Quakers are the truest Catholick Church in the World," with their "President in their Synod, which place they say is supplyed by the Holy Ghost, &c. This is the great Foundation upon which the Church of Rome build their Faith . . . as such, they are to be indispensably obeyed, as was the Precepts of the inspired Apostles; this they [the Quakers] deny; and none hold it but the Papists and Quakers."[93] Others in early modern England also recognized the similarities between the Quakers and their Catholic brethren: not just in their architecture, gravestone iconography, and theological and soteriological views established here, or in the church episcopacy described by Croese, but also in their acceptance of women in the religious realm, which is the topic of the next chapter.

4

∾

Women and Religion

In a popular English text of 1658 an anonymous author railed against the Jesuits who were, in his mind, taking over the western world. The author warned that "most of the Noble Families about Europe" had been infiltrated by this hated Roman Catholic order, for few families were "without one or more of them." These spies relayed important information to the pope as they "intermedle[d] in matters of State" from their elevated positions within influential families instead of busying themselves with the "safety of their own & others souls, having to that purpose retired from the world." According to this author there were "four sorts of Jesuits" strategically positioned to take over the western world: the wealthy "Citizens and rich Merchants" acting on Jesuit orders; Jesuit priests posing as laypeople and influencing wealthy and noble families; the Jesuit clergy; and the dreaded "Jesuits-Polititians" bent on advancing "their Company to a perfect Monarcy." Members of the "first sort" were by far the most insidious, because the Jesuits controlled large numbers of laypeople through the manipulation of the daughters, wives, and widows of high-ranking families. The author was convinced that these women were "under a blind obedience, governing themselves in their particular actions, by the counsel and advice of the father Jesuits." The Jesuits sought to undermine the patriarchal order of the household by manipulating female family members. They also threatened the very fabric of society when they "usurpt the sustenance of Widows, leaving the kindred in very great misery, by enticing and alluring to their fellowship, those of the greatest families that frequent their School and Colledge." For this author, women played a prominent role in the popish threat to the political and social order. Wealthy females—young and old—influenced their male kin to carry out the Jesuits' "evill" plans and, worse yet, they funded the Jesuits' militant attempt to reconquer Europe by relinquishing family property that had been left to them in their widowhood. Consequently, these women turned the patriarchal social order on its head when they acted as historical agents ushering in a popish revolution. The author concluded with a warning that the western world faced the "most dangerous and evill consequence" if governments did not recognize this immediate threat and initiate a "speedy and powerfull remedy" before all was lost to the Roman monarchy.[1]

Another author shared this anxiety about women's penchant for destroying the known social order in his *The Life of Donna Olimpia Maldachini, Who Governed the Church, during the time of Innocent the X, which was from the Year 1644–1655,* an English translation of an Italian original. Here the author (or the translator) argued that Pope Innocent X allowed his sister-in-law to make his decisions for him and in so doing paved the way for her to control the entire Roman Catholic Church for more than a decade. Indeed, the pope "never entered upon any affair publick or private, but first acquainted his Sister-in-law with it; whose advice he took his measure by." The author summed up the story with advice that "the Churchmen [i.e., clergy] of the Roman Faith, will do any thing with a Woman, but Marry her."[2] The natural order of things, in this author's view, placed women as obedient wives under the direct control of male patriarchs. Roman Catholics, however, did not conform to the natural order of the world when they allowed a female to dictate church policy and other "publick or private" papal matters. This potent anti-Catholic rhetoric, emphasizing the folly and ineptitude of the church's most revered leader, drew at least some of its power from the male fear of women controlling men and their spheres of influence. These conspiracy-minded authors were not alone in their concern over the extent to which women participated in religious affairs in early modern England. In 1641 another anonymous English author was mortified to discover "Six women preachers in Middlesex, Kent, Cambridgshire and Salisbury." Faced with an inadequate supply of qualified male preachers, Anne Hempstall, Mary Bilbrow, Joane Bauford, Susan May, Elizabeth Bancroft, and Arabella Thomas—all self-proclaimed "vertuous women"—took it upon themselves to preach to female gatherings "such things as the spirit should move them."[3] The author was horrified by these unschooled women interpreting and disseminating important religious doctrine. In this author's view, it was better to forego religious instruction altogether than to have a female assume a ministerial role and preach to the English country-folk.

These examples of inversions of the patriarchal social order, initiated by Roman Catholic and Protestant women alike, may have existed only in the imaginations of these male authors. Yet collectively these popular diatribes point to a persistent and pervasive fear of women in the male-dominated world of religion—and not without provocation. Women, in fact, played a vital part in English Roman Catholic and Protestant denominations in early modern England, to such an extent that contemporaries—like these anonymous authors—could not ignore their presence. In England, particularly during the Civil War and the Interregnum, women preached, proselytized, debated religious issues, and published religious treatises on an unprecedented scale. Women like Susannah Hopton successfully challenged the male domination of religion by publishing popular devotional books, while other women chose to preach directly to a public audience.[4] Historian Patricia Crawford has argued that "male refrains of 'attend to the spindle and distaff,' and 'go home and wash your dishes'" in response to women's active role in the spiritual sphere "led women to formulate positions which justified female political action." Further empowered and justified by Christian teachings and their new authority in the religious world, women "refused to accept the view that the secular political sphere was an exclusively male domain." Crawford suggests that the gendered battle for power and authority in English religious groups allowed women to make substantial gains during the seventeenth century.[5] Perhaps English women arriving in Maryland carried with them these ideas and practices.

Described by one of her descendants as "the most beautiful and charming girl of her generation," Henrietta Maria Neale began her life as a member of a wealthy Roman Catholic English family that traveled extensively during her youth, finally settling permanently in the English Roman Catholic province of Maryland in 1661.[6] Her parents, Captain James Neale and Ann Gill, both served the crown under Charles I and his Roman Catholic queen, Henrietta Maria. Showing her great affection for her maid of honor, the queen agreed to be her namesake's godmother. When she reached maturity, Henrietta Maria Neale married Richard Bennett, who met an untimely end when he drowned in the Wye River, leaving her with an infant son to care for and a plantation to manage. She later married Anglican gentleman Philemon Lloyd and bore him several sons and daughters before he died.[7] In his last will Philemon asked his Catholic wife Henrietta Maria to educate their children in the Anglican faith. He wrote, "I will yt my children be brought up in ye Protestant Religion and carryed to such church or churches where it is profest & to noe other dureing their minority & untill such years of discretion as may render them best capable to Judge what is most consenant to ye good will of Almighty God unto w[hi]ch I pray God of his mercy direct them."[8] Philemon knew full well that his wife taught her children the Roman Catholic doctrine at home and he wished to counterbalance this with an Anglican religious experience for his children in the hope that they might better choose their faith as they grew older.

Blessed at birth with wealth and land, Henrietta Maria Neale entered both of her marriages with considerable power and moved freely within the civic arena as well as the church. Her activities in the province of Maryland were as varied as they were numerous. For instance, she served as the executrix of her good friend John Londey's will, legally responsible for distributing his property to his heirs in addition to collecting and paying off his debts.[9] She also built a Roman Catholic chapel on her property and maintained an important position within the Catholic community throughout her life. The Calvinists—who gained control of Maryland in 1689 as a consequence of the Glorious Revolution in England—recognized her position in the Catholic community and her ability to launch a military campaign against them when they raided her storehouse of firearms and ammunition.

Henrietta Maria's piety found its last expression in her generous bequests to her favorite priests. When she died in 1697, her son Richard Bennett inscribed his mother's tombstone with words expressing his admiration for her. The stone slab reads

> Shee that now takes her Rest within this t[omb]
> had Rachell's face and Lea's fruitefu[ll womb]
>   Abigall's wisdom Lydea's Faithfu[ll heart]
>   with Martha's care and Mary's be[tter part][10]

Richard's inscription demonstrates his extensive knowledge of Old Testament female biblical figures, more than likely the result of the religious education he received from his mother when he was growing up. He put his knowledge to good use when he selected the biblical females to compare his mother to, including Laban's daughters, Rachel and Leah, in the second line.[11] Leah's lovely eyes attracted her suitor, Jacob, who served her father for fourteen years in order to win her hand in marriage. Both daughters married Jacob, and "fruitefull" Leah gave birth to six sons and a daughter. Significantly, the beautiful Rachel was an aggressive woman who sought to have her own way. She stole the symbols of familial leadership—the "household gods"—that legitimized her father's claim to the clan's property. The third line refers to Abigail, who successfully negotiated with David to spare the life of her traitorous husband, Nabal. David had found Abigail's intellect so appealing that he asked her to be his wife after Nabal's death. Richard also knew of the New Testament women Martha, Mary, and Lydia, the latter a businesswoman who was a "dealer in purple cloth" and a faithful believer in God. Martha worked hard while her sister, Mary, sat at the feet of Christ listening to His teaching. Later, both sisters acted as intercessors on their brother's behalf when they successfully implored Christ to save Lazarus. It seems plausible that Richard carefully selected the names of Old and New Testament women to represent the characteristics of beauty, fruitfulness, cunning, sagacity, piety, and power that, in his mind, were his mother's most remarkable qualities. Perhaps his final tribute to Henrietta Maria Neale also stands as a permanent memorial to her effective religious teachings.

Henrietta Maria Neale's power in her family and in the Roman Catholic community was principally predicated upon her ability to maintain and control real estate. As with all other adults in this early modern province, Henrietta Maria's status in her community, her church, and her family rested upon her ownership of land. Indeed, she purchased several parcels amounting to more than sixteen hundred acres during her lifetime that added to her already extensive holdings provided by her father and two husbands. Illustrating her authority over her dominion, Henrietta Maria named her tracts of land "Henrietta Maria's Discovery" and "Henrietta Maria's Purchase." As a consequence of her status as a major patron, the priests sought her counsel, she was accepted as a trusted associate in legal and business transactions, and her husband, her children, and the generations that followed respected her as the family matriarch. As a landholder she entered both her marriages as a financial partner, expecting to be consulted by her husbands in decisions regarding land and labor usage and the allocation of property to their children. Additionally, she shared in the disciplining of their children and in decisions regarding their education. When Henrietta Maria wrote her last will and testament, she left both her sons and her daughters real estate, perhaps so that they too could secure positions of authority in their community, their church, and their families as marital partners.

Free Will Christian English women in Maryland, like Henrietta Maria, were integral members of their religious groups, and their menfolk seemed relatively unthreatened by their positions and their actions. Like their English counterparts, Maryland females educated their children (and others) in the doctrines and central tenets of their church in order to ensure the group's continued survival. Additionally, wealthier women used their resources of both land and money to build and maintain chapels, while they also supplied and cared for communion plate. Men sought women's input and assistance in acquiring and maintaining adequate clerical care for their communities. And when faced with death, women bequeathed to clergy and the poor goods, land, and money as a final token of their deep and abiding piety. The duties and responsibilities that Free Will Christian women embraced as pious church members in Maryland were much the same as those they had experienced in England. As in England, the wealthiest women in Maryland enjoyed more power and authority in their churches and communities than their poorer counterparts, yet even women from middling families were able to construct their own spiritual spheres of influence in the province.[12]

The scarcity of priests and ministers in the newly settled province strengthened the role of women as religious educators. For most women, their role as religious teachers remained firmly fixed within the home. Catholic John Parsons asked his wife Mary "to maintaine and Educate my said Children bringing them up in the fear of God and the Holy Catholick Religion not at all doubting of her love to and tender care over them."[13] This behavior was also described by Arminian Anglican Thomas Stockett, who wrote, "I Surely trust [my wife] will not neglect any Endeavour that shall be tending to [the children's] good both in Religious Education and for the advancement of their temporall ffortunes which I beseech the Lord of Heaven to give his assistance unto."[14] Women shared their husbands' concerns regarding the importance of religious education, so that when widows left wills providing for young children they often included specific directions regarding their children's instruction. Widow Deborah Davis left a will indicating that her six-year-old daughter was to be placed in the custody of Reverend William Hampton until the girl reached seventeen. Davis stipulated that Madam Hampton "shall teach or cause her to be taught to read the holy Bible & do what other kindness to my daughter she shall see fitt and in case of mortality to dispose of her as she pleases."[15] Davis left her child in the care of her minister and his wife because she wished the spiritual teaching she had already begun with her daughter to be continued. Significantly, it was Madam Hampton's responsibility rather than the reverend's to instruct Deborah's daughter. This important stipulation in Deborah's last will indicates that even in families where the father was an ordained minister and the spiritual leader of his community, the duty of inculcating religious beliefs and teaching small children to read the holy scriptures belonged to the female authority figure in the family. Deborah's daughter and most other children in the province received at least a rudimentary education, predicated on religion, from mothers. Children from families that did not depend heavily upon their added labor often attended a school for one to four years of formal education provided by clerics, or occasionally by female teachers, generally beginning at age twelve or thirteen.[16] Free Will Christians encouraged the instruction of children at home by women during the formative years of child development, a practice that strengthened women's positions in the propagation of doctrine.[17]

Women taught their husbands doctrine as well. Walter Smith, a faithful Arminian Anglican belonging to All Saints Parish in Calvert County, left us evidence of such behavior in his will when he died in 1711.[18] Walter had married Rachel Hall, a member of a prominent Maryland Quaker family, in 1686, and in his testament he used the word "Spirit" as if he had been a pious Quaker, indicating that he had absorbed some central Quaker tenets during his marriage and had melded them with his own Arminian Anglican convictions.[19] Of course, it is impossible to say whether or not Rachel encouraged her husband to attend Quaker Meetings or if his Quaker understandings were inculcated only in their home. We do know that Walter attended the Quaker wedding of Richard Tayller and Ann Trasey in 1687, so he must have felt at least somewhat comfortable with Quaker rites and rituals very early in his marriage.[20] We might assume that Rachel had many different opportunities to influence her husband's religious beliefs, both at Quaker gatherings and in their home.

In addition to educating children and husbands in their faiths, some women, like Henrietta Maria Neale and Mrs. Brooks, built and maintained chapels in their homes or on their plantations.[21] Anne Ayres Chew, a Quaker, also chose to provide her community with a building for worship and enough land for a graveyard. Anne donated both the land and labor for the Herring Creek meetinghouse, to be constructed on the property that had been given to her by her father in 1658.[22] Arminian Anglican Susannah Gerrard, on the other hand, asked for and received the cooperation of her husband in the construction of sacred space on the family's property. Susannah convinced her Roman Catholic husband that a new chapel on their plantation could serve both the Arminian Anglicans and Roman Catholics in their community, and it did so for many years.[23] Elizabeth Baker, by contrast, donated merely the land so that a church could be built close to her home. Elizabeth devised one hundred acres to her parish—enough land to support a church, rectory, school, and graveyard.[24] Perhaps it was this female propensity for donating land to their churches that prompted Lord Baltimore to initiate legislation limiting such bequests to two and one-half acres unless sanctioned by the Assembly. Maryland is the only state or colony ever to pass such a law, and it is still on the books today.

Women who were wealthy patrons of their churches and the sponsors of new sacred spaces probably enjoyed greater authority within their religious communities than others.[25] Property holding also entitled wealthy Arminian Anglican and Roman Catholic women to purchase, house, and protect the treasured religious accouterments, including communion plate, sacred priestly robes, and altar coverings used in worship services. While Jane Brent Green protected the sacred vestments and communion plate, she also contributed "Tenn pounds Sterling" to "ye building or use of the Chappell of Port Tobbo[cco]."[26] Jane was not as wealthy as Henrietta Maria Neale, who could afford to sponsor a Roman Catholic chapel, but she still wished to donate as much as she could so that with the help of other donors a new chapel would be built. In fact, Roman Catholic priests had traditionally encouraged women to enter into joint ventures that lessened their individual financial burden for the purpose of constructing new churches and refurbishing the old. In Cecil County Mary Ann and Margaret O'Daniels pooled their resources to donate three hundred acres of land to Jesuit priest Thomas Mansell to establish a church at St. Xavier.[27] Women's ability to sponsor and maintain sacred spaces in addition to purchasing and protecting religious equipage ensured their authority within their religious institutions as substantial benefactors.

Colonial Maryland women's wealth and acquired status appears to have led some men to accept their authority. Perhaps it was Mary Taney's status as the wife of Calvert County's sheriff that allowed her to wield authority not only in her community but also across the Atlantic Ocean, influencing high-ranking political and religious leaders in England. Agitated over the lack of spiritual guidance by an ordained priest in her frontier community, Mary wrote to both the king of England (as Supreme Governor of the Church of England) and the archbishop of Canterbury to seek their assistance. She asked for the enormous sum of five hundred pounds sterling to erect a church and to support an Arminian Anglican priest, as well as requesting religious texts and Bibles. In her letter to the archbishop she pointed out that her family and her community were loyal "subjects of the King of England," and therefore he had an obligation to protect them and their estates. More importantly, he was to protect "what is far more dear to us, our religion."[28] Both Charles II and the archbishop of Canterbury accepted Mary as her community's spokesperson. They rewarded her for her service with a large shipment of Bibles (and other devotional books), followed by the money needed to build a church and support the Reverend Paul Ber-trand. Thus Mary Taney's family and community, and England's most pow-erful spiritual (and political) leaders, affirmed her position as an effective voice and intercessor in consequential religious matters.[29]

Even women who did not enjoy Mary Taney's high status influenced the practices and leadership of their religious institutions. A 1715 letter from the Baltimore Arminian Anglican congregation of St. Paul's Church to its En-glish bishop requested that the priest, William Tibbs, "be removed and that your Excellency out of Pity will Institute another in his place that will sh[o]w better Example and not fail to Admonish his Auditory to a more stricter Course of Life." The congregation accused Tibbs of being "a comon Drunkard" and often "drunk on his taking the Sacrament before it can be supposed that the bread and Wine is dijested in his Stomach." Moreover, they claimed, "he demands and receives mon[e]y for Administring the Sac-rament of the Lord's Supper when [he] gives it in Private houses." And, much to their chagrin, "he refused to go to private houses to baptize Chil-dren that are Sick and not able to be brought to the Church without being paid for it."[30] The evidence against Tibbs rested largely on the accusations of two women, Mary Boone Merriman and Rebecca Colegate. Both strongly felt that a priest should primarily concern himself with the salvation of souls rather than fattening his purse. Obviously the vestrymen of the church assumed the testimony from these ordinary women would further their cause against an unpopular cleric.[31]

Free Will Christian women in Maryland wielded power and authority in their religious communities as educators, patrons, intercessors, and deci-sion-makers. Accordingly, when they faced death women of means sought to provide their parishes or Societies with a final remembrance of their spirituality and their concern for the poor and for the continuation of their particular religious group. Some husbands acted in conjunction with their wives in making these charitable gifts. William Bretton deeded a parcel of land to the Jesuits to build a Catholic church with his wife's permission and support:

> Know ye that I William Bretton of Little-Bretton in ye County of Saint Mary's in ye Prov[ince] of Md. Gent[leman] with the hearty good lik-ing of my dearly beloved wife Temperance Bretton have given and do herby freely give forever to the behoof of the said Roman Catholic in-habitants and their posterity or successors, Roman Catholics so much land as they shall build ye said church or chapel on with such other land adjoining to said church or chapel convenient likewise for a church yard

wherin to bury their dead containing about one acre and a half of ground.[32]

Perhaps reflecting the English legacy of religiously active women, Temperance Bretton readily performed pious functions as a matter of course in conjunction with her partner. Both William and Temperance sought to express their spirituality (and possibly secure themselves a place in heaven) through the use of their ample estate.

Some historians have suggested that, as a group, women were more inclined than men to make charitable bequests to their churches and to the poor.[33] Yet this was not the case in seventeenth-century Maryland, where both men and women left parts of their estates to the poor or their church approximately 7 percent of the time. Gender differences in bequests were evident, however, between the Predestinarian and Free Will Christian cohorts. Roughly one out of every six Free Will Christian males and females left something to the poor, individual priests, or the church, while only one out of every thirty-three male Predestinarians did so. Strikingly, Predestinarian women never left portions of their estate to the poor or their church. This discrepancy between the two religious groups can be accounted for in large measure by the two cohorts' distinctive theological tenets. While good deeds were considered to be signs of one's election, Predestinarians did not have to perform good works to gain their salvation; their destinies were already determined. Long before they were born, God had decided who would be saved and gain eternal peace in heaven and who would be damned to an eternal life in hell. Good works, such as leaving money to the poor or the church in a will, would not alter a person's condition as one of the damned or one of the elect and chosen saints. However, both the Roman Catholic and Arminian Anglican churches encouraged traditional requiems and a gift remembrance of the poor at the time of one's death. Catholic women in England—such as Catherine Petres, who sheltered her wealth in a Paris bank—gave money and other items regularly to convents in other countries so those nuns would say prayers for them.[34] Quakers also were inspired by the Spirit to do good deeds for the preservation of their souls. All of these Free Will Christian testators believed that material contributions to the poor and their religious communities assisted their entrance into heaven. Thus we are not surprised to see that the female benefactors in Maryland were Arminian Anglicans, Quakers, and Roman Catholics rather than Predestinarians.[35]

While religious ideology contributed to Free Will Christians' inclination to bequeath property to the poor or the church, other factors also came into play. Roman Catholic men often bequeathed their wives large portions of the family's real estate for life. Occasionally, husbands gave their wives land in freehold (in addition to movable goods), allowing them to divest the property as they thought just.[36] This provided Roman Catholic women— who made up the bulk of female benefactors—with the means to make charitable donations. Not surprisingly, all of the female benefactors were women of means. Unlike their Predestinarian counterparts, Roman Catholic women who left money to the church—including Elizabeth Diggs, Jane Green, Elizabeth Lindsey, Henrietta Maria Neale Lloyd, Ann Gill Neale, and Frances Sayer—did so primarily to ensure the salvation of their souls.[37] Additionally, Quakers like Elizabeth Balding and Arminian Anglicans like Elizabeth Rigbye also bequeathed portions of their estates for the benefit of the poor of their communities or the support of their church.[38]

These examples point to some possible connections between religious ideology and a general willingness on the part of males in the church and the larger community to accept the active role Free Will Christian women played in seventeenth-century Maryland religious communities. In addition to a common belief in the importance of good works for their entrance into heaven, Free Will Christians also shared a fundamental acceptance of female authority figures within the church and the family. Unlike Anne Hutchinson and other Puritan women, who were banished from John Winthrop's Calvinist colony for propagating their beliefs, and the predominantly female victims of witch-hunts all across Calvinist New England, English Roman Catholic women were encouraged to act as spiritual leaders by establishing religious orders. Moreover, the seventeenth century saw the surprising rise of the Virgin Mary to a status equivalent to that of Jesus Christ as the *"alter Christus"* in English Roman Catholic devotional literature, which signified a magnified role for Catholic women in general.[39] Arminian Anglicans joined the Roman Catholics in their embrace of the Virgin Mary, paying her respect in their daily observances, which followed the religious calendar that Catholics and Arminian Anglicans shared. Arminian Anglicans adopted the Roman Catholic acceptance of female spiritual leaders on earth as well. Similarly, the Quakers extended virtual religious equality to their womenfolk by expecting them to serve as ministers during Sunday services and in converting others outside their community.[40] These powerful female intercessors among and for the English Arminian Anglicans, Quakers, and Roman Catholics provided positive female models of behavior for both men and women. Confident assertive women were not witches, as they were in Calvinist New England; they were saints.

Historian Elizabeth Reis's gendered analysis of Puritanism points to the inherent contradiction between the position of men as active, powerful patriarchs and the notion that their submissive souls had to passively wait for Christ to carry them to heaven. Women also faced a paradox; their souls could be either godly in their passivity or inherently "ungracious, wicked [and] self-hating." Puritans' conception of the soul led them "to imagine that women were more likely than men to submit to Satan. A woman's feminine soul, jeopardized in a woman's feminine body, was frail, submissive, and passive—qualities that most New Englanders thought would allow her to become either a [good] wife to Christ or a drudge to Satan." The only aggressive women in the society were witches. Reis argues that the witches were "[t]oo impatient or too weak to wait passively for Christ's advance," and they "allowed their bodies and souls to choose, actively, the seductions of the devil."[41] Although Arminian Anglicans and Roman Catholics also referred to the soul in feminine terms, they did not share the Puritans' insistence upon its passivity. The Puritan conceptualization of eternal salvation differs completely from the vigorous, aggressive attempts on the part of Arminian Anglicans, Quakers, and Roman Catholics to use free will to accept Jesus Christ and perform good works throughout their lives in order to obtain eternal salvation.

In stark contrast to their Free Will Christian counterparts, Calvinist women were frequently reminded that they were descendants of the first (and most abhorrent) sinner, Eve. When ministers used biblical females as examples in their didactic writing, they chose "scoffing" women such as Michal to remind women that they can often be devils disguised as saints. Women, according to Calvinist ministers, had to take heed and willingly subject themselves to their husbands' dominance if they were to be prevented from committing sins or surrendering completely to Satan.[42]

Unlike Calvinist women, assertive Free Will Christian women were often saints, teachers, and patrons. English Roman Catholic women, both laywomen and nuns, provided their church with devoted service as spiritual leaders. Almost a generation ago John Bossy suggested that early modern English women continued to practice their Catholic faith at home while the men converted to Anglicanism in conformity with state mandates. Men and women justified this bifurcation by claiming that women's intellect was frail and arguing that concessions should be made to accommodate them. Bossy noted that early modern English Catholics belonged to an "upper class sect" allowing such women to control private ritual and assume authority within the family. Although women were excluded from the formal structure of the church, one might argue that they acted as the lynchpin of religious continuity by preserving religious ritual and behavior in the home, and thus held

intrinsic positions of authority in the family.[43] Other historians have since
modified Bossy's work on English Roman Catholics, but historians continue
to see Roman Catholic women as essential historical agents propagating
their faith. Alexandra Walsham's work on "Church Papists," for instance, argues that the increased severity of anti-Catholic legislation in England and
the government's zealous enforcement provided fertile soil for the growth
of Roman Catholic female agency within families. She suggests that a "husband's concentration on protecting the family's resources and reputation"
by becoming a state church member "could both enable and necessitate his
wife's assumption of a more energetic role in safeguarding" the family's Roman Catholic "spiritual integrity." In fact, "female recusancy seems just as
often a natural division of labour in the management of dissent." Walsham
points out the irony of Roman Catholic women's new status, for "a woman's
inferior public and legal identity afforded her superior devotional status,
fuller membership of the Roman Catholic Church—at least in the eyes of
its hierarchy."[44] Notwithstanding the importance of wives in the continuation of the church, single women also acted on behalf of their faith without taking vows or entering convents, such as the very famous "Shepherdess," Isabel Vincent, who sang "Psalms, Prayed, Preached, and Prophesied
about the Present Times, in Her Trances."[45] Other, less well known Roman
Catholic women took it upon themselves to proselytize in their neighbor-
hoods. Consequently, some English men were outraged when two young female Roman Catholics "Seduced" their nineteen-year-old neighbor, Ann
Ketelbey of Ludlow, into converting while her parents were out of town. The
two neighbors' efforts were further rewarded when Ann fled from her parents to join a convent on the continent.[46]

     While laywomen preserved and fostered the growth of their faith by
proselytizing, educating their own families, and observing Catholic rituals
in the home, daughters of wealthy English families opted to enter convents
in order to express their piety. Becoming a nun permitted a woman to live,
work, and pray under the governance of other females. During the seventeenth century, the anti-Catholic environment forced women to leave England if they chose to dedicate their lives to Christ by joining an order. Of
necessity Catholic women established a variety of convents on the continent
exclusively for English women. Women decided which convent to commit
to largely according to their social status, their family tradition, and sometimes their location. The noble Copley family in England, which provided
Maryland with one of its most influential Jesuit priests, Father Thomas Copley, sent its female kin primarily to St. Ursula's at Louvain, until Thomas's
great-aunt—the prioress of St. Ursula's—established another convent in 1609,

called St. Monica's Convent of English Canonesses of St. Augustine, in the same city.[47] Many American-born women from landed Maryland families such as the Brents, Brookes, Youngs, Gallaways, and Darcys chose to join the English Dominican nuns in Brussels.[48] But it was the English Carmelite nuns, educated in the Netherlands, who eventually returned home to establish the first permanent convent in Maryland in the late eighteenth century.

When Maryland women entered into the religious life they molded their particular orders to suit their special needs in "family" groupings, as is evident in the Carmelite Order. Thus the Carmelites in Hoogstradt and Antwerp who eventually returned to Maryland were decidedly idiosyncratic. The women who joined the English Carmelites had more in common with their Jesuit cousins, brothers, and uncles than they did with other Carmelites (such as the Spanish Order of Carmelites). We know that English-speaking women had been educated in the Catholic monasteries of both Antwerp and Hoogstradt in the Netherlands, in response to the changing degrees of tolerance of Catholicism in England. The phenomenal one hundred pounds sterling dowry of Clare Joseph in the eighteenth century attests to the high entrance costs that the Antwerp, Hoogstradt, and Maryland monasteries required.[49] High dowries enabled them to remain homogeneous and elite for three hundred years. These Carmelite monasteries began as pious havens for wealthy English-speaking women interested in intellectual contemplation, and remained dedicated to these ideals well into the twentieth century.[50]

The founders of the Carmelite monastery in Baltimore were descendants of Maryland's first families, such as the Boarmans, Bennetts, Bradfords, Brents, Brookes, Jarboes, Lowes, Matthewses, Mudds, Neales, Sewalls, Smiths, and Whartons. While it was the vision of Mary Margaret Brent (1731–84)—the grand-niece of the famed Margaret Brent—to establish the first female monastery in America, her premature death meant that this founding would be in the hands of her two nieces, Susanna and Ann Teresa Matthews, and her close friend and cousin Anne Matthews. These three gentry Catholics—who when they took their vows adopted the names Mary Eleanora, Mary Aloysia, and Bernardina, respectively, along with Clare Joseph Dickinson, established the new republic's first convent, in Port Tobacco, Maryland, in 1790. A contemplative order that drew its members from the local Catholic elite, it sustained itself on the income derived from the nuns' dowries in silver, slaves, and Maryland's agricultural products.[51]

The English Carmelites, influenced by the Catholic Enlightenment, took an experimental approach to knowledge.[52] Engrossed in personal academic endeavors, prayer, contemplation, sewing, and weaving, the Carmelites opted not to open a formal school for local children. Bishop John Carroll (the first American Catholic bishop and a close relative of the Maryland nuns) wrote to the cardinals in Rome in 1792, expressing his ardent desire for the Carmelites to open a school for girls. Carroll wrote, "The Carmelite nuns, who, about two years ago, came from Belgium, have located in Maryland. A house and a small farm were given to them by a pious Catholic man [a relative]. Four came; some novices [also relatives] have joined them. Their example, a novelty in this country, has aroused many to serious thought on divine things. They will be far more useful if, according to their rule, and with the background of experience, they undertake the education of girls."[53] The nuns, however, resisted this episcopal appeal and did not utilize their superior educations to educate the masses until a desperate financial situation arose in the 1830s. They chose instead to read in English, French, German, and Latin, contemplate theological questions, and write devotional tracts, poetry, and histories. In keeping with their valuation of intellectualism, these Carmelites desired control over their monastery. The English Carmelites secured a papal dispensation in 1626 allowing them to name their own confessors, who acted as chaplains and advisors on spiritual matters. This papal bull provided the nuns with a unique autonomy, allowing them to maintain their distinctive English Catholic character, in part by naming English or Maryland Jesuits as their confessors.

English Roman Catholic nuns, whether on the continent or in Maryland, served their communities as spiritual leaders and gave succor and guidance to both men and women. Gertrude More went so far as to publish her thoughts about how nuns and "single & married lay people may make very good" Christians if they followed the advice and spiritual exercises she laid out in *The Holy Practices of a Devine Lover*. This popular "pocket" book, and many others like it, was to be carried around by women (and men) to be read, contemplated, and prayed over at various times throughout the day. Gertrude also provided a supplemental reading list of Christian texts—"A Catalogue of such Bookes as are fitt for Contemplative Spirits"—including a plethora of works by or about women. She recommended that all devout Catholics read a wide assortment of texts that highlighted assertive females, such as "The Colloquies of S[aint] Catherine of Siena," "The Workes of S[aint] Dorotheus," "The Revelations of Saint Gertrude and Saint Brigitt," and "S[aint] Teresa Her workes, & Her life written by Herselfe." Catherine of Siena was a fourteenth-century mystic whose piety attracted many followers, including clerics, noble laity, and the poor. She mediated between the papal government and rival Italian city-states before she represented Pope Urban's interests and served as his consultant during the "Great Schism," and was later named a doctor of the church. St. Dorothy is an early (fourth-century) example of female preaching. In fact, it was Dorothy's persistent proselytizing that eventually led to her execution and established her as a pious martyr. The highly educated Gertrude devoted her life to writing about spiritual matters that had a significant impact on medieval Christianity, and St. Bridget of Ireland—the patron saint of scholars—founded a religious community while maintaining a strong presence in the church. Like St. Catherine, St. Teresa of Avila was declared a doctor of the church in the twentieth century. She put her spiritual experiences and philosophy down in writing and founded the "discalced" (barefooted) Carmelites, establishing seventeen convents in the sixteenth century. While Gertrude More believed that these female texts rendered vital spiritual guidance, she devoted even more pages to the "Exercise of Devotion to our Blessed Lady Mother of God," the supreme intercessor, who teaches, directs, helps, cherishes, and protects her devoted followers.[54] These female saints all had a significant impact upon religious life, the teachings of the church, and even the church's survival. Perhaps early modern Catholic women used these examples as models to construct spiritual, pious lives for themselves.

Indeed, for English Roman Catholics most of the many female saints provided positive female models for both men and women as patrons, educators, protectors, intercessors, and spiritual leaders. English Catholic women's writings, such as Katherine Digby's, illustrate how these assertive female models permeated the daily lives of early modern Roman Catholic women. Katherine possessed a manuscript of spiritual exercises handwritten by a number of scribes spanning several generations of females from the eminent Buckinghamshire family. This collection of devotional literature included stories of the lives of saints, such as the famous cross-dresser Marina and the ascetic Catherine of Genoa (1447–1510). Marina dressed as a man, joined a monastery, and was called Brother Marinus by the men in her order for her entire adult life. After many years of living in close quarters, her fellow monks only discovered her secret when they prepared her body for burial. Catherine—a wife and anorectic mystic—devoted most of her life to helping the poor and the sick.[55] The volumes of writing that bear St. Catherine's name have influenced religious thought concerning spirituality, purgatory, and Eucharistic devotion. Marina and Catherine transcended common gender ideals by choosing to adopt a male identity, in Marina's case, and taking positions in the church that were reserved for males as spiritual leaders. These stories and the other parables and biographies copied into this collection were meant to be both didactic and inspirational.[56] The book's well-worn leather binding and the careful notations made on its pages lead us to believe that this was a pious work preserved, read, and reread by generations of Digby females.

Early modern English devotional literature in printed and manuscript form focused on a variety of powerful female saints, both real and imagined. Saint Ann, the "Mother of the Mother of God, and Grandmother of Jesus Christ," for instance, has no biblical foundation to speak of, but she enjoyed a particularly elevated status in seventeenth-century literature that sought to emphasize a mother's (and grandmother's) prominent, authoritative role in Catholic families. Authors argued that the Virgin Mary was unable to refuse her mother anything, much as Mary's son was unable to refuse His mother; thus Ann became an important intercessor for Catholics. Humbly asking Ann to relay one's message to Mary was thought to "be less Presumpt[uous]" than asking the Virgin directly. The authors reminded readers of Ann's authority and power over "the Angels and Elect," who "do homage to her" and "give her the Badges of Soveraignty over Men, Archangels, over Nobles, Thrones, over Kings, and so the rest." After all, "the Blessed Trinity congratulates" and pays tribute to the "Grandmother of Jesus Christ" for her role in creating the holy family. The prayers of adulation to Saint Ann emphasized her esteemed position as "Mother and Head of this [Holy] Family" in her "Offices of Grandmother," which ultimately entitled her to the "Right and Power in Heav'n, to give Souls to Jesus, and to Mary." Accordingly, "In Homage of the Right and Power which [Ann] had of Mother over [her] Daughter, and of Grandmother over her Son, and of their Submissions and Reverences which they render'd," Ann could "bind and unite" souls to Jesus Christ just as ordained priests could.[57] Perhaps these excerpts give us a glimpse into the role of grandmothers in early modern English-speaking Catholic families and the power mothers and grandmothers might be authorized—by example—to exert.

Like St. Ann, the Virgin Mary also took on greater importance in seventeenth-century Roman Catholic devotional literature. It is hard to say whether Ann's renown preceded or followed the rise of the cult of the Virgin Mary. Regardless, the early modern English manuals of devotion reveal a significant shift in gender construction in the post-Reformation era. By 1620, the Virgin Mary had become an autonomous intercessor with a will of her own. Largely independent of her role as Christ's mother, Mary was referred to as the *alter Christus*, humbly called upon by sinners to intercede on their behalf.[58] Believers assumed that Mary negotiated directly with God to help repentant sinners gain entrance into heaven. Of course, the daily recitation of the Hail Mary also reinforced this notion that she could be relied upon to intercede directly with God on a daily basis or, perhaps more importantly, "at the hour of our death."

The elevation of Mary's role in Roman Catholicism can also be found in other English recusant literature. The English translator of a work by the Roman Catholic Alexis de Salo, writing in 1639, explains the Virgin Mary's role as "the daughter to God the Father, Mother of his Sonne, & Spouse of the holy Ghost, and consequently daughter, mother, and spouse of the holy Trinity, considering her alliance and con[j]untion with God, and namely with the humanized Word of God the Sone, whom this great [Catholic church] acknowledges for King; of her being Queen can be no doubt al[l]." De Salo (or his translator) explicates the Queen's authority and power with "Let us then conclude, that she being Queene of this Universe, hath over it an absolut[e] command, and that al[l] are to obey her, and render her that honour and [obedience], which from Vassals is due to those who are over them."[59] Other English Roman Catholic treatises, prayers, and hymns attested to the Virgin's power to perform miracles on earth and her ability to grant a sinner entrance into heaven. Hundreds of hymns for the period include sentiments like "O Glorious Virgin, who art aloft among the Stars, . . . thou openest the Gates of Heaven, that penitents might enter in thou art the Gate of the great King, the bright Palace of light." Similarly, pamphlets stipulated the Virgin's power, such as the one in which Roman Catholics were told that the thirteenth-century Holy Elizabeth and her daughter Sophia often called upon the Virgin to heal the sick. As the patron saint of Halle, the Virgin purportedly protected the city from destruction in 1489 and again during the "bloody Netherland-Wars." Other women called upon the Virgin for assistance during floods, to have death sentences repealed when they had been falsely accused, and to bring babies back to life temporarily in order to be baptized.[60] Mary merited a place next to God, and her elevated status at this time suggests a magnified role for Catholic women in general—a notion Roman Catholic immigrants brought with them to Maryland, if the numerous religious medals depicting the Virgin Mary are any indication.

The sermons Father Peter Attwood delivered in Maryland exhibited a general sense of female dignity and worth while paying tribute to the Virgin Mary as a model for mothers here on earth. Attwood expressed the Virgin Mary's ability to help purify sinners when he suggested, "we might find in her person a mediative, and advocate to god." He added that "ye Eternal father can refuse nothing to [this] son, [this] son can refuse nothing to his mother." As the principal Catholic intercessor, Mary continually petitioned

God on behalf of humans, and Attwood asked his congregation to cease being vain and full of pride, so as not to provoke her. He warned parishioners not to belittle Mary, "w[i]thout whose help no Soul can hope for a crown of glory and whose Smiles bring [with them] a paradise of Spiritual consolations in this, and Eternal happiness in ye [life] to come." Attwood invested mothers in general with the power of intercession, and he demanded that children show respect for their mother's authority.[61] Images of Mary on medals worn around the neck for protection, allusions to Mary in sermons, and references to dates in the medieval calendar (such as that of the Feast of the Annunciation of the Blessed Virgin Mary) indicate that the cult of the Virgin Mary arrived intact when colonists settled in Maryland and that Maryland Roman Catholics accepted Mary as the *alter Christus*.[62]

While Attwood held up the Virgin Mary as a model for families, Father William Hunter tended to use his sermons to admonish the Maryland colonists for their sinful behavior. Yet in his stern reprimands we can uncover much about the freedoms women possessed in the province. Women involved themselves in "licentious discourses, indiscreet libertiys, immodest looks, dangerous curiositys, readings, conversation, and diversions unbecoming a [Christian], excesses against temperance, & a soft & sensual life. He means, ye Daughters of ye world, those studyed & affected aims, those freedom, in conversation, & even in ye accesses to y[ou]r Persons; freedoms destructive to Purity & entirely unbecoming ye modesty of y[ou]r Sex."[63] Clearly Attwood and the greater community held different views of human nature than Hunter, for Hunter says quite baldly, "ye world looks upon [these transgressions] as harmless." Yet this excerpt is particularly revealing of the world Roman Catholic women lived in during the seventeenth century in Maryland. These women engaged in unrestrained discussions (probably with men as well as women), presumably touching on "unbecoming" contemporary topics such as economics, politics, and religion in addition to the more traditionally "feminine" ones of love, children, and fashion. Their "indiscreet" habits of reading and actively participating in the public arenas equipped them with the rhetoric and knowledge needed for such behavior.

Back in England, the Roman Catholic devotion to the Virgin Mary as the *alter Christus* did not go unnoticed by outsiders. Some Arminian Anglicans were uncomfortable with the cult of the Blessed Virgin, which, in their minds, transformed her into a deity on a par with God. Yet in the literature asking people to be careful not to worship her as a deity, Arminian Anglican authors acknowledged that men and women ought to continue to celebrate her name, commemorate her virtues, benefit from her example, and honor her in prayer and song. As head of the Church of England Charles I added his thoughts to the vigorous printed debate when he published a treatise in 1643 clarifying his views. He explained that the Virgin Mary "is blessed amongst women; and that all generations shall call her blessed. . . . And I freely confesse, that shee is in glory both above Angels and men; her owne Sonne (that is both God and man) onely excepted. But I dare not mock her, and blaspheme against God, calling her not Diva, but Dea, and praying her to command and controll her Sonne, who is her God and her Saviour. . . . In Heven she is in eternall glory and joy, never to be interrupted with any worldly business; and there I leave her with her blessed Son our Saviour and hers, in eternall felicity."[64] Even with Charles's curiously oblique distinction between Mary as "Dea" and not as "Diva," Roman Catholics probably would not have found much to quibble over in this Arminian Anglican treatise.

Unlike the Arminian Anglicans, Calvinists spewed hostile criticism of the popular Marian devotional tracts. Adam Widenfeldt, for instance, called Roman Catholics "Indescreet Worshippers," claiming their Marian devotion was really just "Slavery to Mary" and the medals they wore with her image were merely "little Chains of Gold or Silver as marks of this Slavery." The cult of the Virgin, in his estimation, led to huge "numbers of Men and Women Worshippers, & yet possibly there was never so few true Christians." Because there was no scriptural foundation for this "Slavery to Mary," Widenfeldt argued that Arminian Anglicans and Catholics alike were violating the Ten Commandments' restriction upon worshiping false gods with "the false Worship" of the virgin goddess. Widenfeldt warned against "those who Pray to the Holy Virgin as if she had more goodness and mercy than Jesus Christ, and so put more confidence in her intercession than in the Merits of her Son." Widenfeldt warned that "those who pa[id] their Homage to the Holy Virgin as to some inferiour Divinity" and who erroneously believed "that without her, there [was] no approaching God, even through Jesus Christ himself" were making a terrible mistake. For Widenfeldt and other Calvinists, the Arminian Anglicans and Catholics who worshiped the Blessed Virgin as their "Mediatrix between men and Jesus Christ" and as an "equal with God and with Jesus Christ" were committing a great sin.[65]

Unlike the Calvinists, Arminian Anglicans shared many traits with their Roman Catholic sisters. Much as in the Roman Catholic gospel of hope, anyone could be saved, and Arminian Anglican women were not severely disadvantaged as Puritan women were. Sanctification rested upon a process in which individuals, through free will, chose to have faith in God, do good works, and hope for God's grace in granting absolution for their sins. Significantly, they continued to use the medieval calendar of feast and fast days—retaining powerful female intercessors, with a special reverence reserved for the Blessed Virgin Mary. Although they may have been uncomfortable with elevating Mary to the status of a "Diva," they continued to honor her and cite her as a positive model for women. Patricia Crawford also tells us that Anglican women under the Puritan regime "had helped the Anglican faith to survive through the 1640s and 1650s," much as their Roman Catholic counterparts had done during periods of persecution in England. These pious women "had sought out Anglican ministers for the baptism of their children and for their marriages, and in many cases had attended Anglican services wherever possible." When priests could not be found, women used the Book of Common Prayer "for their private devotions, and kept Anglican faith alive in their households."[66] Surprisingly, some Arminian Anglican women also accepted the notion that women should be able to completely devote themselves to their religion, and consequently they established at least one "Arminian Nunnery."[67]

In 1641 an irate man published a report he had delivered to Parliament that detailed the existence of an Arminian nunnery at Little Gidding in England. At Little Gidding pious women lived under the direction of an old "Gentlewoman" referred to as the "Matron of the House," who was much like an abbess in a Catholic convent. The Matron's "Batchelour" son appears to have served as their confessor in the Roman Catholic tradition. The forty-two-year-old "Batchelour" was described as a "jolly pragmaticall and Preist-like fellow," educated at Cambridge, who had taken "Orders of a Deacon" and had visited Rome. The Matron, the confessor, and his "elder Brother a Priest-like man in habit and haire" lived quietly with their sister and approximately fifteen other nuns wearing black gowns or "Friers grey" and "Monmouth Capps," in addition to a manservant and two or three maid-servants. These devout Arminian Anglicans adhered to the Roman Catholic "Canonicall houres" of prayer and contemplation throughout the day and night and regularly observed the fasting days of the Roman Catholic calendar. They prayed six times a day—twice a day "publikly" in the chapel and the other times in the house using the Book of Common Prayer, rising at four o'clock in the morning to do so. The decidedly Calvinist observer also noted that the women (many of whom were virgins) practiced "night-watching": certain "nuns" would stay up praying until the others rose in the morning, just as the "English Nunnes at Saint Omers and other Popish places" did. Their "Crosses on the outside and inside of the Chappell," the "Altar richly decked with Tapestry, Plate and Tapers," and "their Adorations, genuflections, and geniculation" were interpreted by the Calvinist observer to be "strongly" indicative of their "Superstition and Popery." These pious Arminian Anglicans, who based their lives on fasting, prayer, and contemplation, also offered hospital services to the poor and fed them just as the old Roman Catholic monks and nuns had.[68] The existence of this Arminian nunnery, much to the chagrin of the Calvinists, reveals the deep-seated need for a place where women could devote themselves to their faith under the direction of an older female.

Women like Mary Astell believed that there ought to be more Arminian Anglican nunneries in England. Astell published *A Serious Proposal to the Ladies* in 1694, calling for a "Monastery" where women could pursue their religious devotion in addition to "learning themselves or instructing others." Attesting to the popularity of such an idea, her treatise went through four editions over the course of seven years. The need was felt much earlier than Astell's compelling plea, however. Men like Robert Burton called for the establishment of Anglican nunneries in 1621. Burton's *Anatomy of Melancholy* was followed by Lady Lettice's call in the 1630s, Thomas Fuller's in 1655, Anna Maria Schurman's in 1659, the duchess of Newcastle's in 1662, Edward Chamberlayne's in 1671, Clement Barksdale's in 1675, and an anonymous author's in 1678.[69] In each of these petitions for pious female space the authors argued that women ought to have the privilege of seeking an education, teaching others, and caring for the poor and sick, as well as space and time for devout contemplation, prayer, and worship. Nunneries, like that at Little Gidding, provided an opportunity for women to control their household government, provide medical care to the community, act as apothecaries, offer shelter and food to the poor, procure an education for themselves, teach others, discuss theological tenets and church doctrine, and avoid marriage and childbirth.[70]

In 1675 a pamphlet called for the establishment of a "Colledge of Maids, Or, A Virgin-Society" to provide pious women with "decent employments and excercises, both Divine and Humane (with moderate Recreation) in a convenient House." This "Colledge" would give women a place "where they may have Lodging and Diet together, and be under Government, somewhat like the Halls of Commoners at Oxford." In the tradition of a Roman Catholic convent, families might put up "caution-money" when their daughters entered; girls would be under the tutelage of a "Pro-Governess" much like a Roman Catholic abbess. The governess was to provide for her charges "a method of private Reading and Devotion" and the virgins would spend their time reading history, poetry, and books on "Practical Divinity and Devotion" in Latin, English, and other modern languages. Many of them might wish to study philosophy, "especially Natural and Moral," by doing "some of the easier Experiments in Natural things." Their religious devotions "On the Holy dayes" would require them "to go orderly to the Parish-Church near their House, where they have a private Gallery fitted for them."[71] Many early modern Arminian Anglicans, like the author of this pamphlet, felt the need for convent-like spaces for women to worship, learn, and teach under the guidance of an elected female "Governess."

Of course, Arminian Anglican women did create spaces for educating others while providing themselves with an opportunity to express their pious faith. In addition to Little Gidding, Arminian Anglicans established the "Ladies Charity School-house" in London, where women with intense religious sensibilities taught boys to read, write, and "cast accompts" as part of their dedication to performing good works here on earth. For in the words of these pious females, "Temporal Life flies away, but Eternal Life never ends; and Charity leads to that under Christ." These women, who were devoted to the Blessed Virgin, ran the school, read Aristotle, Seneca, and Tertullian, taught their charges, and spent some of their time praying for the souls of the wealthy benefactors who had funded the pious venture. These women extended their influence over the lives of their noble benefactors by issuing a "short, brief, and harmless Pocket-Book" that they "humbly entreat[ed] your Noble Ladyships to peruse, and view over and over, in some serious leisure Hour" so that they might become more pious.[72] Following closely the Roman Catholic tradition of founding convents for pious women, Arminian Anglican women established a variety of female spaces in which to worship God, serve their communities, and foster the growth of their faith. In sum, Arminian Anglican women—supported by the preponderance of female saints as positive models for female authority within their faith—took advantage of some of the same options that their Roman Catholic sisters did as teachers, patrons, intercessors, and spiritual leaders in their homes and communities.

Quakers took women's roles as teachers, patrons, intercessors, and spiritual leaders to new heights when they openly encouraged female ministers to preach in their communities and travel abroad to proselytize. Their vital role in fostering the growth of the Society of Friends began with the first person George Fox proclaimed "convinced"—a fifty-one-year-old woman named Elizabeth Hooten. In fact, Fox's future wife, Margaret Fell, served as his organizational assistant in the group's developmental stages, and recent studies of Quakerism have suggested that women's organizational skills—like Fell's—contributed more to the rise of Quakerism than did George Fox's leadership.[73] Indeed, it was a woman, Elizabeth Harris, who first brought Quakerism to Maryland in 1655, and there it flourished for at least a decade without any significant infusion of ideology or practices from an English male sponsor.[74] This new religious group quickly took root in Lord Baltimore's religiously tolerant province, and it attracted single, married, and widowed women from a variety of backgrounds in an effort to satisfy their quest for spirituality, just as it had in England.[75] Perhaps much of the Quakers' gender-inclusive behavior was derived from their reliance upon powerful female figures from the Old and New Testament as models of behavior, just as this reliance led Arminian Anglicans and Catholics to support women's authority.

Quaker men's acceptance of female preachers was more than some men could tolerate back in England. Gerard Croese argued that the Quakers threatened the natural order of things when they allowed "Women to Teach and Usurp Authority, in their distinct Womens Meetings." Worse yet, Quakers permitted women to "hold a Court or Synod distinct by themselves, have a Clark [clerk], a Book [accounts and minutes], a Purse, and the management of Church Government once a Month, to meet in the County Town about the tenth hour, &c. according to the Order and Institution of George Fox."[76] Treatises like Croese's prompted some of the most eloquent Quaker ministers of the era to respond in print, including Richard Richardson. Citing biblical text in support of female preachers—especially Gal. 3:27–28—Richardson explained away the biblical passages that explicitly prohibited women from preaching, such as 1 Cor. 14:34 and 1 Tim. 2:12, by suggesting that detractors misunderstood these verses. Demonstrating that scripture prohibited all women and men who speak for themselves from preaching, he pointed out that male and female Quaker ministers spoke for God and thus had His authority to do so. Indeed, they were not speaking for themselves when they publicly revealed God's word.[77]

The well-documented Quaker reliance on female ministers shows up in Maryland's colonial records. William Richardson, a distinguished Quaker in the province, applauded the missionary activities of five prominent women in his 1682 letter to George Fox.[78] Many female ministers from Maryland traveled to other colonies in America and also to Europe in their effort to convert others to their faith. When a woman had received the Light, male and female members of her Society expected her to evangelize at the women's meeting, in the weekly worship sessions attended by both men and women, at home with her children, and, perhaps, even across colonial borders in the hopes of starting new enclaves of Quakers. Anne Ayres Chew, who had provided her community with a meetinghouse for worship, also spent a good deal of her time, money, and energy traveling with a group of Quakers to convince others to start their own Societies. In the provincial records Ann Galloway also stands out as a particularly notable Quaker minister. Recognizing her importance to the community, her religious knowledge, and her position within the Society of Friends, the members of the yearly Women's Meeting in 1694 decided "that an Epistell be writ unto our friends and sisters in London and it is agreed by the consent of the said Meeting that our friend and sister Ann Galloway should write it."[79] While there are many other examples of prominent Quaker women teaching, preaching, and convincing others abroad, most women faced less monumental tasks. The duties and responsibilities associated with their chosen faith kept them firmly fixed in their homes and communities as teachers, ministers, and patrons.

Quaker women relied on the models biblical females provided just as their Arminian Anglican and Roman Catholic sisters did. In England Katharine Whitton published the *Epistle from the Women's Yearly Meeting at York, 1688, and An Epistle from Mary Waite*, which points to the many positive female models that influenced Quaker women's actions, such as Lydia, who was "open hearted to God" and to others. Lydia was a wealthy woman whose business in purple dye brought her to Macedonia, where, after meeting St. Paul, she and her whole family converted to Christianity. Quaker women also revered Dorcas, another woman of the New Testament who was "careful to do . . . good." Because of her good works and acts of charity, St. Peter restored Dorcas to life after she fell ill and died. Quaker women also chose women from the Old Testament to emulate, such as Deborah and Jael. Deborah, "concerned in the common wealth of Israel," had been chosen by God to lead His people as a prophetess, a judge, and a military leader of the Israelites. Deborah told Barac to ready his army for battle and she accompanied him to attack Sisara, King Jabin's general. Following her great victory, she composed a canticle that has been preserved in chapter 5 of Judges. This warrior, prophetess, and poet organized a national resistance against the religious, cultural, and political inroads of the Canaanites to successfully free the Israelites from King Jabin's control. Notwithstanding Deborah's prowess, Jael, who was "zealous for the truth" and "praised above women," also contributed to the downfall of the Canaanites. Jael drove a tent stake through General Sisara's head after he sought shelter in her tent just as Deborah had prophesied. Each of these female biblical figures— Lydia, Dorcas, Deborah, and Jael—underscores the Quakers' reliance on Christian female models as they constructed roles for themselves within their faith and in their homes.[80]

These active historical agents from both the Old and New Testaments provided Quaker women with models for their own behavior as preachers, warriors for God, and saints who made sure that "the hungry may be fed, the naked cloathed, the weak strengthened, the feeble comforted, and the wounded healed. So that the very weakest, and hindermost of the flock, may be gathered into the fold of rest and safety, where no destroyer can come, where the ransomed and redeemed by the Lord have the songs of deliverance and high praise in their mouths." Like the biblical females they chose to emulate, Quaker women's writing reveals their militant tendencies, which were much like those of the Roman Catholic Jesuits. Women were roused to "be faithful in the work of your day, be valiant for the Lord and his blessed truth; come up in the nobility of his life, and stand faithful witnesses for him." After all, these women believed they were ushering in a new era: "for we are the city set upon a hill, yea battle axes in God's hand, though our weapons are not carnal, but spiritual and mighty, through the power of God, to the pulling down [of] the strong hold of sin and satan." These women did not neglect their duties and responsibilities closer to home, either. Quaker women advised all parents "not [to] wink or connive at any sin in your children, as you tender their everlasting well being; let no sin go un-reproved or uncorrected." Good Quaker parents knew that "Folly is bound up in the heart of a child, but the rod of correction must drive it out, and he that corrects his child shall deliver his soul from death. So, friends, train up your children in the blessed truth and fear of the Lord, so may you have hope they will not depart from it when they are old."[81]

In sum, early modern Free Will Christian women in Maryland exercised the power and authority that Patricia Crawford found among women in English religious groups during the seventeenth century.[82] It seems likely, then, that English women arriving in Maryland carried with them ideas and practices from England. Unlike Anne Hutchinson and the other unfortunate women banished from John Winthrop's Puritan colony for propagating their beliefs, as well as the numerous victims of witch-hunts in Calvinist New England, Roman Catholic women were permitted to act as spiritual leaders by establishing religious orders. Moreover, we saw the remarkable rise of the Virgin Mary to a status equivalent to Christ's in Roman Catholic devotional literature, providing a model for females exerting authority within their homes, communities, and churches. Arminian Anglicans joined the Roman Catholics in their embrace of the Virgin Mary by paying her respect in their daily observances of the religious calendar. And the Quakers extended virtual religious equality to their womenfolk by allowing them to serve as ministers during religious meetings and in converting others. The Free Will Christians also encouraged the education of children at home by women, thus firmly cementing the female's role in the propagation of doctrine for the future growth of their chosen denominations.

Arminian Anglican, Quaker, and Roman Catholic women in early modern Maryland used their religious institutions to validate their private and public acts of piety as patrons, catechists, mothers, wives, nurses, preachers, and nuns. While the women of each of these faiths undoubtedly experienced limitations and disappointments within their institutions, families, and communities, they transcended these restrictions to create meaningful spiritual lives for themselves and others. In large measure, the women in each of these groups emulated strong, authoritative female saints and biblical figures in constructing pious lives. Whether these women chose to identify with warriors and judges such as Deborah in the Old Testament, or the Virgin Mary as a "Diva" or a "Dea" in the New, Free Will Christian women relied on powerful historical agents of change as models for their own behavior.

This chapter also underscores the fact that Arminian Anglican and Quaker Protestants had more in common with their Roman Catholic sisters than they did with other Protestants. Religion played a key role in the lives of most Marylanders; it informed their behavior in general, and in particular it contributed to their attitudes toward their womenfolk. Yet we need more evidence to support the hypothesis that religious beliefs and gender suppositions are, in fact, directly related to one another. Specifically, can we discern distinctive differences between the Calvinist Predestinarians and the Free Will Christians in their gendered inheritance practices?

5
⚬⚬

Religion, Property, and the Family

U nder English common law, a woman's legal identity was subsumed by her husband's when she married. Being figuratively "covered" by her husband in *coverture,* a married woman could not enter into any legal contracts by herself and no one could sue her as an individual. As a *feme covert,* a wife ceded to her husband control of the property she had brought to the marriage (her dowry), and when he died she was entitled to one-third of her husband's estate (her dower) to use during her lifetime. English common law further limited widows', daughters', and younger sons' ability to hold and control land, as it insisted on primogeniture, favoring the eldest son in distributing real estate.

Yet most people in England did not actually follow common law, opting instead for a more family-centered paradigm based on canon law. Using data from approximately five hundred early modern English parishes, Amy Louise Erickson has found that most property distribution patterns adhered to the spirit of canon law—just as we found in chapter 2 in regard to mate selection, marriage rites, and separations.[1] Church law regulated the division of personal property, following the older Roman civil law, and both were considerably more egalitarian than English common law because they "advocated a form of community property within marriage and the equal division of parental wealth among all children."[2] Generally speaking, ecclesiastic laws dictated an equitable distribution of movable goods—one-third to the wife and the rest divided equally among the children (regardless of gender). Still, the actual application of such laws was even more egalitarian.

While daughters—in this land-poor society—did not regularly inherit land if a son was available, Erickson found that daughters tended to inherit a relatively larger portion of the family's estate in personal property to offset a brother's apparent advantage. And English ecclesiastic courts favored widows and often provided them with much more than one-third of the estate even after the 1670 Act for the Better Settling of Intestates' Estates that sought to restrict widows' rights to family property. In most cases, church courts granted widows nearly 66 percent of the family's personal goods. Erickson also discovered that "in practice wives maintained during marriage substantial property interests of their own."[3] In sum, the English largely disregarded the common law's insistence on primogeniture and limitation of widow's rights to one-third of the family's estate while they supported the rights of women to control their own property both during and after their marriages. This popular and ecclesiastic resistance to civil laws mandating female *coverture* and economic dependence in favor of canon law's insistence on property equity, marriage partnerships, and balanced parental authority in the family is principally what we find in early modern Maryland.

As in the Old World, Marylanders held onto the notion that widows and daughters ought to inherit their fair share of their family's property. In Maryland this meant that colonial widows would often inherit most of the family's real estate and a large portion of the movable goods. Despite the difficulty of determining how communities actually distributed property when men died intestate, there is evidence to suggest that courts allowed women much more than one-third of the family's holdings. On St. Clement's Manor, for instance, the courts leet proclaimed that after a "Releise" was paid to the lord of the manor, Richard Upgate's widow, Annie, would control the family's entire estate.[4] Marital partnerships—with their duties and responsibilities—typified the family structure in seventeenth-century Maryland, where 72 percent of the 1881 married men who left wills between 1634 and 1713 shared their property with their wives as partners. The majority of married men revealed their partnership with their wives by bequeathing them more than one-third of the family's land and personal goods while simultaneously reiterating a wife's ability to manage the property. Further, these testators underscored their partners' central position in the family by acknowledging their continuing responsibility to control the behavior of offspring and other dependents as well as their portions of the family's property during the dependents' nonage.

Using samples of wills across the province, historians have recognized that a majority of widows in early Maryland were given more than their third of the family's property when their husbands died. These scholars, however, attributed this phenomenon primarily to frontier conditions in which the scarcity of women increased their value during the farm-building stage of provincial development. Unlike their counterparts in New England, seventeenth-century Chesapeake men, living in an area where land was relatively abundant, left their wives large portions of their property. This argument that the environment and skewed sex ratios encouraged men to leave their wives much more than one-third of the estate was predicated on the notion that English people who could—like those in New England, where sex ratios were similar to those in England and land was not abundant— adhered to English common law. Maryland, then, was the anomaly.

Certainly the abundance of land, high mortality rates, and skewed sex ratios did have an impact on life in early Maryland. But this argument fails to provide a completely satisfactory explanation for the inheritance patterns found in Maryland in light of Erickson's work and the fact that 28 percent of the married male testators chose not to leave their wives in control of large portions of the family's property. Why, if women were so highly prized in this frontier society, would three out of every ten married men act like strong patriarchs heading families all too familiar to historians? These men refused to leave their wives real estate over which they could exert control even when their sons were young. Stranger still, these patriarchs consciously chose not to distribute their property in accordance with accepted English practice that continued to rely on the spirit (if not the letter) of canon law. Lois G. Carr hinted at a possible connection between religion and inheritance patterns when she noted a disparity between Somerset County, where widows were less likely to inherit real estate, and St. Mary's County, where landholding widows preponderated.[5] Significantly, Somerset County supported a substantial Calvinist population and Roman Catholics tended to congregate in St. Mary's, the birthplace of English Catholicism in the New World.

The Maryland men who chose not to leave their wives in control of large portions of their estates distributed family property much like the Calvinist men who had settled in New England. John J. Waters's research on inheritance patterns in New England found that Calvinists followed the patriarchal favoring of the first son inherent in the Law of Moses. In an effort to maintain family continuity, poorer families followed patterns of primogeniture, in which the eldest son inherited all the land, while in wealthier families the eldest received twice as much land as younger sons. Daughters and wives, for the most part, inherited movable goods rather than land. In keeping with this patriarchal family structure, eldest sons generally accepted the responsibility of providing for their mothers.[6] Kim Rogers, in her study of New England during the farm-building stage between 1640 and 1680, explained why some folks chose to deviate from these normal inheritance patterns. Rogers found that when widows were given significant portions of both land and personal goods, they exerted little control over the inherited property. Furthermore, when men died with grown children, widows merely received room and board from the eldest son. The rare exceptions to this pattern were childless merchants and ministers who, in the absence of any male heirs, often gave complete control over their estates to their widows.[7] The ravages of war also provided the opportunity for some women to control land. William Ricketson has suggested that King Philip's War (1675–76) resulted in an extraordinary number of young men with small estates dying intestate, which created an atmosphere of legal innovation in Massachusetts. War widows were presented with a greater than normal amount of control over property, yet Ricketson reveals that they frequently chose not to accept this power. Instead, widows opted to make contracts giving land usage rights to men in return for a yearly annuity.[8] These New England patterns suggest that New World Calvinists, in their efforts to define themselves as the antithesis of all things Catholic, tended to shun traditional English practices based on canon law, and in so doing they embraced inheritance practices that favored male property ownership.

The similarity between the land distribution practices of Calvinist New Englanders and the 28 percent of Marylanders who resisted bequeathing land to females suggests that religious affiliation might be related to inheritance patterns. I identified the religious affiliations of 1410 married, widowed, and single will-writing males and females and subjected them to a statistical analysis of property distributions. The following discussion is based on analysis of all 3190 of the last wills and testaments Marylanders left between 1634 and 1713, as well as other sources, such as probate inventories, family histories, church records, and letters.[9]

A statistical analysis of two cohorts, based on testators' soteriology, revealed two distinctive family strategies for estate distribution in the wills of married males: Predestinarian men tended to prefer to give land to sons while Free Will Christian men left their wives large tracts of land to manage during their lifetime and enjoyed the rights and responsibilities of a marital partnership.[10] Approximately 80 percent of Free Will Christian husbands left their wives large tracts of land to manage during their lifetime. About half of this group placed their wives in charge of the entire estate, indicating complete confidence in their wives' abilities to manage the affairs of their families and maintain their positions as authority figures after their hus-

Men's Bequests to Wives

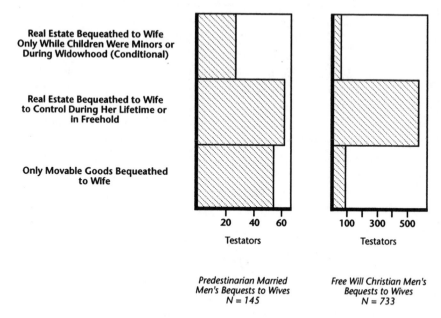

Real Estate Bequeathed to Wife Only While Children Were Minors or During Widowhood (Conditional)

Real Estate Bequeathed to Wife to Control During Her Lifetime or in Freehold

Only Movable Goods Bequeathed to Wife

Predestinarian Married Men's Bequests to Wives N = 145

Free Will Christian Men's Bequests to Wives N = 733

5. Predestinarian and Free Will Bequests

bands died. Thirty-six percent of the Free Will Christian wives held their land in freehold; that is, they had complete legal power to mortgage, sell, or lease it.

While an overwhelming number of Free Will Christian wives controlled large tracts of land, indicating their status as authority figures in the home, the majority of Predestinarian male testators—more than 57 percent —left their widows with only movable goods or a very small amount of real estate. Less than 43 percent of the Predestinarian men left their wives sizable pieces of property for life, and only 22 percent allowed their wives to hold any real estate in freehold. The details of some specific families may provide some clues as to the significance of this data as it relates to the power relationships that existed between a man and a woman in a seventeenth-century Free Will Christian or Predestinarian home in Maryland.[11]

The Free Will Christian notion that widows were entitled to control real estate for the rest of their lives, which can be seen by looking at some specific Arminian Anglican families, indicates an acceptance of their independence

and centrality within the home. This reliance on female partners in marriage was typical in England as well. Amy L. Erickson suggests that during the sixteenth and seventeenth centuries in England—where Anglicans
dominated—marriage was portrayed in terms of "economic partnership
and religious companionship."[12] As economic and religious partners, Arminian Anglican women in Maryland held a considerable amount of power
within the household and many received more than their third of the estate
when their husbands died.[13] Arminian Anglican men tended to return to
their wives not only what they had brought to the marriage, but also a portion of the estate that, in the words of William Burrows, "[she] helped work
for . . . as well as he."[14] John Hammond, who died in 1707, typified this pattern when he gave his wife back her dowry of land and additionally bequeathed their dwelling plantation to her without limiting her ability to sell
or mortgage the property.[15]

Significantly, Arminian Anglicans interpreted the common custom, and
later the law, as giving a widow the rights to one-third of the family's holdings in both real and personal estate.[16] Thus Michael Taney gave his wife
life interest in the large dwelling plantation "in full recompence of all her
Dower right, title & Interest and other demands whatsoever, which She may
have or make to all or any part of my Lands [and] Tenements."[17] Henry
Hanslap went a step further and suggested that his wife Elizabeth sign a
contract relinquishing her rights to one-third of their real estate in exchange
for a five-hundred-acre tract. The Hanslaps distributed the rest of the sizable estate to their grown children and grandchildren.[18] The Taney and
Hanslap examples indicate an awareness by each of the partners of a wife's
entitlement to much more than what these husbands left their wives; thus
it might be reasonable to assume that they discussed the division of the
property, taking into consideration the needs of the entire family. It hardly
makes sense to write a will leaving a wife less than what she is entitled to
unless both parties agree to the arrangement.

Arminian Anglican women exerted authority in the household as partners in their marriages. Husbands consulted them about the important
matter of the dispersal of wealth through the family, as in the examples
above, but also about substantive donations to the church. For example, after John Contee died in 1708 from the "bloody flux," four witnesses testified
that he had refused to sign his last will and testament until he was convinced
that his wife "was Sattisfied" with it. Doctor J. Pearson declared that John,
himself pleased with the wording of the will, "asked his wife if there was
any thing She Disliked saying it should be altered" if she so desired. Another
witness, John Fraser, gave testimony about an item left blank in the will

"Concerning a Donation to the ministry which was to be filled up when he advised with his wife."[19] The language used by Arminian Anglican Thomas Dent of St. Mary's County also vividly illustrates this recognition of a marital partnership. He wrote, "I do give the Said land [in Charles County] unto my Deare wife Rebecca and her heires to dispose of for the good of her Children or otherwise to keepe it and at her decease or during her life to bequeath or give to any Child or Children as She in her discretion shall think fitt. . . . I give the remaining parte of my estate moveables and Immoveables whatsoevr unto my deare wife and yoak fellow Rebecca Dent to dispose of as shall best please her."[20] The term "yoak fellow" does not conjure up romantic visions of marital fulfillment, as its imagery is of an equitable economic partnership, with Rebecca and Thomas jointly investing their labor and equally sharing in the profits from that work. And at the same time, the phrase "yoak fellow" also serves to remind us that the Dents, as joined partners, were equally committed to meeting their familial, community, and proprietary obligations.

The partnerships described here were predicated on the idea that both husband and wife participated in managing the family fortune. In many instances, the wife's business acumen and physical capabilities were acknowledged, in addition to her authority over the children both before and after their father's death. Arminian Anglican Walter Beane of Charles County died in 1670, leaving his wife in control of the family's four-hundred-and-fifty-acre dwelling plantation for her life. Walter qualified all of the sizable legacies bequeathed to their three daughters and son with "Provided allwise that my wife Ellinor shall have liberty to sell or dispose of all or any of the aforesaid horses or Cattle for the said John's benefite," he being their only minor child. Ellinor was also to have the "liberty to Sell or Carry away any sort of timber growing upon the said plantacon for her own."[21] And in order to protect from probate the property Ellinor had controlled during their marriage, Walter specifically mentioned some livestock and "one Negro woman called Mingoes wife" as belonging to Ellinor in his will. Walter took for granted Ellinor's ability to manage, maintain, and increase the value of their estate after his death. And while she did not own her children's shares, Ellinor continued to exert control over their estates in addition to her own.

Roman Catholics exhibited similar sentiments regarding marital partnerships.[22] Husbands and wives, like the Arminian Anglican "yoak fellows," shared the duties, work, risks, and profits involved in running their estates. Leonard Greene of St. Mary's County willed to his wife Ann her dower plus their dwelling plantation for life, asking only that their son Thomas be allowed to begin working for himself on a small piece of the property when he turned eighteen. Leonard added, "I give unto my said loveing wife the use & service of a negroe Woman called Ena . . . [until their son turned eighteen] . . . and alsoe all the Estate shee brought to mee to be returned in kind & what of itt is disposed of to be allowed the vallue thereof out of my Estate," as well as leaving her some livestock. He assumed that his wife was entitled to her fair share of the family's estate over and above the property she originally brought to the marriage. Ann would continue to support her minor son and herself, though she had grown children who could have taken on the responsibility of caring for their mother and younger brother, as did Ellinor Beane in the previous example. Leonard asked his eldest daughter to remain with her mother, though he gave her two hundred acres. He detailed the reciprocal relationship that he hoped the two could agree upon, urging his daughter to "be dutifull & helpful" to her mother as long as "shee carefully provids for her" or until his daughter wanted to work for herself. Assuming that Ann was capable of long-term planning for her future labor needs, her husband provided only a temporary work force—their minor son, a grown daughter, and Ena. Leonard acknowledged that both the adult females in the household could make rational economic decisions and that they were able to provide for themselves and their dependents.[23]

Much like their Arminian Anglican counterparts, Roman Catholic husbands frequently left their wives some property in freehold as well as an entailed parcel, suggesting that the land held in freehold had been their contribution to the marriage. Cuthbert Fenwick of St. Mary's County, who died in 1654, left his wife Jane a tract at "St. Cuthbert's Neck" in freehold as well as their dwelling plantation for life.[24] Others followed a more common pattern of allowing the wife to hold the entire estate for the duration of her life, as did Thomas Swearington. He entailed all of the estate on his son "& his heirs for ever lawfully begotten of his body or to be begotten & never to be sold or Changed nor Embecill'd away on any account but to go from Heir to Heir during Life" only after his "Dear & Loving Mothers Decease."[25] Of course, not all marriages were blissful partnerships. Catholic John Evans of St. Mary's County left his daughter two-thirds of his entire estate when she turned sixteen. He often referred to his daughter Mary as "loving," yet he never mentioned his wife by name, nor did he use any terms of affection in speaking of her. This can hardly have been an oversight on John's part, and we can only guess at the reasons behind his deliberate choice of words. Still, John felt compelled to recognize his wife's right to one-third of both the real and personal property that they shared.[26]

Negotiation played an important part in Roman Catholic marriages, reinforcing the idea of an equitable marriage arrangement. Richard Gardiner, a professed Roman Catholic and, interestingly, a vestryman for the Arminian Anglican All Saints Church, gave his sons equal tracts of land, and his wife, Elizabeth, a large parcel in Virginia "to her and her heirs forever," in addition to the profits from their grist mill during her widowhood. If she chose not to move to Virginia, she could select a tract on which to settle in Maryland. Elizabeth and Richard had discussed the issue of property many times in the past and her acceptance of her husband's last will and testament would nullify the older contracts between them.[27] Richard had given Elizabeth land and other property in both written and verbal agreements prior to his death. Elizabeth had come from a wealthy family, and it seems logical to assume that these pacts with her husband may have been about the land that she brought to the marriage and, more than likely, additional property over the course of time.

Both written and verbal contracts show that Roman Catholic partners worked together in the management of their estate in much the same way that Arminian Anglicans did. This tendency crossed ethnic boundaries in Maryland; we see that Richard Moy from Flanders also followed this pattern. A Roman Catholic innkeeper, Richard named his wife, Elizabeth, his executrix. Faced with the realities of high mortality and remarriage rates in Maryland, he wrote "that if it should please God that she shall happen to mary again she will take such care as to make some settlement of what part or portion of my estate she shall think convenient upon my dear Son Daniel Moy not doubting but that she will deal tenderly and with a motherly love toward my said son."[28] In a codicil written during his final illness in 1675, Elizabeth received the estate for life; it would pass to their son after her death. Elizabeth died shortly after her husband, leaving a will that reiterates Elizabeth and Richard's joint ownership. She wrote of "the Reale and personal Estate to which it hath pleased Almighty God to bless my dear and Loving husband and my Self with all and which my Said husband hath by his last will and testam[en]t Left wholly to my dispose."[29]

Some Roman Catholics limited the second wife's rights to the estate in an effort to preserve it for the children of the first marriage or, frequently, because the wife already owned property from a previous marriage.[30] The practice was not universal, however; Garrett Vansweringen gave his second wife the entire estate for the duration of her widowhood and stipulated that his children and sons-in-law were not to interfere with her management of the estate under any circumstances.[31] The limited control a second or third wife usually held may account for at least some of the instances of Free Will Christians' not leaving their wives more than one-third of the personal and real property; others may be explained by a wife's unwillingness or inability to perform such an onerous task. Not surprisingly during these years of high mortality rates, some wives were just as sick as their husbands when the men composed the family will.[32]

Yet, if Catholic partnerships were as equitable as this evidence suggests —and the ownership of realty extended a widow's familial authority—then why did testators also name overseers or guardians in their wills? We know that in 1699, Roman Catholic Charles Egerton left two thousand pounds of tobacco to Jesuit priest John Hall—one thousand upon his death and the rest on the anniversary of his death. Egerton added,

> And [I] do desire that my adjacent friends and acquantenances may be at the celebration of my anaversary day of my death. Further I desire and ordain, for guardians to my children, Mr. John Hall . . . [and several other males], hoping that they will be so kind, that if any diferances should arise among the mother or the childdren, that they would be pleased to set it to rites, without any further trouble—also I order, all the moveables and stock [in addition to the dwelling plantation] that I have at St. Jeromes, to be at my wifes disposell.[33]

This particular example of an anniversary requiem reveals the Catholic propensity for leaving full control of large tracts in the care of the wife, indicating her central status in the family. Yet it also raises the question of the nature of guardianship and overseers. A Catholic (or other Free Will Christian) husband who named a guardian or overseer did not presume to question his wife's authority or her ability to manage their estate. Rather, faced with the very real possibility of volatile arguments developing over property within the family, they hoped that intercessors would provide a means of settling disputes out of court, thus preserving the family's capital if disagreements arose.

Yet another use for guardians and overseers appears in these wills. Catholic Baker Brooke of Calvert County died in 1679/80, leaving his wife Anne executrix of the will and giving her several tracts of land for life. His sons, Charles, Leonard, and Baker, and his daughter, Mary, all received their shares of the real and personal estate. Baker named Anne's uncle, Philip Calvert, overseer. Philip's responsibility may have been in part to mediate family disputes, but more importantly, he protected the children's interests, particularly since the Assembly had not yet enacted laws requiring remarrying widows and their new husbands to post bond to ensure the children's estate would not be ill managed. Note that the overseer was Anne's relative, not her husband's, although Baker had several kinsmen in the province at the time.[34] This typical Free Will Christian pattern allowed a wife some flexibility, as relatives generally held the interest of their kin as their primary concern. Thus an overseer was not named because the wife needed someone to look after her, and the wife did not inevitably relinquish control to her new husband or to the guardian or overseer, though that may sometimes have occurred. Rather, some women might have otherwise cheated their children out of their legacies. For as late as 1717 we find evidence of women exercising control over their property as freeholders at the expense of their children's inheritance. A letter from lawyer John Playton, written to Robert Brent, voiced his concern over the lack of legal safeguards for "the Son of Wm. Brent by Sarah Brent." Sarah Brent interested herself with "her own Estate & takes no notice of her Son's interest in the Lands."[35] Sarah, in control of the family estate during her lifetime, focused on her own financial and personal well being at the expense of her son's future legacy.

Quakers also named overseers in their wills to ensure that the estate was not "imbezled."[36] Richard Beard gave his wife Rachel "her Life in my now dwelling Plantation and she is to have the Orchard only to her self so long as she Continues a widdow but in Case She should marry then—she is to have but one half of the fruit of the said orchard and my Two Sons Richard Beard and John Beard is to have the other halfe. . . . I do give unto my wife Rachel Beard—Liberty to Cleer as much Ground as she hath occasion for dureing her natural Life and She is to Clear as much into one of my Sons Land as the other this also She is to do without Molestation."[37] Richard did not want Rachel to cheat his sons and their wives out of her portion of the estate before she died by divesting the land, so he named trustees to ensure that the land would remain in the family without anyone being forced to appeal to a court for justice. Simultaneously, he recognized his wife's right to her third of the estate to be used at her discretion, unencumbered by an overseer's judgment.[38] Like the Roman Catholics, Quakers also wanted to avoid the onerous cost of lawsuits in the settling of estates, so they frequently named the Quaker meeting as an advisory/arbitration board, as did Thomas Bincks. Thomas gave his executors full authority to manage his estate but warned that "in case any difference or difficulty doe arise or happen among or with my Executrs of this my will about the manageing or well ordering of the same then they or any of them that then is shall lay itt before good friends [Quaker meeting] to assist them and end the matter or difference that they may end the thing or matter soe happening and not to goe to law to waste my estate left to my wife & cousins."[39]

Quakers—like the Arminian Anglicans and Roman Catholics—acknowledged a wife's right to at least one-third of the real and personal estate and her right to the dowry, in recognition of her contribution toward its acquisition. The wealthy James Berry of Talbot County gave his wife Elizabeth a life interest in all the real estate. Elizabeth's father, John Pitt, had given her five hundred acres as a dowry and Berry's first wife, Sarah Woolchurch, also had brought substantial property to their marriage. Thus Elizabeth got not only the real estate that she had brought to the marriage, but James's and Sarah's too.[40] And since wealth came from the productivity of the land, Elizabeth could have become a wealthy widow from the production of staples without having to own her land in freehold.

Of course, a few Quaker marriages did not follow these patterns. Dr. Peter Sharp died in 1672 and left his friends John Garey, W. Berry, William Stevens, Jr., and William Sharp executors of his large estate. In order to preserve all of his estate for his family, Peter instructed them to administer the will "without the Councell or advice of the Learned att the Law." He bequeathed his wife "one third of all my Choice Moveables plate Money or What Else & also a third of all bills bonds Debts Due by accompts or what Else now due . . . [and] one third of Cattle or horses . . . for the Comfort of her and my Children," provided that she live with his young children and be "a tender nurseing Mother towards them."[41] Peter concerned himself mainly with his children's future and their rights to the land, primarily because this was his second marriage and apparently a childless union. Peter's wife had also been married before and presumably she and her children inherited their estates from her first husband, though Peter did leave them a substantial sum of tobacco.

The majority of Quaker marriages were equitable unions similar to the Catholic partnerships. Quaker husbands and wives discussed their families' future while drawing up the family will; John Rousby of Calvert County made this discussion explicit, stating, "I give and bequeath the same equally amongst my children aforesaid borne and unborne but this I thus Explain upon second thoughts and my wifes desire concerning my debts and the said Legacy of one hundred pounds Sterl[ing] shall be secured paid and taken out of my whole personall Estate."[42] We see that John's wife, Barbara, had her own concerns about the disbursement of the family's wealth; she aired them and her husband responded to her suggestions. This cooperation permeated the language of husbands' wills, indicating a confidence in their spouses' management abilities. Thus prominent Quaker Colonel Samuel Chew died in 1677, leaving wife Anne, his executrix, to manage their six-hundred-acre plantation at Herrington for her life.[43] Furthermore, Anne was responsible for maintaining and producing profits from the thousands of acres that her children would eventually inherit as they came of age. Samuel spelled out his desires: "my Will & minde is that my said dear & Loving wife Anne Chew shall have the Governance Custodie, use, benefits & profits of the portions of all my said Children during their Minorities . . . towards their Educations & bringing up in Learning."[44] Samuel instructed Anne to provide the boys with capital with which to begin their enterprises as well as a laborer when they reached twenty-one and inherited their tract of land. He also named overseers to settle any quarrels that might arise among the children or between Anne and the children. Samuel implied that Anne was more than capable of efficiently handling such a large estate, and they both hoped that she would increase the value of their children's portions.[45]

Overwhelmingly, Free Will Christian widows appear to have lived separately from their grown children, presumably by their own choice. And their husbands acknowledged their independence in their patterns of bequests. These wills indicate that women held authority in their families throughout their lives, as is seen in their ability to negotiate with a spouse. Holding real estate increased a woman's authority, as children frequently had to wait until their mother died to inherit their father's legacy. This did not prevent grown children from marrying, but they depended on their mother's beneficence for a plot on which to establish their own home. At times, these children had grown families before they could claim title to their inheritance. The case of Quaker John Meeres illustrates how a man might have to wait until his stepmother died to complete an unbroken succession of property. He left to his only daughter, Sarah, all of the realty and movable goods given to him by his father and a parcel of land that was "by my Said deceased father given to my Mother in Law [stepmother] for her Lifetime and then to return to me with its appurtenances—and be mine and my heirs for Ever."[46] The wife's control of land enabled her to control her labor force more effectively. Widows had their children's labor until their daughters were sixteen and their sons twenty-one, generally speaking. In addition to their servants or slaves, they may have garnered further labor from their adult offspring. Children eager to start families might have agreed to continue to work for their mother if she provided them with a piece of property.

Particular Baptist, Presbyterian, and Puritan women faced very different prospects when their husbands died. Calvinist male testators preferred to leave their real estate to sons or other male relatives. They frequently left their wives less than one-third of their holdings and severely limited their ability to exert much power over any realty bequeathed to them. Significantly, Predestinarians tended to interpret the custom, and later the law, of a widow's "thirds" differently than the Arminian Anglicans, Quakers, and Roman Catholics. Thirty-eight percent of Predestinarians—compared to a

mere 12 percent of Free Will Christians—believed a wife was only entitled
to a portion of their personal estate, to the exclusion of any real estate, indicating her lack of authority and power to control her own destiny within
the family. Predestinarians assumed that males should inherit realty and females personalty, much like their counterparts in New England. Francis
Finch of Maryland, for example, left all his land to his son, Samuel, giving
his wife only one-third of his movable goods. Finch bequeathed two-fifths
of the remaining personal estate to Samuel and what was left went to his
three daughters. Although he named his wife executrix, she had limited
power to control her children since she held so little of the family's holdings.
Her position within the family before her husband died appears to have
been less authoritative than that of her Free Will Christian counterparts
when we consider that her husband denied her the custody of her children
if she decided to remarry.[47]

Predestinarians such as Denum Olandman, Sr., followed a typical testamentary pattern in which the favored son received twice as much property as the other sons, though the estate was quite large. His wife received
only movable goods, probably resided with her married son, and relied on
him for her maintenance until she died.[48] William Hitchcock of Calvert
County bequeathed his wife, Mary, one-third of the personal estate and his
two minor sons got equal shares of the family's one hundred acres when
they turned seventeen. Only if both of the boys died without heirs would
Mary, his executrix, inherit the land. William named Richard Statlings and
Robert Gerves "to be Guardians to my wife and children."[49] William dealt
with his wife's future as he did his children's—in a sense treating her as another child. As a powerful patriarch in the family, William protected his dependents from the uncertainties of life by naming several male guardians.
Guardians and overseers played a central role in administering Predestinarian wills, as Predestinarians were more likely than Free Will Christians
to deprive widows of the custody of their children—nearly 11 percent of the
Predestinarians took their children out of the care of their widows.

Some Predestinarians left their wives less than "their thirds" of the personal estate, as we see in the case of James Nutthall, who gave his wife only
a fifth.[50] John Allford of Dorchester left his eldest son, John, five hundred
and sixty-six acres and his second son, Matthias, four hundred and thirty
acres. The youngest son, Joseph, received a portion of the livestock, and
John's widow got some tobacco and corn in addition to the privilege of a
crop if she chose to stay in the area for another year. The testator named his
two eldest sons joint executors, indicating that his wife had no leverage
within the family at all.[51] However, not every Predestinarian refusing to be-

queath his wife realty did so because of religious values that emphasized a woman's dependence upon a patriarch. Thomas Thorp left his son William all of the family's land and his wife nothing, because of her infidelity. He wrote, "I disposses my rebellious wife Elizabeth Thorp of any parte of my reall and p[er]sonall Estate because she is in another country with James Carle and have carried a great parte of my goods along with her and lives in adultery with him."[52]

Those Predestinarians who did bequeath their wives real estate often severely limited their ability to manage the property. Nineteen percent of the Predestinarians stipulated that their wives would control the land either during the minority of the children or merely for her widowhood. This manipulation on the part of Predestinarian testators worked against the widow's right to her third of even the movable estate. Presbyterian Robert Hopkins, for example, gave his wife the dwelling plantation and all the personal estate until she remarried. When she did, the realty was to be equally divided among his sons and the personal estate among his daughters, leaving his widow with absolutely nothing.[53] Robert Houston of Somerset County bequeathed his wife one-third of the dwelling plantation during her widowhood. If she remarried, she would receive "only a bed" and the accompanying blankets and pillows.[54] Houston gave his sons land and stipulated that it pass only to each son's "male procrate of his own body and so to Continue from heir male to heir male Entailed for Ever."[55] Houston's naming of two male friends to execute his will is also telling. Since his wife might only control her third of the plantation for a short time (women frequently remarried quickly), the executors could have consistent authority over his sons' legacies from the time of Houston's death until the boys inherited the land. Occasionally, the widow faced a double jeopardy, losing control over the property left to her when either she remarried or the children came of age. Thus, when Neale Clarke died in 1678, he left his wife the large estate during her widowhood or until her sons turned twenty-one; if Neale's wife chose not to remarry in order to maintain control over the property, she incrementally relinquished her power as each of her sons came of age.[56]

These examples clearly illustrate male dominance within the dynamics of the Predestinarian family. William Crosse's preference for male heirs, regardless of their blood relation to him, over his own daughters illustrates this point succinctly. Crosse died in 1677, leaving his small estate to his only son William and a stepson. William received the bulk of the real estate, the stepson a small tract, and his three daughters and wife shared merely in the personal estate.[57] Maryland Predestinarians tended to embrace the patriarchal family relationships of their New England counterparts rather than the more equitable marital partnerships exhibited by the Arminian Anglican, Quaker, and Roman Catholic wills. The Predestinarian patterns may indicate a lack of confidence in the business acumen of their wives, but more likely they depict the fundamental cultural view of a woman as the bearer and nurturer of sons rather than an authority figure within the family.

One might expect that the differences between the wills of Predestinarians and Free Will Christians could be attributed to the age of the testators' children. In the past, historians have assumed that women with small children needed property to support the family and that husbands' wills reflected this need. Yet a close examination of some testators suggests that this factor was not the primary motivation for early modern Marylanders. For the most part, Free Will Christians and Predestinarians closely followed the patterns described regardless of whether their children were infants or grown with children of their own. Many of the previous Predestinarian examples were of young wives who were caring for small children but who did not inherit realty themselves, such as William Hitchcock's widow in Calvert County. The Predestinarians could have specifically given their wives the entire estate in order to provide for their small children, but they very often bequeathed their property to the male children and named a male overseer or guardian to manage the estate until the boys came of age.

Free Will Christians also made specific land bequests to children—both sons and daughters. Yet they reserved a significant portion for their wives and gave them full control over it for at least their lifetimes, just as the spirit of canon law demanded. Catholic John Clark, for example, gave his wife, Sarah, their estate in freehold.[58] Sarah did not have any small children to care for at home and she may have been getting on in years herself. Yet John acknowledged her independence when he bequeathed her the estate to do with as she wished rather than giving it to their grown child and insisting that Sarah be maintained. Similarly, Arminian Anglican George Betts, a grandfather, left his wife the plantation she lived on for the duration of her life. His married daughter received land through the bequest and an unmarried daughter was already living away from home on the three hundred acres that her father bequeathed her.[59] No one assumed that the son-in-law should take responsibility for the women in the family and George allowed his wife the opportunity to continue living on her own. Likewise, Quaker Francis Billingsley gave his wife, Susanna, and eighteen-year-old married daughter, Rebecca Birckhead, half of the family's large estate each. When Susanna died her half would revert to Rebecca. If Rebecca died before Susanna, without any living heirs, Susanna was to manage the entire estate, and it would pass to several cousins when she died.[60] None of these widows had small children to provide for; they lived by themselves and presumably wanted to continue to do so. Free Will Christian widows had this option because they held their own real estate.

While suggesting that distinctions can be made between Free Will Christian and Predestinarian family structures, these examples also bring up the question of wealth. Certainly George Betts and Francis Billingsley were not poor struggling farmers. What if most of the Predestinarians were amongst the poorest of the will-writers and the Free Will Christians, like Betts and Billingsley, were the wealthiest members of the society? Surely, if this were the case, class would be the crucial variable rather than religion. In order to test this hypothesis I used Historic St. Mary's City's inventory data for six counties—collected by a team led by Lois Carr, Russell Menard, and Lorena Walsh—to analyze 340 testators (53 Predestinarians and 287 Free Will Christians—approximating the overall ratio for the population studied) from three wealth categories. Keeping in mind that total estate values (deflated for comparisons across time) only take into consideration movable goods, these figures can offer us a means for examining testators with small (valued at less than 48£), medium (48-226£) and large estates (greater than 226£). The graphic evidence—seen in figures 7 and 8—was striking.

The vast majority of married Free Will Christian testators left their wives land regardless of the size of their estates. This remarkable consistency suggests that the one out of five Free Will Christian testators who treated their wives differently did so for particular reasons that had nothing to do with wealth. Since the colonists faced high mortality and remarriage rates during the seventeenth century, we can safely assume that some of these Free Will Christian widows were second wives who did not receive real estate to use for the rest of their lives or in freehold because they already owned estates of their own, as did Garrett Vansweringen's and Peter Sharp's widows, discussed above. And since some dying testators acknowledge that their wives might be on their deathbeds as well, we can also assume that this small group included a number of old or infirm women who were unable or unwilling to manage the family estate when their husbands died. Quaker William Harris, for example, wrote his will while he and his wife Elizabeth were very ill, so he divided up the estate as if they both would die soon. However, he stipulated that "in Case it pleaseth God my Wife Elizabeth Harris live longer then I do make this my last will null and voyd & I also do Make her my full and whole Executor and do give unto her all my Land Cattells and goods with all things I possesse and Enjoy in as full power and

Testators	No Land/ Conditional	Land for Life/Freehold	Number
Predestinarian--small estates	64%	36%	14
Predestinarian--medium estates	46%	54%	28
Predestinarian--large estates	36%	63%	11
Free Will--small estates	19%	81%	42
Free Will--medium estates	20%	81%	138
Free Will--large estates	22%	77%	107

6. Percentages of Testators in Three Wealth Categories

authority as I my self do enjoy them for her to dispose of them as she shall thinke fitt."[61]

Predestinarians, on the other hand, varied their bequests inversely. As their wealth (and arguably their status) increased, they were more likely to give their widows control over some land, in keeping with the dominant Free Will Christian pattern.[62] Yet even when these Predestinarians amassed large estates they did not leave their wives land as frequently as their Free Will counterparts. While approximately eight out of ten of the wealthiest Free Will Christians left their wives large tracts of land for at least their lifetimes, only six out of ten of the wealthiest Predestinarians chose to allow their wives this much freedom. What might explain this statistically significant difference? If, in fact, these Predestinarian families co-opted elite behavior—established by the Roman Catholic Calverts and their kin—in an effort to find inclusion in the ruling class, they must have done so with some reluctance, as such behavior gave women a position of authority in the family.

While it seems clear that married men, generally speaking, followed these two patterns, we might well wonder whether or not Maryland women readily accepted these two marriage models. Since women (and men) had little time to record their thoughts and daily routines in diaries, and few other documents expressing distinctly female views have survived, the 211 female testaments left between 1634 and 1713 provide us with an invaluable source for recovering the voices of previously ignored female historical participants. These wills reveal that Predestinarian women accepted their positions as obedient wives under the control of powerful patriarchs and that Free Will Christian women embraced the responsibility and duties associated with their demanding positions as "yoak fellows."

Significantly, Predestinarian women whose husbands were still alive

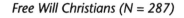

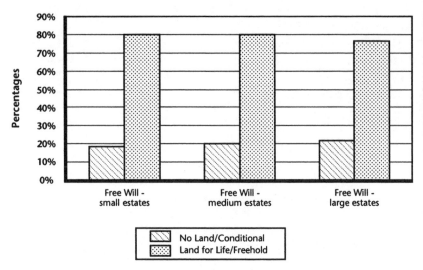

7. Free Will Christian Men with Small, Medium, and Large Estates

never left wills. Since much of their marital duty revolved around producing healthy sons, they left their families' financial affairs in the hands of the male head of the household. It was the husband's duty to manage and maintain all of the family's property. If a wife brought real estate to the marriage, the land became her husband's property and it was his responsibility to allocate these resources to his heirs when he died.[63] If a Predestinarian wife knew that she was dying, she might have given the little personal property that she claimed as her own—such as clothing, jewelry, cookware, dishes, etc.—to other women or to her daughters. Having no debts of her own or significant property to bequeath, a Predestinarian wife could settle her affairs with a simple verbal request on her deathbed. If, however, she failed to make her last wishes known, perhaps her protector (her husband) would give her cherished belongings to an appropriate heir.

One out of every four of the Predestinarian women who wrote wills was single and the remaining three-quarters were widows. Yet we should remember that few widowed or single Predestinarian women in Maryland had a pressing need to write wills, hence their small numbers. Most Predestinarian women possessed only meager estates in personal goods, and their husbands allocated any dower they brought to the marriage to their

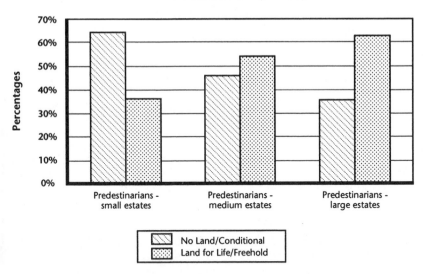

Note: *Figures 6, 7, and 8 represent the percentage of married male testators leaving their wives land for the duration of their lives or in freehold versus bequests to wives that did not include land or only allowed control over land during widowhood or until the eldest male child reached maturity [Conditional].*

8. Predestinarian Men with Small, Medium, and Large Estates

eldest sons. Those women who felt a need to write a will in order to name a guardian for their children or an executor of their husband's will often disbursed the household items, slaves, and clothes to their children and other relatives, as did Widow Ann Smith and Widow Elizabeth Eareckson.[64]

The few Predestinarian women who held real estate in their own names left the administration of their estates to a male executor and the land to male friends or relatives, as did James Browne's widow Ann and the widow Mary Aldry.[65] And since these widows believed that land should return to its proper place in the male domain, daughters and other females mentioned in their wills nearly always received personal and household goods in the form of clothing, cookware, dishes, and livestock rather than land. Thus Predestinarian widows concurred with their fathers, husbands, and sons that females ought to inherit personal goods rather than realty and males, in general, ought to have control over real estate as executors and administrators. A Predestinarian woman's lack of control over her family's most valuable property—land—indicates her overall lack of authority and power within the family. Moreover, individual Predestinarian women's pervasive reluctance to leave this property to their female heirs indicates that they too believed that the patriarchal family model was both natural and desirable.

Free Will Christian women tell a very different story. Their testaments indicate that they shared their male counterparts' ideas about marriages between "yoak fellows." A man and woman were joined together as a working team managing their servants, children, and property. As partners they shared the work and risks associated with running a plantation during the early years of settlement, facing soft tobacco prices, the high costs of purchasing and providing for servants who might run away, and unpredictable weather. Simultaneously, some partners enjoyed the benefits too. In a Free Will Christian family, status and power within a family had more to do with age than gender. In a society in which death often diminished the size of a family quite quickly, the older a child became, the more likely he or she was to reach adulthood. Consequently, birth order rather than gender often determined how much of the family's wealth would be left to a particular child. Older daughters, like the eldest sons, generally received sizable portions of the real estate while younger siblings received considerably smaller shares. Consequently, these daughters grew up and became wives who brought their sizable estates to their new unions and, significantly, these women tended to maintain control over their natal estates while they were married.[66]

Thus we are not surprised to find Free Will Christian wives exerting their authority within the family, manifested in their ability and inclination to write a last will and testament. Since Free Will Christian husbands thought of their wives as partners with land of their own to control, approximately one of every five Free Will Christian women leaving a will was married. While Predestinarian married women had no reason to write wills, some Free Will Christian wives who owned and controlled significant parcels of land during their marriage wanted to bequeath their separate estates in their own wills when they died. Husbands readily accepted this action as a matter of course in these families, or Free Will Christian wives would not have left wills, as the Predestinarian wives did not.

Like their Predestinarian counterparts, nearly three-quarters of all Free Will Christian female testators were widows, but unlike the Predestinarian women they used their wills in such a fashion that we are inclined to accept the notion that they held authority in their families when their husbands were alive and continued to do so after they became widows. Free Will Christian women tended to hold real estate in addition to personal goods throughout their lives. Widow Sarah Harris thought of herself as an "unproffitable servant of God" and wrote her will while "in perfect health and memory (praised be God) yet considering the certainty of death and the uncertainty of the time when it shall please Almighty God to call mee doe willingly and with a free heart render my Spiritt into the hands of my Lord God and Creator." Sarah had outlived at least three husbands—Walter Jenkins, Thomas Brookes, and Mr. Harris. She indicated in her will that Walter Jenkins had purchased the one-hundred-acre tract that she willed to her grandson John Ingram. Sarah bequeathed her daughter Hanna and Hanna's husband Christopher Goodhand the three-hundred-acre parcel purchased by the late Thomas Brookes. Sarah assumed that the business acumen of her male and female heirs was largely equal when she named her daughter and son-in-law joint executors. Therefore, she gave her daughter the onerous responsibility for administering her will and the ownership and management of her own real estate.[67] Free Will Christian women, like Sarah, typically named female and male beneficiaries in equal numbers. These female testators also gave their daughters, granddaughters, and other females real estate as often as they gave it to male relatives, indicating their marked propensity for following the typical male Free Will Christian testamentary patterns.[68] Free Will Christian males and females thought that the ability to manage real estate had little to do with gender.

Unfortunately for comparison purposes, many of the wills in England for this same time period do not contain the elaborate pious preambles found in Maryland, making it much more difficult to ascertain whether a testator was a Predestinarian or Free Will Christian. Perhaps hired scribes who based their rendering of wills on formulary books were more common in England than in Maryland during the seventeenth century. Or it is quite possible that testators avoided expressing their religious beliefs in these legal documents when political and religious upheavals plagued the era. Indeed, religious preambles seem to fluctuate with the times. Before Henry VIII's break with Rome, most testators bequeathed their souls to God, the Blessed Virgin Mary, and all the saints in heaven in elaborate preambles. After the English Reformation, testators simplified their statements, leaving their souls to God and trusting to be saved through His goodness, in order to conform to the mild Protestant reforms being embraced by the Church of England. English wills in the seventeenth century often omitted religious preambles altogether, perhaps indicating testators' anxieties over the possible persecution of surviving kin in light of the shifting political and religious ground throughout the period.

Despite this obstacle, William Stevenson has identified a few Quakers in Huntingdonshire, Cambridgeshire, and Bedfordshire based upon other sources, and his work permits a comparison with the Maryland wills. Although Stevenson is primarily interested in proving that "nonconformists of all sectarian persuasions were drawn from a very wide cross-section of society," including "the very poor as well as the prosperous and wealthy," his detailed descriptions of some of the dissenters' wills provides at least a few examples from which to draw some preliminary conclusions.[69] A wealthy Huntingdonshire Quaker by the name of Nurse Parnell bequeathed his wife seven houses to take care of until their son reached his majority. For her own use, Nurse left his wife a "dovehouse"—which Stevenson explains was a "traditional symbol of gentry status"—along with two acres of meadowland. Over and above this "symbol of gentry status," Nurse gave his wife another eighty acres of land in various locations. Altogether, the widow controlled more than forty-five percent of the family's land for her own use. Less wealthy Quakers in Huntingdonshire, such as William King and Thomas Emerson, also left their wives—and daughters—significant portions of the families' estates in both land and movable goods even when the families had at least one son who could have inherited all the land.[70] Perhaps these few examples suggest that Free Will Christians in Maryland followed English inheritance patterns.

Other sources, including genealogical records, help to identify some English Arminian Anglicans and Roman Catholics. These English Free Will Christians also followed the inheritance patterns found in Maryland. Arminian Anglican Robert Dawbeney, from the town of Sudbury in Suffolk County, left his "dear and loving wife and faithful yoke fellow" all of the houses and land he possessed in Norwich, his tenement in Walshames, and the Hinderclay farm for her life. After naming her his executrix, he also gave her "all my goods and chattels, bonds and bills after my legacies have been discharged."[71] Likewise, Arminian Anglican John Gryme—a yeoman from the same county—bequeathed his "loving wife" his "freehold messuage" (manor house) with the extensive land that surrounded it to use during her life. The couple's son, John, would have to wait until his mother died before he took control of the family's property. John the elder also asked his wife— his sole executrix—to keep "all the rest of my goods and chattels," make sure that he was "decently buried," pay the family's debts, and maintain the family's houses in a "husbandly manner" that precluded her from felling too many trees.[72] Roman Catholics, such as Henry Fermor, Bullen Reymes, Jr., Augustine Petre, and Josias Arundell, also followed the typical Free Will Christian inheritance pattern.[73] Whether gentry or simple "clothier," these English Roman Catholic men left their wives most (if not all) of the family's houses, manors, and land to use during their lifetimes.[74]

Predestinarian dissenters in the parish of Fenstanton appear to have adhered to the practices of their Predestinarian counterparts in Maryland. Henry Browne, for instance, was a fairly wealthy shoemaker when he made up his will in 1659. His movable estate was valued at an impressive 225 pounds sterling. Despite his wealth he decided to leave his wife the house they shared only for as long as she remained a widow. If she chose to remarry, "she was to receive forty shillings per annum," which was much less than a woman would need to support herself and far less than the one-third of the family's estate that she was entitled to according to English common law. Although we cannot reconstruct the trials and tribulations this woman must have faced after her husband's death, we do know that she was worse off, at least financially, than she had been when her husband was alive. In 1684/5, Browne's widow had only eleven pounds sterling worth of movable goods to her name.[75] Henry Browne appears to have treated his wife in much the same manner as some of the poorer Predestinarian men in Maryland treated theirs. In Maryland, a wealthy Predestinarian man worth 225 pounds sterling would have been more inclined to adopt the more egalitarian Free Will Christian inheritance patterns that dominated early Maryland's society. Thus Henry Browne's will might suggest that wealthy Predestinarians in England were less willing than their Maryland counterparts to adopt Free Will Christian practices, if this particular example is indicative of the larger English Predestinarian population.

Devonshire, the longstanding stronghold of Calvinist non-conformists, offers more fertile ground for identifying Predestinarians through their testamentary preambles, which illuminate the Predestinarian view of womanhood. In the town of Exeter in Devonshire there were at least five Calvinist meetinghouses by 1691, and historians have estimated that by 1715 Calvinists made up approximately one-third of the town's population—some three thousand people.[76] The other Devonshire towns had similar Calvinist populations. Thomas Tucker, who died in 1694, was one of these seventeenth-century dissenters living in Devonshire. The wealthy Tucker left his wife Elinor twelve pounds sterling per year for her maintenance for as long as she remained a widow. If she chose to remarry, her income dropped by more than 15 percent. In the house they once shared Elinor was to have the use of "the halle, and all those two rooms on that side the entry," along with "the upper garden." She also had "for her yearly burning 200 well made faggots of wood," some furniture (including a bed), and linen. All of these bequests would return to the true heir (their son Thomas) when Elinor died. Thomas Tucker named his son the executor of his will and beneficiary of the entire estate. The Tucker will suggests that after her husband died Elinor did not hold a position of authority in the home. As executor, Thomas the younger did not need his mother's consent or her approval in financial matters. The living arrangements further underscored Elinor's dependent position within the family. In stipulating that Elinor had the right to use two rooms and the "halle," her husband seemed to say that her presence was to be tolerated by her son. Living under Thomas the younger's roof only entitled Elinor to rooms in which to eat and sleep. Thomas the younger may have looked upon Elinor's right to living space in his house as an infringement upon his right to the property and perhaps his bride might have shared this resentment.

Surely, this living arrangement emphasized Elinor's position as a dependent of the new patriarch; she was not an authority figure in the home.[77] Thomas Melinuish, from Barnstaple in Devonshire, put his wife Joan in a similar position when he laid out provisions for her. He left Joan eight pounds sterling, a bed, and a chest from their "parler," in addition to access to the small orchard on the west side of the moor. The bulk of the estate, however, went to the couple's son John, who also acted as Thomas's executor.[78] Both the Tucker and Melinuish examples illustrate the Predestinarian notion that women were dependents in need of male protection and, as such, they ought to be taken care of by their sons after the death of their husbands.

Perhaps Bulstrode Whitelocke would have agreed with this assessment. Whitelocke was a lawyer, Parliamentarian, and scholar, an ambassador to Sweden, the father of seventeen children, husband to three wives, and a pious Puritan. When he prepared his will in 1675, he neglected to firmly state his beliefs in a religious preamble, choosing instead to use the space to attack his critics for their "hard usages of me," since he had suffered great injustices at their hands. Still, the rest of his will indicated that he too understood that males were better suited than females to managing real estate, even if the property in question originally belonged to the female. Although his third wife, Mary, brought a "great estate" to the marriage, he left his "worldly estate both real and personal" to his son Carleton. He knew his wife was entitled to much more than "such of the [movable] goods as she shall think fit to make choice of," but he hoped she would understand his decision to leave the estate to his son. Whitelocke closed the document with the request that his children "be dutiful and respectful to my wife and loving to one another. And I commend them all to the blessing of our most gracious God, whom I counsel them to follow fully in all things." Surely, having to show Mary "respect" was not the same as having to yield to her authority in financial matters. Without control over substantial portions of the family's estate, a widow like Mary would have little influence over an heir. In this case in particular, Mary had no authority over Carleton, since her husband had appointed several men to control Carleton's legacy until he came of age. There is little doubt that Carleton had to acquiesce to the dictates of his male supervisors in all his financial dealings until he became an adult, but Mary's advice or consent would not be necessary (or even perhaps desirable). Additionally, Carleton's responsibility to "be dutiful" to Mary was directly related to her dependent position in the family. As the newly appointed patriarch, who would assume the family's estate, Carleton also assumed his father's duty to protect Mary and provide her with the basic necessities of life—firewood, food, and a place to sleep.[79]

Certainly, English Calvinists can be found subscribing to the Maryland Predestinarians' conception of womanhood, as in the cases cited above. Yet other English Calvinists are not so easily categorized. For instance, Richard Wayman (an "Ironmonger" from Birmingham) clearly displayed his Calvinist beliefs in his will when he bequeathed his "Soul unto the Lord God of Heaven, whoe elected mee before the world began, trusting and assuredly beleeving that by the Death and bountyfull blood sheding of his deare sonne, my onely Saviour and Redeemer Jhesus Christ, after my mortall Life is dissolved, and my filthy body then mortally diseased, that my soule shall pr[e]sently enter into the Celestiall Joyes." As a true Calvinist, he believed that before the beginning of time God had selected him to take his place among the elect and chosen saints. Richard also summed up a typical Puritan characterization of humanity as both "filthy" and "diseased." And yet this pious Calvinist of the middling sort displayed a Free Will Christian inheritance pattern when he left the majority of his estate to his wife. He did, however, behave more like his Calvinist Maryland counterparts when he recognized that his wife would not welcome the position of executrix: "I knowe it will be great trouble and vexation for my said wife to gather in all my debts." Thus Richard "appointed Richard Carrles of Birmingham, Yeoman, and Wm Seeley of the same, woollen draper" to settle his estate as executors of his last will.[80] Yet we are still left to wonder why Richard bequeathed so much of the family's estate to his wife. Did Richard think of his wife as his "yoak fellow," sharing the work, risks, and responsibilities of managing the family's financial situation, in the same way that most Free Will Christians did? Or is it possible that Richard was adopting the Free Will Christian inheritance pattern to conform to a Free Will Christian community's practice, as his wealthier Predestinarian counterparts did in Maryland? The possibility also exists that Richard might have been merely returning to his wife the dowry that she had originally brought to the marriage. Ultimately, however, the answer to this query has been lost; only Richard or his wife could adequately provide an answer.

Richard Wayman's will reminds us that inheritance patterns were not absolute. Clearly, not every Predestinarian or Free Will Christian in Maryland adhered to the patterns described above. Thus we should be cautious about focusing on a few English wills that neatly fit into the practices laid out in this chapter. A sample of English wills from a variety of locations might be more helpful in uncovering any connections between English and Maryland inheritance patterns. After identifying twenty-seven male Predestinarians and fifty-one male Free Will Christians from a variety of social classifications—ranging from lowly husbandmen and yeomen farmers to wealthy gentlemen—we can say with greater certainty that Maryland inheritance patterns may have been based on English practice. Twenty of the English Predestinarians sampled (74 percent) believed that women were dependents and thus gave them merely a small portion of the family's movable goods to control. Tellingly, only three of the Free Will Christians (6 percent) exhibited this Predestinarian propensity. The Predestinarians underscored their insistence that women were dependents when merely seven of them (24 percent) named wives or other females as the executors of their wills. This fact is particularly important because other historians have pointed out that, as a whole, English men named their wives as executors roughly 80 percent of the time. Unlike these Predestinarians, English Free Will Christian men overwhelmingly believed that women could and should manage the majority of a family's estate after the death of a "yoak fellow"; forty-eight out of these fifty-one (94 percent) gave women control over large portions of their estates.

To be sure, this sample of wills cannot be taken as conclusive evidence that English Predestinarians and Free Will Christians established patterns that their Maryland counterparts brought with them to the New World. Certainly a more rigorous investigation might point to significant variations in inheritance patterns related to wealth and status, region, and time, considering the social upheavals during the seventeenth century. It does, however, suggest that a more thorough investigation would be worthwhile, to establish connections that this study implies between the English and Maryland patterns.

Of course, the demographic, economic, and political explanations for colonial behavior offered by other historians provide us with valuable information.[81] Yet the older variable of religion is equally important for illuminating a society in which religion served as a dominant matrix. Most of the Predestinarian and Free Will Christian women of Maryland landholding families did not share a common destiny. Mirroring their New England and English counterparts, Maryland's Predestinarian wives were dependents—like the children they bore—who needed and wanted the protection of a strong male patriarch. A Free Will Christian union, on the other hand, was a bond formed between two partners who shared the risks and benefits of managing the family's estate in addition to power and authority in the household itself.[82] The Free Will Christian patterns described here coincide with Amy Louise Erickson's work on early modern England, where women controlled property, children, and households in ways similar to their Maryland counterparts and where testamentary practices were more egalitarian than those in New England.[83] Consequently, while colonial American historians have viewed the liberties seventeenth-century Maryland women had as an anomaly caused by disparate sex ratios and frontier conditions, their behavior may represent a pattern of normal English (and perhaps western European) family relationships with some minor adjustments. Thus we might begin to reassess the propensity of historians to claim that patriarchy in the family represented a cultural norm in the early modern period. Using religion as a crucial variable of analysis, we are starting to see complexities, family arrangements, and social creativity that recast and enrich our understanding of the early modern period.

6

Ɔ

Free Will Christian
Women's Public Authority

*I*n testament to her love and respect for, and commitment to, her life's
partner, Ursula Burges bid him farewell by having these words engraved on the large stone slab marking his final resting place:

> Here lyeth ye body of W[illiam] Burges,
> Esq., who departed this life on ye
> 24 day of Janu., 1686;
> Aged about 64 years; leaving his
> Dear beloved wife Ursula, and eleven
> Children; viz. seven sons and four daughters,
> And eight grand children.
> In his lifetime he was a Member of
> His Lordship's Council of State; one
> Of his Lordship's Deputy-Governors;
> A Justice of ye High Provincial Court;
> Colon. of a regiment of ye Trained Bands;
> And sometimes General of all ye
> Military Forces of this Province.
> His loving wife Ursula, his Executrix,
> In testimony of her true respect,
> And due regard to the worthy
> Deserts of her dear deceased
> Husband, hath erected this Monument.[1]

In a poignant message to posterity, Ursula, with "due regard" and "true respect," suggests that duty to one's spouse, family, and community and to the proprietor of the province formed the essence of Free Will Christian marriage in early modern Maryland. That intimate bond also represented a union between at least two natal families, as well as the understanding that they would have to work together to meet their obligations and commitments to these families, their community, and the proprietor. They assumed their positions within a newly constructed family as partners sharing common values; that they did so is manifest in their struggle for economic security as well as the continuation of the family and the extension of kinship for political, social, and economic purposes within the known boundaries of early modern life and death.

In recognition of this complex integration of lives, Ursula emphasized her social standing as a function of her husband's noteworthy political achievements. She obviously took great pride in her contribution to her husband's success. More importantly, Ursula draws the reader's attention to her executorship in this epitaph, underscoring the critical shift in her life cycle, her family position, and her community status. Once a partner, she now faced managing her dependents and property without her dead husband's assistance, guidance, and support. We cannot know—solely from this gravestone—if Ursula embraced her new role as an opportunity for greater power and authority, or if she dreaded the added stress and anxiety associated with additional, and perhaps overwhelming, duties and responsibilities. Yet one thing is certain. Ursula took her new position—with its added work and responsibilities—seriously.

Ursula's story raises several new questions. Did early modern English women relish the role of executrix? If so, were there any discernable differences between Free Will Christian and Predestinarian female executors? And did this critical shift in status after the death of a husband represent a genuinely new role for a widow? Or was this new position of authority, in fact, merely an extension of Free Will Christian women's active participation in the public realm throughout their adult lives? Fortunately, additional sources, such as wills, legal testamentary proceedings, provincial laws, and payment receipts provide some clues about the varied experiences of female executors to begin to answer these important questions.

Undoubtedly, some female executors faced unfamiliar duties in the courts, their families, and their communities when they first assumed their new legal positions. First, their obligations began with either collecting witnesses' letters of testimony to submit to the court clerk (if they could not appear in person) or escorting witnesses to court in order to publicly pro-

claim the authenticity of their husbands' wills. Proving a will was a particularly necessary task in this profit-motivated society where a reputation for
credibility and honesty could affect a family's community status for generations. Consequently, at least two witnesses, male or female, were required to
swear an oath in court stating that the testator was of sound mind when he
did in fact "Signe Seale publish and Declare" his last will and testament.[2]
Second, the executrix also took an oath—significantly, the same oath male
executors swore—promising not to embezzle any part of the estate, but to
uphold the testator's intentions in distributing the legacy. These important
legal formalities merely marked the beginning of a widow's responsibility
as executrix. She also had to journey back to her plantation to settle her husband's debts and collect monies due in addition to managing the estate's
property—often while raising several small children and tending the tobacco at the same time.

When a husband died without leaving a will, the duties and burdens
associated with the position of administrator were similar to those of an
executor. Acting as her deceased partner's court-appointed administrator,
Jane Cockshott first appeared in court to swear an oath different in form,
but not in substance, from the one that executors took. She agreed to "truely
Administer the goods & chattles and debts of [her husband] deceased intestate according to the ten letters of Administration to me commited. A
true Inventory of all and singuler his goods Chattles and debts w[hi]ch shall
come to my hands possession or knowledge I will make, & or list account
when thereunto I shall be lawfully called of my Administration I will give
So helpe me god, and the contents of this booke."[3] As she promised, Jane
had the family's large estate inventoried and then submitted the written
document to the court in a timely manner. This action marked the initial
steps toward balancing her husband's accounts, just as it would have for an
executor.[4]

Conforming to English custom, the vast majority—84 percent—of Free
Will Christian married male testators [N = 1881] named their wives to execute their wills.[5] If we can take these men at their word, husbands assumed
that their wives had the practical knowledge and business sense necessary
to settle complicated estates. John Gary, for one, reminded his executrix—
his wife Alice—to act on the family's behalf "as if I were personally present
to Effect the Same."[6] But Roman Catholic Randolph Brandt, a gentleman of
Charles County, perhaps said it best when he "impower[ed]" his wife (and
executrix) with the authority to "recover and sue" his brother's estate in
Barbados and then to "dispose of the same for her and [the children's] advantage."[7] Likewise, Margaret Prior settled an estate her husband had

left heavily in debt.[8] Impeded by the limited funds she had to work with, Margaret paid off the family's many creditors—including Mathias Vander-heijd, who was owed 1200 pounds of tobacco—seemingly accustomed to acting in this capacity.[9] These wives fulfilled their husband's expectations with a degree of expertise that suggests their business acumen was not a newly acquired skill.

This was not true only of elites. Men with marginally profitable farms also believed their wives possessed the necessary talents to effectively handle time-consuming, complex settlements, as did Richard Chaffee. Facing death and knowing that his unprofitable plantation could not possibly provide for his family and his many creditors, Richard asked "that all my Just debts . . . be paid so farr as the Tobbacco in the Tobbacco houses shall pay." When the current crop was depleted he hoped that "my Cr[e]ditors will be so kind to stay till another Season or Year till my Executrix be able to pay ye remainder whose Industry I hope will not be Wanting to Sati[s]fye the Same as Soon as possible." Richard fastidiously listed his creditors in his will and recorded the amount of tobacco owed to each. He wanted to be sure that Ann would meet the family's economic obligations in order to preserve its good name. At the same time Richard's will also ensured that Ann would not be swindled out of property that the family could ill afford to lose.[10] This carefully crafted legal document, witnessed by several people in the community, would serve to verify both the magnitude of the family's debts and its legitimate creditors. Although armed with this legal document, Ann still faced a huge task when her partner died, since the small family farm did not provide an easy means for paying off its delinquent accounts. Yet her husband was sure that Ann would fulfill the promises that he made on his deathbed. Confident in his partner's management skills and physical strength, Richard assumed his wife could and would work the farm, harvest and pack the tobacco, and then satisfy the family's creditors within a year's time.

After their husbands died, executrixes like Margaret Prior and Ann Chaffee often found themselves struggling to settle debts with men and other women as well. As a rule, both Free Will Christian men and women readily recognized the legitimacy of women's managing and settling compli-cated estates.[11] However, on occasion, women had to turn to the courts for assistance; Jane Basha and Jane Cockshott, for example, spent considerable time filing legal claims for property owed to their husbands' estates.[12] Others continued protracted legal battles that had preoccupied their husbands be-fore their deaths. Having taken advantage of Lord Baltimore's offer of land in Maryland, Robert Hewett thought he was entitled to at least eight hun-

dred acres for transporting servants and family members to the new province; but, because Hewett had died before Lord Baltimore formally deeded
the real estate to him, in 1650 his widow Hannah went to court to get it.[13]

Debt collection sometimes required a widow to appear in court as her
late husband's attorney. Others, like Anne Hammond, had served as their
husbands' attorneys even while they were alive. Thus in 1655, two letters of
attorney empowered Anne "to act singly" as her husband's attorney in a
land transaction with Richard Hotchkeys. When Hotchkeys paid the "Just
summe of 5500 [pounds] of good sound Merchantable leafe Tobacco &
caske" to Anne, she was to sell, "assigne & sett over unto the s[ai]d Richard
Hotchkeys" the thousand-acre "Plantacon lyeing on the east side of Brittons
bay." The deal included "all houses edifices buildeings fences fruit trees timber trees Rainges underwood profitts Comoditys & appurtanances whatsoever there unto belonging."[14] Since normally husbands and wives acted
jointly when they bought or sold land in early Maryland, we are left to wonder what circumstances prompted John Hammond to place this particular
deal completely under his wife's control. Did John have to leave the province
for an extended period of time before the land transaction could be completed? Was he already out of the province when a particularly good real
estate opportunity came to his wife's attention? If so, did he send letters of
attorney with two different servants to ensure that one would make it safely
into his wife's hands? Unfortunately, the answers to these questions are not
preserved in the records. Regardless of the reason behind Hammond's decision to grant his wife power of attorney in this instance, he was certainly
not blazing a new trail with his actions. Husbands trusted their wives to act
on their behalf as attorneys in early modern Maryland with some regularity.

Besides acting as attorneys, women commonly appeared in court seeking justice for wrongs done to them. One Jane Fenwick brought a suit
against the Jesuit priest Ralph Crouch for wrongfully detaining her horse.
The horse in question had been found roaming around Captain Cornwaleys's house and, "thinking it was the priests horse," Cornwaleys made it
swim across the "Creek into Mathewes neck of land," where Father Crouch
lived.[15] Presumably after several attempts at negotiating with the Jesuits to
secure her horse's return, Jane turned to the court system to retrieve her
property. Anne Fletcher also sought justice from the legal system after she
left the service of "Sr. Edmond Plyden Kn[igh]t" because he refused to pay
her the wages she thought she deserved.[16] And servants like Sarah Taylor
brought suits against their masters for excessively cruel and inhumane treatment. Sarah's mistress, Mary Bradnox, a medical practitioner, was repeatedly summoned to court to answer her servants' charges of brutality. Per-

haps Sarah was telling the truth about her mistress's frequent abuse, for Mary did not hesitate to strike Sarah with a "rope's end" right in front of the judge.[17] The judge must have taken Sarah's allegations seriously, for he freed her from her "apprenticeship" because the gross mistreatment placed her in "imminent danger."[18] Mary Bradnox had also appeared in court to sue the estate of one of her patients for care received and not paid for, just as Isabella Barnes, Mary Gillford, Mrs. Sprye, and other female medical practitioners did.[19] Irrespective of their wealth or marital status, women used the legal system to sue fellow colonists for theft, mistreatment, and non-payment.

Women also frequently appeared in court as defendants or witnesses. In addition to answering allegations of brutality, women such as Elizabeth Barber were summoned to appear when they were accused of not honoring verbal or written contracts.[20] Both single and married female witnesses regularly appeared before the court to testify against men and were reimbursed for the inconvenience.[21] As a matter of fact, men actually won lawsuits based on women's testimony. Penelope Hall and Elizabeth Darnell testified in court against William Brookes, who was accused of beating Thomas Allanson. Because of the testimony of these two twenty-three-year-old women, Allanson was awarded damages—three hundred pounds of tobacco—in addition to reimbursement of his court costs.[22] As further evidence of women's recognized legal status in the province, the courts did not question the testimony of female witnesses to wills.[23]

In sum, a widow (wealthy or poor) facing the time-consuming responsibilities of an executor or administrator was, in all likelihood, fairly familiar with the legal system prior to her husband's death and might have already acted as her husband's attorney in court while he was still alive. Typically a woman gained legal expertise as she came in contact with the court system and she used this knowledge when she participated in drawing up her husband's last will and testament. Free Will Christian husbands sought the advice and consent of their wives while they drew up their wills in order to both satisfy their wives and secure their positions of authority. After all, a wife's labor and reproductive capabilities and the property she brought to the marriage made her a significant contributor to the family's assets. Her husband took into account her opinions and concerns as he drew up the family will, while also considering other family members' interests. This phenomenon helps to explain why so few women felt the need to write a will themselves during the early modern period. After all, if husbands were willing to consult with their wives and negotiate an equitable distribution of family wealth through at least the next generation, then few widows would think it necessary to draw up their own wills. This was a practice that Free Will Christian families brought with them from England.[24]

Frequently, men and women employed the family will as a contract or a ratification of a written or verbal agreement between a husband and wife. Requiring only two witnesses, drawing up a will proved to be an inexpensive, quick, and effective means of legalizing an oral contract. In fact, testators used their wills as contracts at least 15 percent of the time. This practice might explain why so few prenuptial agreements survive in Maryland, compared to other colonies.[25] Will writers like Samuel Cooper explicitly reveal that wills were used to ratify oral contracts with wives. Cooper made his wife, Jane, executrix of his will and gave her their entire estate "to her heires and assignes forever," requesting only that she "remember what I have Desired of her."[26] Samuel tells us that he and his wife discussed plans for their estate, and Jane agreed to institute them in exchange for full control over the family's property. Since most testators wrote their wills when death seemed imminent, we can assume that Jane and Samuel thought that setting their agreement down in writing, while Samuel was of sound mind and body, was an important step to ensure Jane's authority. Some testators, like Samuel Cooper, named overseers in their wills to see that the executrix carried out the provisions of the contracts judiciously. Indicative of a fairly literate society, wills provided an easy substitute for the complicated procedures of equity law. These wills signaled a wife's authority within the family, granted the wife power of attorney, or were used as pre- and post-nuptial contracts between husband and wife. Colonists' propensity to draw up wills to ratify oral contracts as well as lost written ones suggests that Maryland probably had more prenuptial agreements than other colonies.[27]

Of course, women exhibited similar power and familiarity with the legal system in other official documents of the period. Thus on March 19, 1697, the Prince George's County court clerk dutifully recorded William Sesell's wife's last demand: "I William Sesell *by the Request of my wife* as She Lay upon her Death bed I have Disposed of my Childdren to Marreen Devall and his heires till they are of Age. John Sesell aged Seven yeares the 24th of December Last past Phillip Sesell, aged five yeares the 28th day of this instant Susan Sesell aged two yeares as of January Last these are humbly to Request of your Worships to bind these, Children this Court to the aforesaid Devall and his heires to the age of 21: and the girle att 16 [emphasis added]."[28] Sesell had to travel to the court when it was in session to record his wife's last "Request" and may have had to pay a fee for having such a request duly noted in the county's official books. Similarly, women's control over property found expression in prenuptial contracts. When William Bretton filed his prenuptial agreement with his betrothed, Temperance Jay, in the Provincial Court on July 10, 1651, he promised that after he died his bride would enjoy the "dwelling house in Little Brittaine aforesaid with four hundred acres of land next adjoyning, also one blackbrown cow named Browning, cropt both ears; also one reddish brown cow named Chestnut slit both ears; also one other reddish brown cow named cherry and one black cow named Collier both of my own proper mark." Additionally, Temperance would receive "one blackishe heifer . . . two cow calves . . . [the] best bed with all its furniture [and] also the half of all other my now household goods." And when William Bretton died in 1672, without writing a formal will, the court had no objection to his widow's using their prenuptial contract as his will for purposes of property distribution.[29] Thus in some cases wills served as prenuptial contracts, while in others a prenuptial contract could be used as a will.

Drawing up a family will and naming a wife as executor allowed many Free Will Christian families to formalize oral agreements and allocate family resources in a manner that ensured widows' continued authority and power within their families and communities. Anticipating family chaos if a widow happened to die without writing her own will while the children were still minors, some husbands chose to name a male co-executor of their wills. Samuel Queen, for instance, made his wife Katherine his executrix jointly with his father-in-law Richard Marsham. He assumed Marsham would take over the administration of the estate if Katherine died while their children were too young to manage on their own. Samuel also hoped that his adult son Samuel would take charge of his younger siblings along with another guardian, whom Samuel believed Katherine would select.[30]

Widows, however, did not necessarily view a joint executorship as benevolent insurance for the future good of the family. Indeed, many women, like Susanna Workman, saw it as an abridgment of their authority. Arminian Anglican Anthony Workman had named his wife and John Wells co-executors of his will. After her husband died, however, Susanna decided that she would not share the control and authority of her newly acquired position as executrix. Indeed, she was willing to pay handsomely for the privilege of acting as the sole executor of her husband's will. Accordingly, John Wells—after coming to a lucrative agreement with the widow—signed the following statement renouncing his right to administer Anthony's estate:

Know yea that I ye said John Wells . . . in consideration of ye Summ of thirty pounds Sterl[ing] money of England . . . paid by ye said Susanna Workman . . . do fully & absolutely acquitt & discharge . . . Susanna

Workman her Ex[ecutr]ex & Adm[inistrative] [duties] forever as for divers other good causes & Considerations . . . [I] have renounced & refuse[d] the Executorship and Administration of ye said Last will & Testament & all and Singular The Goods Debts rights Chattells and Creditts of ye s[ai]d Anthony Workman Dec[ease]d as also all the Estate right title interest & Demand which I have or any wise may or might have in & ye s[ai]d goods Chattles rights and Credits of ye d[ecea]s[ed] deed Either by Vertue of ye s[ai]d Ex[ecutor]ship or otherwise . . . [and I] desire that Letters Testamentary & adm[inistrative] of all & Singular ye goods Chattles & Creditts of ye said dec[ease]d may be Soley Granted to . . . Susanna Workman.[31]

Even for a wealthy family, thirty pounds sterling was a lot of money. In agreeing to such a large settlement, Susanna must have believed that total control over her husband's estate as his sole executor increased her status and authority in both her family and the larger community. As a rule, few women had to pay off their co-executor. In deference to a widow's inherent ability to manage a complex estate, many male co-executors relinquished their rights of administration without demanding to be compensated and without having to be dragged before a judge.[32] For example, in 1676 Baker and Roger Brooke refused to serve as executors of Thomas Brooke's will, which left the widow, Elinor Hatton Brooke, to administer the estate alone.[33] On the other hand, some male co-executors had to be forced to give up their rights by a judge. When Margery Warren absolutely refused to share the executorship of her husband's huge estate with her stepson she petitioned the court to make her the sole executor.[34] These Free Will Christian courts tended to support a widow's right to execute her husband's will without the assistance of a co-executor.

A widow willing to fight or pay for her right to wield complete control over her husband's estate must have enjoyed the new status and authority of her position. But she also faced enormous responsibilities, including distributing her husband's legacy to his heirs and paying off creditors. Most widows took these responsibilities seriously and completed their duties in a timely manner. When Jane Smith's second husband, John, died he left Jane a three-hundred-and-fifty-acre dwelling plantation for life that was to pass to John's nephew. Smith bequeathed several hundred acres to others, such as Ellen Mulliken (possibly his goddaughter) and John Prather, his stepson.[35] Three years after his death, Jane wrote her will to distribute her own sizable estate amongst her grown sons and grandchildren. She made it clear that she had already dispensed the property bequeathed by her last husband to his heirs.[36]

An executrix (or administrator) could, however, withhold payments or property for several years (or in some cases indefinitely) as a means of maximizing her own wealth or that of the family—a strategy that men also routinely pursued. As the executor of John Medley's wife's will, Thomas Garrett held onto John's inheritance for several years following his wife's death. In fact, John had yet to recover his legacy when he died in 1662.[37] Court-appointed female administrators also used this strategy. After Thomas Bennett, Jr., died intestate his widow even delayed inventorying the estate so as to continue to reap the benefits of an orphan's property that her husband managed before he died.[38] The courts recognized a widow's right to delay settlement. Governor Leonard Calvert sued Widow Rose Gilbert for three hundred and twenty-six pounds of tobacco that her late husband had promised him. Rose agreed she still owed "fourescore & foure pound weight of tobacco," but successfully postponed the payment.[39] The court extended this right to withhold money, land, and tobacco payments to other female executors besides a deceased's widow.[40] "Gentleman" Margaret Brent, executrix of Governor Leonard Calvert's will, faced an exacting task after the governor's death. In addition to his many commercial debts, the governor had promised mercenaries he would pay them out of his personal funds after they defended Maryland's interests. Calvert's creditors sued Margaret over a period of several years as she skillfully managed to pay them off without bankrupting the estate. The 1649 Assembly was so impressed with her management skills that they wrote to Lord Baltimore praising her financial expertise and suggesting that she "be admitted and declared your Lordship's attorney, by order of Court."[41]

The litigation over Governor Calvert's estate, which preoccupied much of Margaret Brent's time after his death, illustrates how an executrix could and did procrastinate for years in divesting property when she thought it expedient. The Assembly somewhat limited an administrator's ability to withhold property in response to a letter from the proprietor outlining the "succession from the dead to the living" in 1681. Since withholding property was a long-accepted strategy for increasing the estate (or lining one's own pockets), the Maryland Assembly passed a law stipulating a twelve-month administration period, after which a progress report had to be rendered. If "any adm[inistrator] shall faile to give an Acco[un]t within the time . . . the said Judge shall Revoake the ffirst Letters of [administration] . . . & shall grant adm[ini]strac[i]on . . . to some other person."[42] Notwithstanding, the act did not specify an *immutable* time limit on the disbursement of the debts or legacies. It merely stated that an administrator had to appear in court and give a progress report; thus it might limit an administrator's power to withhold property, but it did not prevent the practice entirely. This strategy worked well for maintaining familial authority. A widow, acting as executrix, withheld a child's portion indefinitely—whether a stepchild or her own flesh and blood—if she thought it in either her own or the family's best interest, often extracting additional labor out of grown children who otherwise would not have volunteered their services.

Apparently, both men and women in the community as well as the legal system fully accepted the right of a female executor or administrator to act on her own as sole executor of her husband's will and to delay disbursing land, movable property, and tobacco. When estates went unsettled over a period of years, individuals did not petition the courts to appoint another executor, nor did they question the right of the widow to withhold property. The litigation merely reflects the impatience of creditors to be reimbursed. This strategy of delay was common in the province, prompting some testators to specify in their wills that heirs were to be given their just legacies within certain time periods. Thus when Widow Elizabeth Lockwood died in 1711, she stipulated that some of her movable property had to be distributed by her executor within "Eighteen months after my Decease."[43] Elizabeth may have selected this language because she had been executrix of her husband Robert's last will and testament. We know that in his will Robert had bequeathed his sister Ann Saws, of York, England, one hundred and fifty pounds sterling and stipulated that it was to be paid out within "six months after the same be Lawfully Demanded."[44] This was hardly an innovation. The practice of withholding bequests must have irritated many people in English society who were victims of such behavior. After all, men and women in both England and Maryland occasionally stipulated specific time periods for the disbursement of property to avoid making their heirs (or creditors) wait too long for payment. In fact, the first Lord Baltimore—George Calvert—did just that in his will.[45]

Not every Free Will Christian husband joyfully handed his wife full control over his estate when he died. A few men had misgivings about allowing their wives carte blanche in administering their estate, for a few women did cheat their children out of their portions—often in collusion with a new, much younger husband. We have the sad case of the dead sheriff John Norwood and the quick remarriage of his widow Anne, followed by her son's legal action. Anne's son Andrew, although "loth to goe to law wth his owne Mother," did so because his mother and her young husband "by force of Armes" kept him "out of the possession of his inheritance and turneth him out of Doores."[46] Hoping to avoid just such a confrontation, Quaker Henry Taylor, Sr., appealed to his wife's sense of fairness and her duty as a mother when he reminded her not to cheat their children. Henry left his wife most of his estate during her life, "wholly and Soley to dispose of att her will and pleasure," but he also expressed his sincere desire "that she will not wrong her owne Children dureing her life."[47]

That some mothers cheated their children out of their shares was only part of what concerned John Johnson. He worried that his children might cheat their mother as well. Johnson thought it prudent to warn his family that "iff any of my children to whome I have left a legacy shall sue the Executrix [his wife] either by law or Equity they shall for that default forfet theire legacy to the Ex[ecutr]ex & if the Ex[ecutr]ex shall defraude any one of my children of any part or the whole of theire legacys shall forfeit fifty pounds sterling mon[e]y of England to that child."[48] Henry Taylor and John Johnson understood the risk to their children's portions when they left their wives in charge of the family's estate and both sought to obviate the risk of their wives' cheating their children. Henry used a psychological approach, appealing to his wife's sense of fairness, and John used a more pragmatic one based on indemnity payments should his wife "defraude" her children. And John Johnson was right to worry about the possibility of his own children cheating their mother out of her rightful share of the family estate. Women from even the most powerful wealthy Roman Catholic families, such as Ann Neale, fell victim to such behavior, and Ann felt betrayed when her ungrateful son attempted to seize as much of the family's property as possible.

Ann and Captain James Neale had settled in Maryland after the execution of King Charles in 1648. Queen Henrietta Maria had given Ann an oval pendant encrusted with diamonds and pearls depicting the Assumption of the Virgin Mary, as a token of her great affection for Ann (her maid of honor) and as a symbol of the couple's devotion to her.[49] After arriving in the Roman Catholic province the Neales established themselves as a powerful family by holding political and military positions and marrying into the most important family in Maryland, the Calverts. Captain Neale was a well-off merchant and planter in addition to serving his proprietor as an agent for Governor Leonard Calvert, as a member of both the upper and lower houses of the Assembly, and as a captain in the provincial military. He fulfilled his provincial duties while continuing to assist Charles II and the duke of York as an ambassador to Spain and Portugal. When he died, he left behind approximately 6500 acres of land and an impressive personal estate estimated at over 270 pounds sterling.[50] Unfortunately, he failed to leave a will that satisfied his beloved wife.

Ann Neale challenged her husband's "pretended" will on the grounds that only one witness, John Darnall, had signed it. More importantly perhaps for Ann, the will did not leave the widow everything she felt entitled to. A court clerk recorded on August 18, 1684, that "no persuasion can induce" Ann to swear the executrix's oath because she was convinced that James's will was invalid. Her absolute refusal forced the court to accept, albeit reluctantly, her son Anthony's petition to serve as the estate's sole executor. Ann appeared in court a short time later, declaring that her son was "altogether unmindfull of ye duty hee oweth to yor [petitioner] his mother." Ann objected to his seizure of her cattle, sheep, furniture, and other movable goods for appraisal. Ann was particularly incensed that he confiscated "Even ye Church plate" and the "furniture of my owne [bed]-Chamber" in his zealous attempt to settle his father's estate. His audacity knew no bounds, for he misappropriated Ann's young slave, who, according to Ann, was the "only p[er]son left mee to provide me wood for firing." Her son, then, had left her quite unable to sustain herself by "depriving" her "of all necessary conveniences for her Support & maintenance" in order to "satisfie" his own "Appetite." Ann went so far as to declare that Anthony was deliberately trying to "Ruine" her. Having already been awarded her third of the family's land, she wanted the court to force Anthony to give her the use of her third of the personal estate—including livestock—in addition to her own "Jewells Necklace & other her bodily ornam[en]ts together with ye [silver] plate & Church plate" and the "Negro boy aforesd & one Girle" to wait on her. Totally unaccustomed to living without an abundance of luxuries, servants, and property, Ann maintained that she was "Unable now in her old age to undergo such new hardships" while her son lined his own pockets at her expense. We cannot know with certainty how this Roman Catholic matriarch was perceived in court or her community during this difficult period in her life, but the court clerk's inclusion of her pledge "to take her Revenge of her s[ai]d sonne Anthony Neale" may indicate that men took this old woman's threats quite seriously.[51]

Ann Neale, "now in her old age," continued to fight for her rights for quite some time, although she refused to accept the executorship of the "pretended" will of Captain James Neale. Yet for other women, old age in and of itself was enough to prevent them from accepting their husband's executorship. Elderly Richard Owing left his wife a joint executorship with her grandson, but stipulated that "she ye s[ai]d Jane [was] to have ye sole authority during her naturall Life." Jane, finding herself less than fit for the undertaking, asked the court to allow her grandson to act as sole executor, she having "Resigned my Right unto him." Jane explained to the court, "whereas my deceased husband Rich[ar]d Owing by his last will [and] Testam[en]t made me ye Exe[cutri]x of his Said will w[i]th: my Grandson Rich[ard] Michel but for as much I am very ancient [and] weake I pray that you would be pleased to grant [execution?] of [administration] unto him ye s[ai]d Rich[ar]d wholly in his name."[52] Similarly, aware that his wife's age and health might prevent her from taking on the added responsibilities and worries, James Dashiell asked that his brothers accept the burden if his second wife chose not to administer his estate. James thought her capable of taking on the task, but stipulated "that if my wife Isabell Dashiell Doth not care to Administor or to take Letters of Administration that She may deliver up to my three Brothers Tho[mas,] George and Robert and they to be [executors]."[53]

As a rule, husbands like Richard Owing and James Dashiell named their wives executors of their wills regardless of their wives' health or age. Yet not every Free Will Christian husband appointed his wife to administer his will. In the small number of cases where husbands refused to appoint their wives as executors, male appointees often relinquished their rights to the widow, in keeping with the local custom that held it a widow's right and duty to settle her family's affairs. For example, Zorobabel Wells named John Chairs and John Haimor executors of his will in 1696. Both Chairs and Haimor surrendered their authority, being "assured of the Prudent fidelity, Care & Deligence of Catherine Wells the Widdow." They gave the widow her "right of Admin[istration] to the Estate of the s[ai]d Testator and all the Right title & Int[e]rest & Trust" while agreeing to assist her in any land transactions at her request.[54] This was fairly common when a husband named someone other than his wife to execute his will, as did Thomas Paine, who named his three friends Nathaniell Garrett, John Reynolds, and John Smallpiece. Dissatisfied with her exclusion from the executorship, his widow, Jane, asked the court to demand that her husband's executors appear before a judge to prove the will, whereupon a clerk recorded that John Smallpiece "Immediately appeared without Citation and then Immediately for himself renounced the Execution" of Paine's will. Smallpiece also produced a written statement from Garrett renouncing the same, and accordingly John Reynolds relinquished his right, too. The judge then "ordered that administracon of the said Deceased be Comitted to Jane the Widdow of the Said Thomas Paine and that she have letters of administration with the will of the said Thomas thereunto annexed to her granted."[55]

A husband's refusal to name his wife executrix could be interpreted as a calculated effort to undermine her authority in the family and circumscribe her power in the public arena, as we see in the case of Thomas Courtney. History remembers him primarily for removing the ears of his young female mulatto servant—an action that spurred the government into passing a law against the mutilation of servants and slaves. The court had decided to free the servant—who was serving a thirty-one-year term at the time of the incident—because of Thomas's gross mistreatment of her. More to the point for our purposes, however, in Thomas's will he did not mention his wife although he clearly had a spouse when he wrote it. His executor (and cousin), Peter Watts, refused to undermine the widow's authority in a deposition after Thomas's death, stating he was "unwilling to intermeddle therewith" and would "renounce all my right to the said executorship," giving his "Right of the Exectorship unto Mary Courtney the widdow & relict of the said Thomas Courtney."[56] Regardless of Thomas's intent to keep his widow from administering his estate, Peter Watts, Mary Courtney, and the court believed it was her right and responsibility to do so.

Sometimes, however, a husband's failure to name his wife executrix of his estate was merely a mistake, or so we are told. Two witnesses argued in court that Quaker Edward Keene had left in such a hurry to fight the Indians that he erroneously named two friends as executors instead of his wife. Keene had remembered to bequeath his wife, her daughter, and his two daughters equal shares of the family's land and personalty, but in the confusion before he left Keene made an important mistake. The two witnesses argued that Keene really meant to name his wife executrix and his friends should have been named overseers.[57] In other words, Free Will Christian widows, the courts, and members of the community believed that a widow ought to administer her husband's estate before all others as both her natural right and duty. Clearly then, Free Will Christians expected their womenfolk to actively participate in the public realm—at least in protecting and administering domestic matters.

In sum, the testamentary evidence suggests Free Will Christian men and women associated an executrix with real power and authority within the family because she was the distributor of familial assets. In the public realm, she acted as the deceased's lawyer, satisfying creditors and suing for any debts owed to the heirs as part of the testator's legacy. Why then would eight out of ten Predestinarian husbands also accept the idea that widows ought to serve as executors of their wills? Predestinarian women, as pointed out in the previous chapter, thought of themselves as dependents in need of protection rather than as authority figures in the family controlling the family's most valuable asset, land. As indicated by their bequest patterns, Predestinarian husbands overwhelmingly agreed with this social construction. Naming their wives executrixes of their estates seems inconsistent with the Predestinarian patriarchal family model presented in the previous chapters, so why did Predestinarians follow the typical Free Will Christian pattern in naming their wives executrixes? Assuming that both power and authority were linked to the executorship of wills, we must ask whether Predestinarian women embraced the power—as the Free Will Christian women did—or relinquished it regularly.

Kim Lacy Rogers's work suggests that we can distinguish between religious groups according to acceptance of the responsibilities associated with an executorship. In Rogers's study of New England Puritan women, she found that they regularly declined the opportunity to control the dispersal of property.[58] Mary Beth Norton's research tends to confirm Rogers's findings. Norton argues that "[e]ven if a husband's will left his wife relatively unencumbered by restrictions," Calvinist widows in New England "often had to obtain a court's permission to take certain necessary steps with respect to their husbands' estates." Abridging their power and authority as executrixes, some New England courts went so far as to supervise "widows' payments of legacies to their children." Norton also points out that, "[s]ignificantly, the General Court itself devoted a considerable amount of time to discussing widows' petitions, and approval of their requests was not automatic."[59] Documentation left by Free Will Christian women in Maryland, on the other hand, suggests that the provincial courts and larger society accepted powerful female executors in the public sphere. These women not only embraced the challenge of settling complicated estates, but they successfully fought to gain control over the administration of wills denied to them by their husbands. Consonant with the Calvinist practices in New England, Maryland Predestinarian women—as dependents rather than authority figures in their families—relinquished administrative authority more often than their Free Will Christian counterparts.

The evidence suggests that Predestinarian women were six times more likely to relinquish their authority and control over an estate than were their Free Will Christian counterparts. The widow of the Presbyterian William Hatton is a typical example. William appointed his wife to serve as co-executor along with their son Joseph. In keeping with her family position as a dependent, the Widow Hatton refused the position, yielding authority to her son, the new family patriarch.[60] The more complicated case of Widow Townehill and her son-in-law, Richard Snowden, serves to underscore the pervasiveness of this pattern. Calvinist Edmond Townehill and his family had lived in Anne Arundel County for some time. As a wealthy landowner,

Edmond had employed many indentured servants, including Richard Snowden, who had completed his labor contract and then married one of the Townehill daughters before the death of the family patriarch. When Edmond died, he left his wife, as executrix, in control of the estate until their eldest son reached maturity. Unable or unwilling to cope with the position of authority in the family, the widow quickly gave the executorship of her husband's estate to her son-in-law, Richard Snowden. Snowden's avaricious ambitions eventually put him at odds with the Widow Townehill, who grew concerned about her son's legacy. Undoubtedly the widow would have allowed him to continue to manage the family's property until her eldest son became an adult and could take his rightful place as the head of household had Snowden not been so greedy.

The reluctance to take on the role of executor shown by Widow Townehill, and the willingness to relinquish the power to another, were fairly common among Predestinarian females. Only when the true male heir's land was placed in jeopardy would a woman like Widow Townehill step into the public sphere, in order to protect her son's interests. The court clerk recorded that the widow believed that her children were "in danger of loosing their Childrens part unless the Exec[utri]x [Widow Townehill] by letters testamentary be impowered to Sue for their rights."[61] Since the court supported the prevailing Free Will Christian notion that a widow had both the right and responsibility to administer her husband's will, the court allowed the widow to regain the control she had bestowed so eagerly upon her son-in-law years earlier. The Widow Townehill had not relinquished her right to administer her husband's estate because she was suffering from a serious illness or simply old age, as did Free Will Christian widows. As a Calvinist woman, she accepted the principle that patriarchs—even if they were not her blood relatives—naturally ought to concern themselves with the family's financial affairs, while as a mother she was responsible for the nurturing of sons. Only when her minor son's land was in danger of being embezzled—and there was no patriarch to protect his claim to the property—did she assert her right to control the family's estate.

Women from Predestinarian families tended to depart from the norms of the dominant Free Will Christian group and relinquish the position of executor to the new family patriarch. Conversely, the vast majority of Free Will Christian women in Maryland embraced the authority and power accorded them by the executorship of their husbands' wills. An executrix acted on behalf of her deceased husband—legally in his stead—in the public sphere. She sued for property in court as her husband's lawyer, as did Quaker Nehemiah Coventon's widow, Ann, when he appointed her his "true and Lawfull attorney."[62] An executrix settled unpaid debts for goods in the marketplace as if her husband "were personally present to Effect the Same." The authority and power she exerted in the public sphere were matched by an equally impressive force in the private arena as well. The control and disbursement of at least some of the family's realty and personalty offered a woman influence over both her minor and grown children. The executorship of her husband's will fortified her already strong position of authority as the ultimate distributor of family property.

The impressive power and authority of female executors and administrators was a significant component of Free Will Christian women's public lives. Nevertheless, we need to appreciate the fact that these temporary positions in the legal system represented only one facet of early modern women's extensive participation in the larger public arena. As busy as these women must have been giving birth, educating children, and maintaining a home, they found time to appear in court as witnesses, litigants, lawyers, and administrators and executors of wills. And, not surprisingly, in keeping with the Free Will Christian belief that women ought to be active and influential family members, women expanded their sphere of influence to include the economic and political realms as well.

Free Will Christians knew their women to be willing to participate in the economic sphere by assisting the family in accumulating, or at least maintaining, wealth and social status. Indeed, women supported themselves or contributed to the family coffers as commercial shippers, teachers, landladies, medical practitioners, and apothecaries, in addition to countless other occupations.[63] In fact, a Mrs. Spry enjoyed a good reputation as a cheese maker in the province and her renown extended as far away as England.[64] Since women were active participants in business affairs, it is not surprising to see them as "Owners or Traders" of slaves as well. In London, the Public Record Office clerks noted that several women, such as Mrs. Smith and Mrs. Bascow, brought hundreds of slaves to Maryland as the demand for African labor increased and the supply of white indentured servants fell. According to one of Maryland's nineteenth-century historians, women provided 45 percent [N = 1029] of the total number of slaves [N = 2290] recorded entering the province between 1705 and 1707.[65] To be sure, English Free Will Christian women from all levels of society were active participants in the business world.[66] The duchess of Marlborough, for instance, served Queen Anne by keeping the Privy Purse and Robes accounts and she took pride in managing this great responsibility. Though others criticized her, she felt that she had "saved the crown" a great deal of money "by my good management." To support her assertion, the duchess recorded several long lists of payments made to shopkeepers and other "trades people," including many females.[67]

From the very top echelons of English society down to the growing ranks of shopkeepers and "trades people," Free Will Christians on both sides of the Atlantic expected female kinfolk to contribute to the family's financial well-being and enhance the family's social standing. A popular marriage manual of 1683 outlined the responsibilities of a wife as her husband's helpmate in "Shop-keeping." It argued that joint "Shop-keeping" was one of the ways in which a marriage could grow and prosper. Young women were instructed, "through love and care, herein [to] be assistant to your husband oftentimes . . . and so by degrees learn to understand the Shop, and converse neatly with the customers . . . help the customers, and give them pleasing answers, insomuch that you oftentimes attain to as perfect a knowledge of the Trading, as your husband himself." In turn, a wife could run the shop by herself when her husband suffered from a "headake" or was "very dull and sleepy" from overexerting himself in the marital bed, or even when he left town to attend to business. The author assures us that husbands "will appreciate the partnership" and women find real satisfaction in their new role. Indeed, working in the shop made women "happy, yea ten times over happy . . . and that not only so, your husband, but principally for your self." A wife's business acumen would also come in handy because "if that mischance might happen to you, that death should bereave you of your husband, you find your self oftentimes setled in a way of Trading, which you can manage your self, and set forward with reputation."[68] Needless to say, running a shop in her husband's absence could provide a wife with more freedom than her husband anticipated. Take for instance Langley Curtis's wife, Jane, who was prosecuted for "Publishing and putting to sale a Scandalous Libel" while her husband was "a hundred miles off" in Lincolnshire.[69]

Women's active participation in the business world included managing property long before they became widows. To begin with, the naming of land in Maryland seems to indicate a broader acceptance of female land ownership in the province than has previously been acknowledged. Indeed, married women's ownership of property can be found in the naming of tracts. Oral tradition tells us that the secretary of the province, Henry Sewall, and his wife built their manor home as partners, and for generations after it was referred to as "My Lady Sewall's Manor-House." Women managed their property from as far away as England, for in 1713 Lord Baltimore gave his wife, Lady Margaret, ten thousand acres to control. He thoughtfully charged her only one barrel of corn as an annual quit-rent for the huge tract called "My Lady's Manor."[70] The frequent use of female names—both religious and secular—for cities, counties, plantations, rivers, and towns in Maryland substantiates the claim that women had a strong influence on their culture. For when we look at Calvinist New England we find a dearth of feminine names at the local levels.

Historians argue about the significance of men's naming places and possessions with female names. In fact, Anne Norton convincingly posits that territories with feminine names were an "empty sign for things political" because women held no political power themselves.[71] Yet Maryland's situation seems different. Parcels of land in Maryland were often named for their intended use, such as "Doe Park," "Mary's Dower," "Paying Debts," and "Pasture Point." Other times, titles described how the land came to the family, such as "Digges' Purchase," "Doctor's Gift," "Indian Field," "Mother's Gift," and "Proprietor's Gift." On occasion, colonists revealed their bitterness in place names such as "Would Have Had More," "Misfortune," "Worthless," "Mistake," "Cuckold's Mess," or the cautionary "Thief Keep Out." More often than not, however, property names in Maryland merely stated ownership: "Powell's Lot," "Robertson's Addition," "Stevens' Meadow," and "Thomas & Anthony's Chance." Therefore, when a tract possessed a female name it requires no stretch of the imagination to assume the name was an indication of possession or the anticipation of possession by women, as illustrated simply by George Ashman when he left his daughter, Charity, "Charity's Delight" in 1699.[72] Hundreds of tracts like "Ann's Choice," "Betty's Desire," "Betty's Enlargement," "Fanny's Inheritance," "Henrietta Maria's Purchase," "Judith's Garden," "Margaret's Hill," "Mary Pope's Land," "Mary's Portion," and "Sarah's Lot" suggest that women's position in this culture was better than is commonly assumed about colonial society. We know that these women often inherited the land named for them, and the land titles indicated possession and ownership by women. Names were not Norton's "empty sign"; naming patterns held much more significance in Maryland than they did in other places.

Last wills and testaments provide additional evidence of married women managing their own estates. Elizabeth Cannin, a well-educated woman of Talbot County, was one such woman, who left her husband "Daniel Canning my now dwelling House in Annapolis with the two Lotts belonging there to which I bought of Henry Mathews with all the rest of Goods and Chattles moveables and immovables not herby given and bequeathed."[73] Often a wife's property had been given to her by her father, as when Arthur Monday bequeathed his two daughters a tract of land "to be Divided between themselves and no other man to have any thing to do with it."[74] Catholic Vincent Lowe, whose wife Elizabeth had inherited the island of

Great Choptanke from her wealthy father Seth Foster, felt compelled to explain—at great length—that he had not misused his wife's property or prevented her from managing it. He wrote,

> And as for Grate Choptanke Island Seath ffoster my father in Law leved to his Eldest Daughter Ellizabeth Low with all the Apportenances there-unto belonging to her & her [heirs] For Ever I doe therefore Declare in the pr[e]sence of Allmighty God that I never did alter ye Property of the Same by Will & Deed Contract bargaine promis or other wise nor never did Impernine my wife to Doe any Such thing soe as itt Came by her father freely to her & her Eares for Ever Soe it must in Law Revers to her after my Discese & as for the Goods & Chattles that are there upon it as Negrowes Servants or Any other Chattle or Chattles . . . being about the Like number her said father Left her which Doe of right be-long to her but how Ever to Cleere all Doubts though I need not make any Disposistion of it, Doe give it all freely to her & her [heirs] for Ever As of Just right to her Death appertaine—But my Request to my wife is that If ple[a]se God, Shee Dy with out Issue of her Bodye that the said Island goe to ffoster Turbut his [heirs] for Ever & soe in the right Lyne but at her Discrestion.[75]

While the law may have allowed Vincent Lowe the use of "Great Choptanke" during his marriage to Elizabeth, Vincent himself wanted everyone to know that he did not "alter ye Property" and that Elizabeth owned it. Moreover, he wanted to clarify that he had not changed the condition or quantity of Elizabeth's chattels, either. Wealthy Catholic women's private ownership of real estate and personal property was not new. Vincent bequeathed land in England "Left me by my Mother Ann Lowe by her last will & Testament & the fifty pounds Sterling Alsoe left me by my said Mother."[76] Separate estates in Maryland must have been at least as common as they had been in England.[77]

In addition to women's active participation in the legal and business realms, there are numerous examples of early modern English women ex-tending their influence into the political arena as well. Elite women in particular—with their ability to publish their thoughts—expressed their po-litical views and attempted to influence male behavior in the political realm. Additionally, we find letters exchanged between husbands and wives that indicate the extent to which women entered the political debates of their times. The duchess of Marlborough ran the family's finances with the assis-tance of "L. Freasorer" while her husband was away from home in 1703 and it is clear from their letters that they discussed politics often.[78] Similarly, in a letter dated March 30, 1644, Queen Henrietta Maria gave King Charles detailed advice concerning peace negotiations with the Puritans.[79] The queen's letters to her husband indicate the influence she hoped to have on his political decisions, and the extent to which they faced a political crisis as partners.

Both stories and surviving letters attest to women's action in the political arena in Maryland. Mrs. Talbot's experience is a case in point; following the arrest of George Talbot by Virginia's governor, Lord Howard of Effingham, for the murder of Christopher Rousby, legend has it that Mrs. Talbot, who believed that her husband's imprisonment was politically motivated, risked her own life by orchestrating his escape.[80] Women acting in the political realm also took other actions as well. Lord Baltimore, for example, appears to have taken his sister's advice often, as well as advice offered by the countess of Tyrconnell, who recommended that he appoint Mr. Butler to the important position of Talbot County sheriff in 1687.[81] And when Lord Baltimore's governor was taken prisoner by the Puritan rebels in 1655, it was the governor's wife, Verlinda Stone, who played a key role in provincial politics. She served Lord Baltimore, the province, and her husband by obtaining critical information as she crossed enemy lines to nurse her imprisoned husband's wounded shoulder. Verlinda's ability to move freely between the Puritan and Roman Catholic territories provided Lord Baltimore with essential information that helped him regain the province. Her transmission of vital information perhaps would have been less likely if Verlinda and her husband had not discussed politics in their home.

Reminiscent of Verlinda Stone's letters to the proprietor during the first Calvinist rebellion, Barbara Smith's correspondence with the proprietor helped Lord Baltimore to argue his case before the Council and Board of Trade in England against the Calvinists who took over his province during the second Calvinist rebellion in 1689. Like Verlinda, Barbara acted on her husband's behalf to inform the proprietor of the insurgents' actions when her husband was taken captive. Barbara reported to Baltimore that "Upon the 25th of March last a rumour was spread" by the Calvinists "that Ten thousand Indians were come downe to the western branch of the said River, whereupon my husband went up to the said Western branch where he found noe Indians but there a strong report that nine thousand were at Matapany and at the Mouth of Puttexent and that they had cutt off Capt. Bownes family." Fearing for their lives, some colonists "therefore rose in Armes to secure the Magazine of Armes and Ammunition and the Protestants from being cut off by the said Indians and Papists." Barbara explained that these colonists were already "very apprehensive of the said Indians" and of the powerful positions that the Roman Catholics held and therefore it was easy for some of them to believe these false rumors. She reported that Baltimore's loyal supporters made a valiant effort to resist the armed men "at St. Maryes in the State House where the Records are kept," but they were soon overcome. The Calvinists, "having thus possessed themselves of the government," arrested her loyal husband out of "fear he should goe for England . . . to give an account of their proceedings." On August 21 Sheriff Michael Taney and Barbara's husband were brought to trial before the new Calvinist Assembly, "Capt. Code and his complices having pretended they had the Kings Proclamation for what they did."[82] Barbara Smith's detailed description of the political upheavals in the province helped Lord Baltimore gain some support in England for his position as the legal proprietor of Maryland. Verlinda Stone, Barbara Smith, and other Free Will Christian women acted in the provincial political realm when events warranted such behavior. In turn, men generally seemed to accept their contributions, and in some cases the lives of their imprisoned menfolk actually depended on their political participation.

While not every woman back in England had the liberties found at times in Maryland, women certainly worked for wages, educated children, took political stands, owned personal property, and appeared in court, as Elizabeth Brooke's eulogy attests. After eighty-two years of serving her family, her church, and her community, Elizabeth died "The Faithful and Diligent Christian." Her priest admired her for "seeing every remaining Branch of her Family largely provided for, and in very good Condition, before her Death . . . and giving both spiritual comfort to friends, family and servants." She was heralded as "a most affectionate, tender Wife, and watchful Mother, restraining her Children from Evil, according to her power, and bringing them up in the Nurture and Admonition of the Lord, most constantly endeavouring to instil into their Minds the Principles of Justice, Holiness, and Charity." On the political scene, Elizabeth had supported Charles I and did not hide her feelings of "disgust" with the Calvinists' "usurping Powers" before the Restoration. In court, Elizabeth endured many "unkind Law-suits" brought against her and yet she still found time to write much about "what a Christian must believe, and practice."[83] Historians have long recognized that women like Elizabeth Brooke moved in the public sphere with some ease because their wealth allowed them to enter it from a position of power. And yet after examining the phenomenon in Maryland, we must also acknowledge religion as a factor in determining women's place in society and their level of participation in the public realm.

To be sure, religion was a deciding factor in the level of women's participation in the economic, legal, and political arenas. Early modern English Free Will Christian and Predestinarian women did not make the same choices regarding female agency in the public sphere. While Predestinarian women regularly shunned opportunities to assume power and authority, Free Will Christian women's willingness to fight or pay for the exclusive right to administer their husbands' estates suggests that they embraced the new position with some zeal. It was a logical extension to their authoritative familial roles, and widows were fairly well prepared to handle it because they had been actively involved in the legal system and business world throughout their married lives. Given the extent to which early modern Free Will Christian women participated in the public realm—in the legal system, the economy, and the political arenas—it is clear that they were not overwhelmed by the new role executorship placed upon them. Indeed, the business acumen of these women went unchallenged by some of the wealthiest men in the province even when these gentlemen had been unpaid creditors for several years. Free Will Christian communities and families fully expected their womenfolk to be knowledgeable enough to deal with complicated business and legal affairs. We now see that the *de jure* authority and power Free Will Christian women wielded as administrators of male wills mirrored the *de facto* influence these women already exercised in early modern Maryland.

~

Conclusion

*T*ree Will Christians—Arminian Anglicans, Quakers, and Roman Catholics—shared a fundamental view of salvation that tended to unify them more often than their professed differences divided them. They believed that all sinners had an equal opportunity to work toward eternal salvation—if they chose to do "good works." Conversely, Maryland Particular Baptists, Presbyterians, Puritans, and other followers of John Calvin's predestinarian beliefs perceived their world as corrupt, flawed, and feigned; these "elect," with their passive souls, awaited certain salvation; they thus saw "good works" as a sign, not a cause, of their election.

This essential theological bifurcation had a decisive impact upon women's freedom in the early modern English world. In Maryland, Calvinists' belief in predestination contributed to their perception that Eve's daughters tended to be wanton, lustful creatures who by nature led their men astray. Thus, Calvinist Predestinarian males had a moral duty to protect society and their families from these "weaker vessels" by favoring hierarchical family structures headed by strong patriarchs; it was their duty to limit a female's freedom. In keeping with this moral imperative, patriarchs tended to treat their wives as dependents in their bequests—by bequeathing them merely personal goods or rigorously restricting their control of any land given to them. The beliefs held by Free Will Christians, on the other hand, encouraged them to construct a definition of womanhood that emphasized women's central role in their families as companions, confidantes, and loving partners. Thus, Free Will Christians supported more egalitarian familial structures that resulted in a more equitable social, political, and economic world for their women. These people fully expected female kin to control land and property, manage it effectively, execute wills, wield power and authority within their families, play pivotal roles in their churches, and have their day in court.[1]

At a time when seventeenth-century Maryland society was dominated by Free Will Christians, many women moved freely in the public sphere. Yet as the society grew and matured a noticeable shift in inheritance patterns occurred. By the middle of the eighteenth century male testators bequeathed significantly fewer female heirs real estate. Since Calvinist Predestinarians did not outnumber Free Will Christians in the society at any time during the colonial period, what could explain the widespread adoption of what I have dubbed a "Predestinarian" inheritance pattern by the mid–eighteenth century? Lois Carr and Lorena Walsh have suggested that a disparate sex ratio, in which men outnumbered women, in the seventeenth century provided an environment in which men tended to accord women an elevated role in society.[2] Under these circumstances, men who sought female companionship may have had to offer more goods, land, and perhaps power to potential marriage partners in order to attract a spouse. Thus, when the sex ratio equalized after 1704, the culture adopted the traditional English bequest pattern of allocating real estate to sons instead of wives and daughters. In sum, an increase in the number of females available for marriage meant that men could decrease the amount of land offered to their womenfolk.[3] Thus, as a community grew and its economy matured, men gave their women less land, particularly when land became less productive and scarcer as planters stripped the soil of nutrients with the overproduction of tobacco. Carr posits that over time families had less land to bequeath children and therefore fathers attempted to preserve as much of the family's land as possible by leaving their land to sons and bequeathing daughters and wives only movable goods.

Surely these demographic and economic interpretations have much to tell us about the behavior of early modern folk. But further investigation might uncover a more complex phenomenon similar to what Amy Louise Erickson found in early modern England, where land was also scarce. In England, while land generally went to sons, daughters did inherit goods of much the same value as their brothers' portions of the family wealth; moreover, many wives inherited more than their third of the estate. Perhaps Maryland females, like their English counterparts, also continued to preserve their own separate estates that were made up of silver, slaves, and livestock. Further research needs to be done to see just how closely Marylanders' eighteenth-century behavior followed Erickson's findings for early modern England. Yet it might be worthwhile to speculate about other factors, such as religion, that may have contributed to the change over time in inheritance patterns, particularly since we have examined religion's pivotal role in the lives of seventeenth-century Marylanders.

We might begin by examining Maryland's "newer" eighteenth-century immigrants as seen in the seminal works of historians Emmett Curran and Jay Dolan, who see a dramatic shift in religious piety as well as new manifestations of devotion directly related to immigration.[4] Perhaps increased immigration and the consequent acculturation that must have taken place when foreigners, such as German Protestants, poured into the province also ushered in significant changes in Maryland inheritance practices. Although French Huguenots had trickled into the province during the seventeenth century,[5] large numbers of French Acadians—evicted from Nova Scotia by the British and from central Pennsylvania by the Scots-Irish—moved to Baltimore Town, where they more than doubled the population "from over six thousand in 1776 to more than thirteen thousand by 1790."[6] Likewise, the first great influx of Scots-Irish Presbyterians and Catholic Irish peasants appears to have been in 1728. There can be no doubt that the number of aliens in the province—increasing exponentially in the eighteenth century—had an impact on the society.[7]

The huge influx of convicted English criminals also presented the province with potential acculturation problems. By 1755 one out of every ten white males in Baltimore, Anne Arundel, Charles, and Queen Anne Counties was an English convict who had opted to immigrate to Maryland rather than face execution in England.[8] Present-minded nineteenth-century historians recognized the similarity between this colonial phenomenon and their own experiences when they detailed the dangers of allowing too many foreigners into Maryland. Sydney Fisher, for instance, deplored the "enormous importation of a low class" primarily composed of "Spaniards, Italians, Dutch, Germans, and Bohemians" in addition to the "twenty thousand criminals" during colonial times. Their "enormous" presence, according to Fisher, had a deleterious effect on the society. The English convicts posed a particularly potent threat to the social fabric because of their total disregard for authority. But the most damaging groups, by far, were the "low class" foreigners and criminals who served as teachers for young, impressionable children and who sought to bring the entire society down to their own level. He explained the power these teachers had over the society: "it is easy to see the degenerating influence which pervaded the masses of the people, on whom, in the end, the character of a community always depends."[9] Obviously we ought to recognize Fisher's biases. Certainly we need to question (and investigate) just how many of these teachers had criminal pasts, and we should also examine the literacy levels of all later immigrants. More importantly, we ought to recognize that the arrival of both Irish and Italian Roman Catholic peasants most assuredly challenged the elite status of the old Catholic establishment. And we might safely assume that many of the newcomers had different ideas about women's roles in society, as well as a more male-centered ideal when it came to the inheritance of family property.

While these new immigrants would ultimately challenge and eventually change the Anglo-American culture of colonial Maryland, the "native" will-writing elite did not disappear. Free Will Christian women continued to inherit property and played influential roles in their families, their churches, and the larger society just as they had in the past. As an example, the provincial government printer, Anne Catherine Hoof Green, published *The Maryland Gazette* during the second half of the eighteenth century, expressing her political beliefs. And in order to prepare their daughters for a rapidly changing world, Maryland elites founded the Georgetown Visitation School in 1799. Still, not every woman in the eighteenth century exercised the liberties that her Free Will Christian predecessors had. The widespread shift to a Predestinarian inheritance pattern in the eighteenth century suggests that many women may have lived in patriarchal families. Economic pressures, including land scarcity, and the mutual adaptations of diverse peasants and the host society may have contributed to the subsequent adoption of a more patriarchal inheritance pattern by the landholding classes in the eighteenth century. Yet we must keep in mind that a majority can become a minority without necessarily losing its own values. Only additional research into Maryland's nineteenth-century evolution will allow us to say what happened when the colonials and the new immigrants created modern Maryland.

While much work needs to be done to explain fully the changes noted in the eighteenth century, the preceding chapters have described the lives of English settlers in seventeenth-century Maryland by searching out their views on property distribution, gender roles, religion, work, personal relationships, life in general, and death in particular. On the whole, this revisionist study seeks to correct the standard Protestantizing reading of early Maryland religious history, and aims to correct simplistic patriarchal suppositions regarding social practice in early Maryland. This study, with its focus on non-evangelical women in early America and its reliance on English social practices and mores as a control for understanding Maryland social practice, offers new views of Maryland society. It also focuses on the use of material culture—everything from the spatial allocations in church buildings, to their style and location, to ritual representations and grave-stones, to land naming practices—to uncover inherent cultural, religious, and theological meaning. Overall, this study addresses three principal questions: First, was religion a causal factor in history? Second, if so, how did people express their spirituality? Third, did the Arminian Anglicans, Quakers, and Roman Catholics share a similar worldview, permitting them to share a common marriage market?

In my mind, there can be no doubt that theological understandings had an effect on provincial mores. The Roman Catholics' adherence to rational systematic discourse manifested itself in their valuation of education, wealth accumulation, innovation, and the control of nature. The theological tenets of all the Free Will Christians placed assertive females at the side of males as partners, in both the mortal and immortal worlds. And as the Roman Catholics and their Free Will Christian in-laws exerted considerable influence upon society, we can assume that their values and behavior had an impact on other religious groups and classes as well. The presence of females in the church and in the work force, educating their children and sharing their opinions with male intimates, illustrates this impact. Most importantly, the Free Will Christians reified their doctrine in their bequests to males and females. Their propensity to rely on females as trusted, intelligent relations contrasted sharply with the Calvinists' view of women as subordinate dependents needing the supervision of a strong patriarch. In sum, religion molded both personal and public identities and goals; it transmitted values and behavior patterns to co-believers and others alike. And in addition to uncovering religious values and social arrangements shaping the lives of English women and determining their place in early modern society, this study also fielded a third question of religious affinity. Theologians and religious historians tend to concentrate upon the distinctions amongst various religious groups. I have argued here for a radical rethinking of the similarities between groups based upon their stated dogmas, para-liturgical behavior, religious architecture, burial practices, and most importantly their marriage customs. Indeed, the evidence demonstrates that the Arminian Anglicans and Quaker Protestants had more in common with their Roman Catholic brethren than they did with other Protestants; and intermarriage took place primarily between these groups.

These early modern people consciously developed notions about earthly concerns, such as property distribution, gender roles, work, and personal relationships, on the basis of a complex web of previous experiences, present environmental, economic, and political conditions, and, most assuredly, religious beliefs. The dying wishes of testators have proved to be a rich source in the quest for new historical actors as well as providing a window into the intents and aspirations of these folk, who can now speak to us from the grave. Most importantly, the evidence collected adds to a sound body of information about English customs, rituals, and beliefs brought to the New World while positing new questions to ask of other English colonies and the mother country. Ultimately, this study suggests that multicultural Maryland—and by inference the mid-Atlantic region—created significant cultural, intellectual, and social norms that in the long run have had more effect than those of colonial New England in shaping the diverse world of the American people.

Notes

ᘐ

Introduction

1. John Leeds Bozman, *History of Maryland: From its First Settlement in 1633, to the Restoration, in 1660* (Baltimore: James Lucas and E. K. Deaver, 1837), 194.

2. Patricia Crawford, *Women and Religion in England, 1500–1720* (London: Routledge, 1993); David Cressy, *Birth, Marriage, and Death: Ritual, Religion, and the Life-Cycle in Tudor and Stuart England* (New York: Oxford University Press, 1997); and Ralph Houlbrooke, *Death, Religion, and the Family in England, 1480–1750* (Oxford: Clarendon, 1998).

3. Marilyn Westerkamp, *Women and Religion in Early America, 1600–1850: The Puritan and Evangelical Traditions* (New York: Routledge, 1999).

4. For this study, Anglican spirituality will be divided into its Arminian— referring to Free Will Christians with Roman Catholic leanings—and Calvinist components. While many historians, such as Peter Lake, have pointed out the problems with using the term "Puritans," Calvinist Anglicans will often be referred to as Puritans in this study strictly for simplicity's sake. Pragmatic Anglicans (for lack of a better term) who attended church functions in England for economic, political, and social advantages had a negligible impact on the society and culture of early modern Maryland.

5. Historians have debated whether Maryland instituted religious tolerance because of pragmatic considerations or because it adhered to a modern philosophy. See Carl Everstine, "Maryland's Toleration Act: An Appraisal," *Maryland Historical Magazine* 79 (1984): 99–115; Thomas O'Brien Hanley, *Their Rights and Liberties: The Beginnings of Religious and Political Freedom in Maryland* (Chicago: Loyola University Press, 1984); John Krugler, "'With promise of Liberty in Religion': The Catholic Lords Baltimore and Toleration in Seventeenth-Century Maryland, 1634–1692," *Maryland Historical Magazine* 79 (1984): 21–43; R. J. Lahey, "The Role of Religion in Lord Baltimore's Colonial Enterprise," *Maryland Historical Magazine* 72 (1977): 492–511; and Maxine Lurie, "Theory and Practice of Religious Toleration in the Seventeenth Century: The Proprietary Colonies as a Case Study," *Maryland Historical Magazine* 79 (1984): 117–125. This debate is not new, for in 1855 George Davis argued against a colleague he called "the Protestant historian of America" and the interpretation of the Roman Catholic colonists' pragmatism, stating that "freedom of con-

science existed, not only in the legislation, but also in the very heart of the colony. It prevailed for a period of nearly sixty years; a real active principle; and the life-guidance of many thousands" (Davis, *The Day-Star of American Freedom; or, The Birth and Early Growth of Toleration, in the Province of Maryland* [New York: Scribner, 1855], 258).

6. Of course, not everything went perfectly well for the early settlers: there were high mortality rates; the number of females in the province remained low throughout the seventeenth century; and, most importantly, labor supplies never met the insatiable demands of the profit-seeking planters. Russell Menard estimates that "seasoning" in Maryland may have resulted in death rates as high as 35 to 40 percent among new arrivals. These figures are for servants who arrived both before 1643 and in 1648–52 (Menard, "Economy and Society in Early Colonial Maryland" [Ph.D. diss., University of Iowa, 1975], chapter 5).

7. Somerset County is referred to as the cradle of the Presbyterian church in America, having first been served by Rev. Francis Mackemie of the Old Rehoboth church. The Labadists followed Jean de Labadie, who held that God can and does deceive men, and that the observance of the Sabbath is a matter of indifference. The Labadists believed that people should pray when "they felt some inward motive for the purpose," and they lived communally. William Penn visited this group and found that women held a position similar to that of Quaker women. Even though at least one of the Labadist women was highly educated, the Labadists were poor record keepers, making any definitive statements difficult. The Labadists seemed to have isolated themselves, and eventually their group died out in Maryland. For a letter describing some of the Labadist practices in 1702 as observed by a Quaker, see Edward D. Neill, *The Founders of Maryland as Portrayed in Manuscripts, Provincial Records, and Early Documents* (Albany: Joel Munsell, 1876), 158–159.

8. See Russell R. Menard, "British Migration to the Chesapeake Colonies in the Seventeenth Century," in *Colonial Chesapeake Society*, ed. Lois Green Carr, Philip D. Morgan, and Jean B. Russo (Chapel Hill: Published for the Institute of Early American History and Culture, Williamsburg, Virginia, by the University of North Carolina Press, 1988); Lois Carr and Lorena Walsh, "The Standard of Living in the Colonial Chesapeake," *William and Mary Quarterly*, 3d ser., 45 (1988): 135–159; Lorena Walsh and Russell R. Menard, "Death in the Chesapeake: Two Life Tables for Men in Early Colonial Maryland," *Maryland Historical Magazine* 69 (1974): 211–227; Russell Menard, "From Servants to Slaves: The Transformation of the Chesapeake Labor System," *Southern Studies* 16 (1977): 355–390; Russell Menard, "The Maryland Slave Population, 1658–1730: A Demographic Profile of Blacks in Four Counties," *William and Mary Quarterly*, 3d ser., 32 (1975): 29–54; and Gloria Main, *Tobacco Colony: Life in Early Maryland, 1650–1720* (Princeton, N.J.: Princeton University Press, 1982). Michael Graham is the exception in assuming that the Quakers and Catholics shared a strong sense of community that provided the foundation for Maryland's success, while granting that Arminian Anglicans, Catholics, and Quakers often found themselves in conflict (Graham, "Meetinghouse and Chapel: Religion and

Community in Seventeenth-Century Maryland," in *Colonial Chesapeake Society*, ed. Carr, Morgan, and Russo, and "The Collapse of Equality: Catholic and Quaker Dissenters in Maryland, 1692–1720," *Maryland Historical Magazine* 88 [1993]: 5–25).

9. Sir Josiah Child, *A New Discourse on Trade* (1665), quoted in Anthony Pagden, *Lords of All the World: Ideologies of Empire in Spain, Britain, and France, c. 1500–c. 1800* (New Haven, Conn.: Yale University Press, 1995), 36.

10. Historians' resistance to the influences of religion runs deep. J. A. Doyle summed it up best in 1882 when he discussed the problems with using Father Andrew White's account of the first trip to Maryland. He wrote, "It gives a vivid and somewhat garrulous account of the voyage, the early life of the settlement, and where religion does not come into play, it is a valuable authority" (Doyle, *English Colonies in America: Virginia, Maryland, and the Carolinas* [New York: Henry Holt, 1882], 275; I would like to extend a special thanks to Stanley Engerman for presenting me with a copy of this book).

11. C. John Sommerville, "Anglican, Puritan, and Sectarian in Empirical Perspective," *Social Science History* 13 (1989): 120. Furthermore, the professed differences among the Arminian Anglicans, Catholics, and Quakers seem inconsequential when the frequency of conversions and intermarriage between them is examined.

12. John Bossy argues that the Elizabethan era marked a decidedly matriarchal period in English Catholicism (Bossy, *The English Catholic Community, 1570–1850* [New York: Oxford University Press, 1976]), and Jo Ann McNamara suggests early Christianity had a positive effect on women's status and life choices (McNamara, "Wives and Widows in Early Christian Thought," *International Journal of Women's Studies* 2 [1979]: 575–592). However, other historians have posited that the practice of Catholicism helped to construct negative female gender roles: Ramon A. Gutiérrez, *When Jesus Came the Corn Mothers Went Away: Marriage, Sexuality, and Power in New Mexico, 1500–1846* (Stanford, Calif.: Stanford University Press, 1991); and Margaret Miles, *Desire and Delight: A New Reading of Augustine's Confessions* (New York: Crossroad, 1992).

13. Anna Sioussat, "Colonial Women of Maryland," *Maryland Historical Magazine* 2 (1907): 222.

14. Sioussat, "Colonial Women," 225. Signatures of some prominent Maryland women can be found in Hester Dorsey Richardson's *Side-lights on Maryland History: With Sketches of Early Maryland Families* (Baltimore: Williams and Wilkins, 1913; reprint, Cambridge, Md.: Tidewater, 1967), 524.

15. The Digges family supplied the first verifiable Maryland nun, Mary Digges (c. 1696–?). In 1721, the Holy Sepulchre in Liege described Mary as a "canoness regular." Her father, William Digges (whose father was Governor Edward Digges of Virginia), married Elizabeth Sewall Wharton, who was related to Lord Baltimore, some time before 1679. In that year he emigrated from Virginia to Maryland, where he held several important political offices.

16. The Brooke family provided the first verifiable Maryland-born priest, Robert Brooke, trained at St. Omer in Flanders and ordained in 1681. When he

died in 1689, he bequeathed his estate to the Jesuits after his mother's death. In the early nineteenth century, the prestigious Catholic Carroll family intermarried with Anglicans who, not coincidentally, were English noblemen. The Carroll family includes some of the most distinguished Catholics in America, including a descendant, Charles Carroll, who, along with a Quaker and an Arminian Anglican (William Fitzhugh and Nathaniel Rochester), established the first city of the new Republic—Rochester, New York—and another Charles Carroll who was the only Catholic to sign the Declaration of Independence. The Carroll family also provided the first Catholic American bishop in 1784, John Carroll.

17. My genealogical study emphasized both individuals' connections to English court circles and the number of interfaith marriages in families. For more Catholic-Anglican intermarriages, see Gerald Fogarty, "The Origins of the Mission, 1634–1773," in *The Maryland Jesuits, 1634–1833*, ed. R. E. Curran, J. T. Durkin, and G. P. Fogarty (Baltimore: Corporation of the Roman Catholic Clergymen, 1976).

18. Some scholars have argued that Calvinist families were not quite as patriarchal as was once thought. See for instance Robert Evans, "Deference and Defiance: The 'Memorandum' of Martha Moulsworth," in *Representing Women in Renaissance England*, ed. Claude Summers and Ted-Larry Pebworth (Columbia: University of Missouri Press, 1997), 175–186; and Margaret Ezell, *The Patriarch's Wife: Literary Evidence and the History of the Family* (Chapel Hill: University of North Carolina Press, 1987), 163.

1. *Maryland's* Raison d'être

1. Relevant secondary sources include John L. Bozman, *The History of Maryland* (Baltimore: Lucas and Deaver, 1837); William Hand Browne, *Maryland: The History of a Palatinate* (Boston: Houghton Mifflin, 1899) and also *George Calvert and Cecilius Calvert, Barons Baltimore of Baltimore* (New York: Dodd and Mead, 1890); James Foster, *George Calvert: The Early Years* (Baltimore: Maryland Historical Society, 1983); William Kilty, ed., *A Report of All Such English Statutes As Existed at the Time of the First Emigration of the People of Maryland* (Annapolis: Jehu Chandler, 1811); James McSherry, *History of Maryland: From Its First Settlement in 1634, to the Year 1848* (Baltimore: John Murphy, 1849); Newton Mereness, *Maryland as a Proprietary Province* (New York: Macmillan, 1901); Hester Dorsey Richardson, *Side-lights on Maryland History: With Sketches of Early Maryland Families* (Baltimore: Williams and Wilkins, 1913; reprint, Cambridge, Md.: Tidewater, 1967); William Russell, *Maryland: The Land of Sanctuary—A History of Religious Toleration from the First Settlement until the American Revolution* (Baltimore: J. H. Furst, 1907); John T. Scharf, *History of Maryland: From the Earliest Period to the Present Day* (Baltimore: John B. Piet, 1879); C. Ernest Smith, *Religion under the Barons of Baltimore* (Baltimore: E. Allen Lycett, 1899); Bernard Steiner, *Maryland during the English Civil Wars*, 2 vols. (Baltimore: Johns Hopkins University Press, 1906–07); and James Walter Thomas, *Chronicles of Colonial Maryland* (1900; reprint, Baltimore: Clearfield, 1999).

2. John Krugler, "'With the Promise of Liberty in Religion': The Catholic

Lords Baltimore and Toleration in Seventeenth-Century Maryland, 1634–1692," *Maryland Historical Magazine* 79 (1984): 25.

3. Edward Shorter uses this dichotomy between "traditional" and "modern" in his work *The Making of the Modern Family* (New York: Basic, 1975).

4. Tobie Matthew, *A true historicall relation of the Conversion of Sir Tobie Matthew to the holie Catholic fayth*, c. 1640, Folger Shakespeare Library, call number V.a.269, pages 7–9 in the postscript. Sir George Calvert's assistance is mentioned on page 196. In a letter to Matthew from Captain Thomas Yong in 1634, we can see that Matthew took an active interest in the establishment of Maryland as a Catholic haven (Clayton Hall, ed., *Narratives of Early Maryland, 1633–1684* [New York: Charles Scribner's Sons, 1910], 58).

5. William Hand Browne, ed., *Archives of Maryland*, 72 vols. (Baltimore: Maryland Historical Society, 1883–1972), 41:146.

6. These plots were blamed on the English Roman Catholics, but the English government may have concocted them to influence public sentiment.

7. Reprinted in Scharf, *History of Maryland*, 35. This clause refers to a county palatine at Durham (and also in Chester and Lancaster) giving the border lord independent authority to secure the frontiers as a defense against outside invasions.

8. Scharf, *History of Maryland*, 49.

9. Quoted in Henry Chandlee Forman, *Jamestown and St. Mary's: Buried Cities of Romance* (Baltimore: Johns Hopkins University Press, 1938), 185.

10. Thomas Vane, *A Lost Sheep Returned Home; or, The Motives of the Conversion to the Catholike Faith, of Thomas Vane, Doctor of Divinity, and lately Chaplaine to His Majesty the King of England, &c* (Paris, 1648), preface.

11. *A Moderate and Safe Expedient To remove Jealousies and Feares, as any danger, or prejudice to this State, by the Roman Catholicks of this Kingdome, And to mitigate the censure of too much severity towards them. With a great advantage of Honour and Profit to this State and Nation* (London, 1646), 3–8, 15 and 16. (A copy is housed at the John Carter Brown Library at Brown University.)

12. Hall, *Narratives of Early Maryland*, 102. James II, in reference to New York's Roman Catholic governor (Thomas Dongan), noted that "once liberty of conscience be well fixed, many conversions [to Catholicism] will ensue" (quoted in J. R. Western, *Monarchy and Revolution: The English State in the 1680s* [London: Blandford, 1972], 191).

13. The Maryland Jesuits devoted themselves "zealously" to the conversion of the English Anglicans and they acknowledged that "God has blessed our labors," suggesting many successes (Hall, *Narratives of Early Maryland*, 119–120).

14. Hall, *Narratives of Early Maryland*, 70, 71, 84.

15. Hall, *Narratives of Early Maryland*, 16, 17, 20.

16. The Jesuits were so successful in Maryland that they began a mission in New York in 1683, headed by Thomas Harvey (alias Barton) as superior, and with Henry Harrison (alias John Smith) as assistant missionary (William P. Treacy, *Old Catholic Maryland and Its Early Jesuit Missionaries* [Baltimore, 1889], 170).

17. Cornwaleys to Cecil Calvert, April 16, 1638, in *The Calvert Papers,* 3 vols., Maryland Historical Society Fund Publications 28, 34–35 (Baltimore: J. Murphy, 1889–99), 1:172.

18. George Alsop, *A Character of the Province of Maryland* (1666; reprint, Freeport, N.Y.: Books for Libraries, 1972), 43–44.

19. The governor of Virginia was anxious to help the colonists, against the wishes of the council, because he needed Lord Baltimore's assistance in recovering a large sum of money from the exchequer in England (Hall, *Narratives of Early Maryland,* 39).

20. Hall, *Narratives of Early Maryland,* 42–43.

21. The headright system was ended in 1683. Many references to feudal patterns appear in the government records. See, for instance, Browne, *Archives of Maryland,* 53:637 and 57:437–439. Robert Brugger points out that Lord Baltimore gave Daniel Dulany subfeudal authority over Frederick County in western Maryland in 1745, and quit-rents continued to be imposed well into the eighteenth century (Robert J. Brugger, *Maryland, A Middle Temperament, 1634–1980* [Baltimore: Johns Hopkins University Press in association with the Maryland Historical Society, 1988], 69).

22. The estates and goods of the rebels Claiborne, Fendall, Godfrey, and Talbot were all declared forfeited to the proprietor, but the judgments were never actually executed.

23. Browne, *Archives of Maryland,* 17:181–184.

24. Browne, *Archives of Maryland,* 2:55–57.

25. Browne, *Archives of Maryland,* 41:94.

26. The oath of fidelity to Lord Baltimore is quoted in Scharf, *History of Maryland,* 201.

27. Quoted in Forman, *Jamestown and St. Mary's,* 267.

28. Browne, *Archives of Maryland,* 41:87.

29. This right was restricted in 1681 when the proprietary narrowed the franchise to freemen with property.

30. James Thomas (citing Chancellor William Kilty's 1811 report to the Maryland legislature on the English statutes in effect during the colonial period) suggests that "nothing of English law was ever in force unless adopted by legislative acts, judicial decisions, or constant usage" (Thomas, *Chronicles of Colonial Maryland,* 175). And in practice, the laws of Maryland always superseded English common law (Steiner, *Maryland during the English Civil Wars,* 2:36). In 1706, while Maryland was under royal control, Governor Seymour bemoaned this fact in a letter to the secretary of state. Seymour wrote that "the severall Statutes of England, unless they expressly mention the Plantations, are not in force here." He went on to say that Marylanders insisted that Lord Baltimore's charter guaranteed them the right to accept or reject all of the English laws (Public Record Office: Secretaries of State: State Papers Domestic, Anne [SP 34/9/5]).

31. Browne, *Archives of Maryland,* 10:213–215.

32. Andrew White translated the Our Father, the Hail Mary, and the Apostles' Creed from English to Piscataway as early as 1640 ("Early Maryland Jesuits' Papers Collection," Special Collections, Georgetown University Library).

33. Early Jesuit missionaries were from noble English families (with some having direct ties to the Calverts themselves) and often followed their names with Esq. Others in the province often referred to them as "Gentlemen." William Treacy suggested that "the Protestant party, helped by the English Protestant or Puritan government, was, from time to time, in power, and finally in the Revolution of 1689, gained complete ascendancy; still the mass of the people always were Catholic" (Treacy, *Old Catholic Maryland*, xi and 17). Edward Neill, who argued against the idea that Maryland was established primarily as a Roman Catholic haven, stated that one of the early Jesuit priests, Father Philip Fisher (alias Thomas Copley), was a member of the Assembly until he refused to take the oath supporting the Act of Toleration (1649) (Edward Neill, *Maryland in the Beginning: A Brief Submitted to the Historical & Political Science Association of Johns Hopkins University* [Baltimore: Cushings and Bailey, 1884], 46).

34. A significant difference did exist, however. These Indians believed that "the issue of the daughters hath more [noble Indian] blood in them than the issue of the sonnes" (Hall, *Narratives of Early Maryland*, 84).

35. Hall, *Narratives of Early Maryland*, 90, 74.

36. The Susquehannock population in 1647 (after a smallpox epidemic) has been estimated at six thousand. "By contrast, Maryland's numbers were little more than 400 by 1642 and were still fewer than 1500 by 1650" (Francis Jennings, "Indians and Frontiers in Seventeenth-Century Maryland," in *Early Maryland in a Wider World*, ed. David B. Quinn [Detroit: Wayne State University Press, 1982], 219).

37. Alsop, *A Character of the Province of Maryland*, 76–77.

38. Browne, *Archives of Maryland*, 1:238–239.

39. Browne, *Archives of Maryland*, 1:246.

40. Scharf, *History of Maryland*, 171.

41. Scharf, *History of Maryland*, 169.

42. Browne, *Archives of Maryland*, 4:441.

43. The Jesuits referred to Puritanism as "the very dregs of all Calvinist heresy" (Hall, *Narratives of Early Maryland*, 135).

44. Scharf, *History of Maryland*, 220.

45. David Ridgely, *Annals of Annapolis* (Baltimore: Cushing, 1841), 47.

46. William George Read, *Oration, Delivered at the First Commemoration of the Landing of the Pilgrims of Maryland* (Baltimore: John Murphy, 1842), 47.

47. Ridgely, *Annals of Annapolis*, 52.

48. The Jesuits wrote annually to Rome; this ordeal is preserved in the 1656 letter, translated in Treacy, *Old Catholic Maryland*, 25–26.

49. Until 1751 the year was considered to begin on March 25 (Lady Day, or the Feast of the Annunciation); what we now think of as January of 1655, therefore, con-

temporaries called January of 1654. I have followed the conventional practice of giving both the contemporary and the modern number of the year for dates between
January 1 and March 25.

50. Browne, *George Calvert and Cecilius Calvert*, 148–149.

51. Scharf, *History of Maryland*, 272–273.

52. In contrast to the controversy surrounding colonial New England's precapi-
talist mindset, no debate over Maryland's commercial origins has taken place. Cur-
rently some social scientists suggest, as did Adam Smith two centuries ago, that the
proclivity of all humans to engage in trade for profit is biologically based (Joshua M.
Epstein and Robert Axtell, *Growing Artificial Societies: Social Science from the Bottom
Up* [Washington, D.C.: Brookings Institution, 1996]).

53. Bernard Steiner, ed., *Rev. Thomas Bray: His Life and Selected Works Relating
to Maryland*, Maryland Historical Society Fund Publication 37 (Baltimore: J. Murphy, 1901), 167–168.

54. Though he neglects to tell us specifically what colonial period he is referring to, Sydney Fisher describes Maryland men and women as conspicuous consumers: "The men and women . . . ordered champagne from Europe by the cask and
Madeira by the pipe, also dressed expensively in the latest English fashions, and
French travellers said that they had seldom seen such clothes outside of Paris"
(Sydney Fisher, *Men, Women, and Manners in Colonial Times* [1897; reprint, Philadelphia: J. B. Lippincott, 1902], 212). The Puritan community of Providence appears
to have been occupied by conspicuous consumers of international goods, with a
particularly strong preference for Dutch goods. They used imported Dutch building
materials, including yellow brick for their chimneys, yellow and green floor tiles, and
delftware decorative tiles. Like the Dutch settlers in Albany, they lined their cellars
with wood. Moreover, several decorative Dutch buttons have been recovered (Al
Luckenbach, *Studies in Local History: Providence 1649—The History and Archaeology
of Anne Arundel County, Maryland's First European Settlement* [Annapolis: Maryland State Archives, 1995]).

55. Regular fare included apples, beef, chicken, corn, crab, duck, eggs, fish,
goose, hominy, oysters, peaches, pork, raccoon, turkey, turtle, and venison. They
used cinnamon and cloves, but preferred the flavors of nutmeg and pepper for seasoning food. For a detailed description of the changes in meat consumption over
time see Henry Miller, "An Archaeological Perspective on the Evolution of Diet in
the Colonial Chesapeake, 1620–1745," in *Colonial Chesapeake Society*, ed. Lois Green
Carr, Philip D. Morgan, and Jean B. Russo (Chapel Hill: Published for the Institute
of Early American History and Culture, Williamsburg, Virginia, by the University
of North Carolina Press, 1988), 176–199. And for information on spice imports see
Margaret Shove Morriss, "Colonial Trade of Maryland, 1689–1715" (Ph.D. diss., Bryn
Mawr College, 1914), appendix.

56. Alsop, *A Character of the Province of Maryland*, 100.

57. Betty Ring, *Girlhood Embroidery: American Samplers and Pictorial Needlework, 1650–1850*, vol. 2 (New York: A. A. Knopf, 1993), 499–522.

58. Maryland Hall of Records (hereafter MHR), Prerogative Court Wills (hereafter cited as Wills), book 1, page 479 (1670).

59. Wills, 5:1 (1676).

60. Wills, 7:100 (1694).

61. Wills, 1:511 (1671).

62. Wills, 4:17 (1683).

63. Wills, 4:55 (1684).

64. Browne, *Archives of Maryland*, 1:171. My thoughts on the differences between traditional Old World and modern worldviews were influenced in part by Mechal Sobel, *The World They Made Together: Black and White Values in Eighteenth-Century Virginia* (Princeton, N.J.: Princeton University Press, 1987). Paul Shackel, in his analysis of timepieces found in Annapolis probate records beginning in 1700, argues that the ownership of these scientific instruments may indicate the society's wish to have "control over nature, legitimizing the elite's control over society" (Shackel, *Personal Discipline and Material Culture: An Archaeology of Annapolis, Maryland, 1695–1870* [Knoxville: University of Tennessee Press, 1993], 96–100). See also Mark Smith, *Mastered by the Clock: Time, Slavery, and Freedom in the American South* (Chapel Hill: University of North Carolina Press, 1997).

65. "Clocks and Watches," permanent exhibit at the British Museum, London.

66. Wills, 10:10 (1679).

67. Wills, 12.2:148–149 (c. 1709). Time is also mentioned frequently in the Provincial Court records. (See Browne, *Archives of Maryland*, 4:182, and Joseph H. Smith and Philip Crowl, eds., *Court Records of Prince George's County, Maryland, 1697–1699* [Washington, D.C.: American Historical Association, 1964], 164 and 318.) The court records are incomplete for the period studied here. Records from the Provincial Court cover 1637–83, and only the proceedings of four of eleven county courts have survived.

68. Forty-five homicide cases came before the Provincial Court between 1635 and 1683; twenty involved masters accused of killing their white servants. In these cases, the court asked medical experts to determine if the servant died from physical punishment or a previous illness. Helen Brock and Catherine Crawford suggest Marylanders' reliance on medical testimony and postmortems "seem[s] to cast doubt upon the assertions usually made about the relative infrequency of medical evidence in inquests and criminal investigations within the jurisdiction of English common law before the eighteenth century" (Brock and Crawford, "Forensic Medicine in Early Colonial Maryland, 1633–1683," in *Legal Medicine in History*, ed. Michael Clark and Catherine Crawford [Cambridge: Cambridge University Press, 1994], 41).

69. Browne, *Archives of Maryland*, 49:308.

70. These men and women—without the knowledge of bacteria—used deadly medicines such as arsenic. The evidence for this particular medicine comes from Historic St. Mary's City in Maryland, where scholars have analyzed hair samples from a seventeenth-century corpse found on the site. The archaeological evidence also suggests colonists—including women and children—smoked too much and had

the unsanitary habit of dumping refuse into pits located under the floorboards of the living quarters in addition to outside back doors and windows. Elite colonists also experienced pronounced dental disease from the sugar they consumed. See Henry Miller, "Mystery of the Lead Coffins," *American History* 20, no. 4 (September/October 1995): 46–48, 62–65; Douglas Ubelaker, Erica Bubniak Jones, and Abigail Turowski, "Skeletal Biology of the Patuxent Point Human Remains," in *Living and Dying on the Seventeenth-Century Patuxent Frontier,* ed. Julia King and Douglas Ubelaker (Crownsville: Maryland Historical Trust Press, 1996), 47–104); and Dennis Pogue, *King's Reach and 17th-Century Plantation Life* (Annapolis: Jefferson Patterson Park and Museum Studies in Archaeology, 1990).

71. *Calvert Papers,* 1:202. Marylanders died frequently from dysentery and malaria (Darrett Rutman and Anita Rutman, "Of Agues and Fevers: Malaria in the Early Chesapeake," *William and Mary Quarterly,* 3d ser., 33 (1976): 31–60). Recent archaeological digs at Historic St. Mary's City have also uncovered evidence suggesting that children died of smallpox, rickets, and infections.

72. Anne Yentsch, "An Interpretive Study of the Use of Land and Space on Lot 83, Annapolis, Md.," *New Perspectives on Maryland Historical Archaeology* 26 (1990): 36–37.

73. If one's thirst could not wait several months for a "Shrub" to blossom, one might prepare the following punch: "The peel of 8 Oranges and 8 Lemons in 1 quart of rum. 3 Gallons of Water boild with 3 lb. of loaf Sugar and the Whites of 8 Eggs. 2 and 3/4 pints of orange juice and 1 and 3/4 Pints of Lemon juice. strain the quart of rum from the Peel and add one Gallon more of rum to rest of the ingredients" (Richard Hooker, ed., *A Colonial Plantation Cookbook: The Receipt Book of Harriott Pinckney Horry, 1770* [Columbia: University of South Carolina Press, 1990], 98 and 139). Colonists of the middling sort drank cider and sack. The 1666 Assembly records indicate that while it was in session, members consumed "Liminade made with Wine" along with brandy, beer, rum, punch, and other drinks made with sugar and "Lyme water."

74. Browne, *Archives of Maryland,* 49:318–319.

75. Browne, *Archives of Maryland,* 10:401–402.

76. Helen West Ridgely, *The Old Brick Churches of Maryland* (New York: Anson D. F. Randolph, 1894), 60.

77. Browne, *Archives of Maryland,* 10:522, 534–545; 41:385, 504. See also Brock and Crawford, "Forensic Medicine in Early Colonial Maryland," 25–44. For further information on English cruentation, see Robert Brittain, "Cruentation in Legal Medicine and in Literature," *Medical History* 9 (1965): 82–88.

78. Browne, *Archives of Maryland,* 49:476, 486, 508 (Bennett) and 2:425–426 (Cowman); Francis Parke, "Witchcraft in Maryland," *Maryland Historical Magazine* 31 (1936): 282–289, 295–296 (Fowler, Edwards, Violl, Prout).

79. Quoted in Raphael Semmes, *Crime and Punishment in Early Maryland* (Baltimore: Johns Hopkins University Press, 1938), 168.

80. Browne, *Archives of Maryland,* 65:39.

81. Treacy, *Old Catholic Maryland*, 26.

82. For a different interpretation of the Associators Revolution, see Lois Carr and David Jordan, *Maryland's Revolution of Government, 1689–1692* (Ithaca, N.Y.: Cornell University Press, 1974).

83. Scharf, *History of Maryland*, 326.

84. Scharf, *History of Maryland*, 313.

85. Browne, *Archives of Maryland*, 22:334–335.

86. Jennifer Thomas Dade, "British TV Crew Turns Up Some Clues to St. Mary's City," *Lexington Park (Maryland) Enterprise*, May 22, 1996. Philip Calvert, Cecil's youngest brother, built St. Peter's.

87. One of the most popular novels was John Pendleton Kennedy's *Rob of the Bowl: A Legend of St. Inigoe's* (Philadelphia: Lea and Blanchard, 1838). Rev. Ethan Allen spoke out during the second half of the nineteenth century on behalf of a Protestant *raison d'être* (Allen, *Who Were the Early Settlers of Maryland: A Paper Read before the Maryland Historical Society at Its Meeting Held Thursday Evening, October 5, 1865,* Maryland Historical Society Pre-fund Publications 2, no. 24 [Baltimore: Printed at the Office of the Am. Quar. Church Review, New Haven, Conn., 1866]).

2. Private Lives

1. William Hand Browne, ed., *Archives of Maryland*, 72 vols. (Baltimore: Maryland Historical Society, 1883–1972), 53:628.

2. Browne, *Archives of Maryland*, 10:464.

3. Browne, *Archives of Maryland*, 10:503.

4. Browne, *Archives of Maryland*, 10:501–504, 555; 41:20, 50–51, 85; 53:4, 33–34.

5. In England and, I would argue, in Maryland as well, estranged wives were legally entitled to one-third of the estate (Colin Chapman, *Marriage Laws, Rites, Records, and Customs* [Dursley, England: Lochin, 1996], 89).

6. Robert Robins appeared in court with Elizabeth Weekes for producing an illegitimate child after the Robinses' separation (Browne, *Archives of Maryland*, 53: 250–251). In England, cases concerning marriage were heard in ecclesiastical courts while Maryland dealt with these in the regular court system.

7. Browne, *Archives of Maryland*, 10:280–282.

8. John Taylor's legal formulary is housed at the Folger Shakespeare Library in Washington, D.C. (Taylor, "Presidents of Assignment, Bonds, Covenants, Letters of Attorney, Releases, Affidavits, Charterpartys, Indentures of Apprenticeship," MSS [c. 1730]).

9. Wills, 6:201 (1699).

10. Mary Keysor Meyer suggests early Marylanders recognized English law in regard to divorce. Thus, men and women could obtain a "divorce from bed and board" (*a mensa et thoro*)—in other words, a legal separation. She cites as evidence Rev. William Wilkinson's 1658 marriage of Robert Holt to Christian Bonnefield while Holt's first wife, Dorothy, was still living. Although Holt was later charged

with bigamy, Meyer insists that a document signed by Dorothy confessing her adulterous activities amounted to a legal divorce from Robert (Mary Keysor Meyer, *Divorces and Names Changed in Maryland by Act of the Legislature, 1634–1854* [privately printed, 1970], iii–iv). In Calvinist New England a deserted wife could file for divorce because an unsupervised woman posed a threat to the social order. Divorce in Maryland, on the other hand, did not occur until the 1790s.

    11. Mary Beth Norton, *Founding Mothers and Fathers: Gendered Power and the Forming of American Society* (New York: Alfred A. Knopf, 1996), 90.

    12. Wills, 4:152 (1684).

    13. I suspect that these types of living arrangements were fairly rare. Mary Beth Norton found a clear case of a woman living with her husband and her lover in the same house (Norton, "Gender, Crime, and Community in Seventeenth-Century Maryland," in *The Transformation of Early American History: Society, Authority, and Ideology*, ed. James A. Henretta, Michael Kammen, and Stanley N. Katz [New York: A. A. Knopf, 1991], 130–131).

    14. Wills, 4:159 (1685).

    15. Wills, 1:101 (1658).

    16. Wills, 2:372 (1675).

    17. Rose Pinner's husband, William, died between November 10, 1684, when he wrote his will, and June 17, 1685, when the will was proved in court (Wills, 4:146 [1684]). Traditionally in England, men were required to wait a month after a wife's death to remarry and women were supposed to wait one year. The longer waiting period for a widow was intended to ensure that she was not carrying her deceased husband's child. Generally speaking, however, women were not encouraged to remarry at all. In Maryland both these prohibitions were largely ignored.

    18. Wills, 4:153 (1684).

    19. Browne, *Archives of Maryland*, 54:127, 186, 205, 206, 211, 212.

    20. Chapman, *Marriage Laws, Rites, Records, and Customs,* 79; and David Cressy, *Birth, Marriage, and Death: Ritual, Religion, and the Life-Cycle in Tudor and Stuart England* (New York: Oxford University Press, 1997), 241.

    21. In another example, maidservant Bridgett Nelson claimed that she was married to her master Quintin Counyer (Browne, *Archives of Maryland*, 41:456–457).

    22. Browne, *Archives of Maryland*, 10:549–551.

    23. Quoted in James Walter Thomas, *Chronicles of Colonial Maryland* (1900; reprint, Baltimore: Clearfield, 1999), 169.

    24. *The Calvert Papers,* 3 vols., Maryland Historical Society Fund Publications 28, 34–35 (Baltimore: J. Murphy, 1889–99), 1:263.

    25. In early modern England, approximately half of all young men and women had lost their fathers by the time they contemplated marriage (James Smith and Jim Oippen, "Estimating Numbers of Kin in Historical England Using Microsimulation," in *Old and New Methods in Historical Demography,* ed. David Rehere and Roger Scholfield [Oxford: Oxford University Press, 1993], 306–308).

    26. Wills, 7:141 (1696, Jane Long), 12.1:212 (1707/8, John Phillips).

27. Wills, 2:332 (1693).

28. Wills, 4:103 (1684). Occasionally, a grandparent entered into the decision-making process, as did Widow Johanna Spry, who bequeathed "milch-Cattell" and featherbeds to her three granddaughters, stipulating that "if either of them prove disobedient and Marry contrary unto their Mothers consent then my will is that She so offending shall have no share nor parts of any Legacy given her in this my will" (Wills, 2:349 [1674]).

29. Joan Scott and Louise Tilly, *Women, Work, and the Family* (New York: Methuen, 1978), 41; and Patricia Seed, *To Love, Honor, and Obey in Colonial Mexico: Conflicts over Marriage Choice, 1574–1821* (Stanford, Calif.: Stanford University Press, 1988), 34–35.

30. George Alsop, *A Character of the Province of Maryland* (1666; reprint, Freeport, N.Y.: Books for Libraries, 1972), 50–51.

31. Patricia Crawford and Laura Gowing, eds., *Women's Worlds in Seventeenth-Century England: A Sourcebook* (London: Routledge, 2000), 139.

32. Browne, *Archives of Maryland*, 10:499, 500, 531–533.

33. Wills, 7:132 (c. 1691).

34. Edward D. Neill, *The Founders of Maryland as Portrayed in Manuscripts, Provincial Records, and Early Documents* (Albany: Joel Munsell, 1876), 152–153.

35. Wills, 4:272 (1686/7).

36. Luis de Granada, *A Memorial of a Christian Life: Compendiously containing all, that a Soul, Newly Converted to GOD, Ought to do, That it may Attain to the Perfection, After which it ought to aspire*, translated from Spanish (London, 1688), 213–214. Father de Granada was a Provincial in the Dominican order.

37. Katherine Digby's manuscript "Spiritual Exercises" (c. 1650) is housed at the Folger Shakespeare Library, call number V.a.473.

38. "American Catholic Sermons Collection," Special Collections, Georgetown University Library.

39. Chapman, *Marriage Laws, Rites, Records, and Customs*, 43, quoting the Beverley, Yorkshire, parish register of November 1641.

40. Catholics did not hold weddings on December 28, Childermas or Holy Innocents Day, since the day commemorated Herod's massacre of children.

41. Wills, 13:224 (1711).

42. Chapman, *Marriage Laws, Rites, Records, and Customs*, 53, 84.

43. Wills, 2:163 (1681). Lorena Walsh has argued that "Before justices of the peace were authorized to perform marriages, many couples simply married themselves, signifying their union by some customary ceremony such as breaking a piece of silver between them" (Walsh, "'Till Death Us Do Part': Marriage and Family in Seventeenth-Century Maryland," in *The Chesapeake in the Seventeenth Century: Essays on Anglo-American Society*, ed. Thad W. Tate and David L. Ammerman [New York: W. W. Norton, 1979], 130). I would argue that Arminian Anglicans, Quakers, and Roman Catholics devised religious ceremonies based on devotional literature.

44. Chapman, *Marriage Laws, Rites, Records, and Customs*, 83.

45. Quoted from the county court records in Harry Wright Newman, *The Maryland Dents: A Genealogical History of the Descendants of Judge Thomas Dent and Captain John Dent, Who Settled Early in the Province of Maryland* (Richmond, Va.: Dietz, 1963), 17.

46. Browne, *Archives of Maryland*, 1:97.

47. "Puretanes" in England expressed their hatred of the "fylthe Canon lawe" as early as 1568 (Richard Fytz, *The Trewe Marks of Christes Churche* [London, 1568]. See also SP 15/20 no. 107, ff. 254 Av-257r in the Public Record Office).

48. See Henry Scobell, *An Act Touching Marriages and the Registring thereof; And also touching Births and Burials* (London, 1653).

49. Since marriage was not a sacrament for Calvinists, New Englanders accepted petitions for divorce when a spouse was abandoned.

50. Browne, *Archives of Maryland*, 2:523.

51. William Smith, *Joyfull tidings to the begotten of God . . . with a few words of counsel unto Friends concerning marriage* (London, 1664), 6.

52. Oswald Tilghman, *History of Talbot County, Maryland, 1661–1861*, vol. 2 (1915; reprint, Baltimore: Regional Publishing, 1967), 527. George Fox ordered in 1662 that "not less than a dozen Friends and Relations be present" when two Friends united in marriage. And later, "At a Quarterly Meeting in Hadenham in the Isle of Ely, 1st of the 10th. Month 1675. viz. It is ordered and agreed upon at this Quarterly Meeting, that no Friends for time to come, may permit or suffer marriages without the consent of Friends at two Mens and Womens Meetings, and the Man and Woman to come both to the said Meetings to receive the answer of Friends" (Gerard Croese, *A Brief History of the Rise, Growth, and Progress of Quakerism; Setting Forth, That the Principles and Practices of the Quakers are Antichristian, Antiscriptural, Antimagistratical, Blasphemous, and Idolatrous from plain matter of Fact, out of their most approved Authors, &c. Containing Also, A modest Correction of the General History of the Quakers* [London: Francis Bugg, Senior, 1697], 154–155).

53. Smith, *Joyfull tidings to the begotten of God*, 5–6.

54. Kenneth Carroll, *Quakerism on the Eastern Shore* (Baltimore: Maryland Historical Society, 1970), 145.

55. Carroll, *Quakerism on the Eastern Shore*, 145.

56. Smith, *Joyfull tidings to the begotten of God*, 6.

57. Francis Shannon, *Several Discourses & Characters address'd to the Ladies of the Age. Wherein the Vanities of the Modish Women are Discovered* (London: Robert Midgley, 1689), 93–94.

58. William Whateley, *A Bride Bush: or, A Direction for Married Persons* (London, 1623), 83–84, 86.

59. Shannon, *Several Discourses & Characters address'd to the Ladies of the Age*, 73–75.

60. E. A. Wrigley et al., *English Population History from Family Reconstitution, 1580–1837* (Cambridge: Cambridge University Press, 1997), 438–439.

61. Peter Coldham, "Index of Tracts," in *Settlers of Maryland, 1679–1700* (Baltimore: Genealogical Publishing, 1995), 203.

62. Wills, 7:94 (1695).

63. Wills, 2:362 (1675).

64. Wills, 11:210 (1702).

65. Clearly, not all marriages fit into this pattern. William Welch, for instance, left his wife Charity "one shill[ing] Sterll[ing]"—an amount typically used to exclude disobedient children from sharing in the family wealth—presumably for her infidelity (Wills 4:197 [1685]). In seventeenth-century Virginia, Edmund Morgan suggests, "the fortunes gathered by those early immigrants during the deadly first half century were not necessarily lost or dispersed. Capital still accumulated in the hands of widows and joined in profitable wedlock the sums that well-heeled immigrants brought with them" (Morgan, *American Slavery, American Freedom: The Ordeal of Colonial Virginia* [New York: W. W. Norton, 1975], 304).

66. Wills, 5:180 (1677).

67. Bodleian Library, Oxford, MS Top Oxon c. 124, ff. 14–15.

68. The conscious desire to build or continue a family line is clearly illustrated by the fine example of Isreal Skelton. His will specified that after his wife died, his daughter (if his son died first) was to inherit his wife's share of his estate and pass it on to her heirs, "whether they be Lineally or Colatterally Desended from her," not just the heirs of her body (Wills, 12.1:37 [1706]).

69. Not every woman wanted a child, as evidenced by several cases of infanticide and abortion in Maryland. Women used opium, savin (from *Juniper sabina*), and other "purges" to rid themselves of both worms and unwanted pregnancies. (See, for instance, Browne, *Archives of Maryland*, 53:387–391 and 41:20.)

70. Robert Schnucher, "Elizabethan Birth Control," in *Marriage and Fertility: Studies in Interdisciplinary History*, ed. Robert Rotberg and Theodore Rabb (Princeton, N.J.: Princeton University Press, 1980), 76.

71. For instance, "with child" appears in Matthew 1:18 and "the child in my womb" in Luke 1:44.

72. Wills, 7:168 (1696).

73. Amy Louise Erickson, *Women and Property in Early Modern England* (London: Routledge, 1997), 49.

74. Less than 16 percent of the colonists who referred to pregnancy used terms like "babe" or "infant." In legal usage, the word "infant" referred to males or females under the age of seventeen (Browne, *Archives of Maryland*, 7:198).

75. Wills, 13:567 (1710).

76. Wills, 12.2:49–51 (page 50 is mislabeled 51) (1709).

77. In the seventeenth century, a quarter of the children born in England died before they reached their tenth birthday. English women could expect to give birth to approximately seven children, of whom only about three would reach adulthood (E. A. Wrigley and Roger Schofield, *The Population History of England, 1541–1871*

(Cambridge: Cambridge University Press, 1989), 249; and Wrigley et al., *English Population History from Family Reconstitution*, 438–439. Traditionally in England, women were "churched" after childbirth. This rite, outlined in the Book of Common Prayer, provided women an opportunity to publicly express thanks to God for delivering them safely through childbirth. It also served to symbolically cleanse a woman and signal her reentry into the community after her lying-in period. Puritans shunned this practice as "popish."

78. Crawford and Gowing, *Women's Worlds in Seventeenth-Century England*, 231.

79. Wills, 12.2:207 (1709).

80. Wills, 12.2:97 (1709).

81. Wills, 4:280 (1687).

82. Sir William Blackstone argued in 1770 that "the duties of parents to legitimate children" included "their maintenance, their protection, and their education . . . suitable to their station in life." He stressed the fact that "No person is bound to provide a maintenance for his issue, unless where the children are impotent and unable to work, either through infancy, disease, or accident, and then is only obliged to find them with necessaries" (Blackstone, *Commentaries on the Laws of England*, book 1 [1770; reprint, Philadelphia: G. W. Childs, 1862], 446, 450, 449).

83. Wills, 6:79 (1698).

84. Wills, 13:235 (1705).

85. Wills, 12.2:37 (1708).

86. Wills, 13:75–76 (1710).

87. In 1770 Blackstone claimed that a father "may indeed have the benefit of his children's labour while they live with him, and are maintained by him; but this is no more than he is entitled to from his apprentices or servants. The legal power of a father . . . over the persons of his children ceases at the age of twenty-one: for they are then enfranchised by arriving at years of discretion." In this commentary Blackstone also suggested a wife held no such power in England, "for a mother, as such, is entitled to no power, but only to reverence and respect" (Blackstone, *Commentaries on the Laws of England*, book 1, 452).

88. Wills, 4:269 (1687).

89. Wills, 12.2:174 (1701).

90. Wills, 4:318 (1688).

91. Wills, 7:304 (1696). Some grandparents who needed additional labor on their own plantations offered legacies to grandchildren in exchange for labor (Wills, 13:9 [1709]).

92. Mary Swain, a widow from Somerset County, asked her son "to bury me according as a son should his mother" (Wills, 13:258 [1710]).

93. Alsop, *A Character of the Province of Maryland*, 93.

94. *Calvert Papers*, 1:277–278 and 283.

95. Wills, 11:130 (1699).

96. Wills, 11:131 (1699).

97. Wills, 11:223 (1701).

98. Wills, 12.1:221 (1707). Sir William Blackstone wrote, "The *duties* of children to their parents arise from a principle of natural justice and retribution. For to those who gave us existence we naturally owe subjection and obedience during our minority, and honour and reverence ever after: they who protected the weakness of our infancy are entitled to our protection in the infirmity of their age; they who by sustenance and education have enabled their offspring to prosper, ought in return to be supported by that offspring, in case they stand in need of assistance" (Blackstone, *Commentaries on the Laws of England,* book 1, 453).

99. In the early years of the province, when mortality rates were particularly high, colonists would often name several sons after their father, in an effort to ensure the continuation of not just the family name but also the essence of that individual. Seventeenth-century governor Francis Howard of Virginia and his wife, Philadelphia, named all three of their children after Francis—the first was a daughter. (See Debra Meyers, "Frances Howard," in *American National Biography* [New York: Oxford University Press, 1997], 301–302.) For a compelling essay on the significance of naming patterns see John J. Waters, "Naming and Kinship in New England: Guilford Patterns and Usage, 1693-1759," *The New England Historical and Genealogical Register* 138 (July 1984): 161–181. See also Jacques Dupaquier, "Naming Practices, Godparenthood, and Kinship in the Vexin, 1540-1900," *Journal of Family History* 6 (1981): 135–155; Gloria Main, "Naming Children in Early New England," *Journal of Interdisciplinary History* 27 (summer 1996): 1–27; Daniel S. Smith, "Child-Naming Practices, Kinship Ties, and Change in Family Attitudes in Hingham, Massachusetts, 1641 to 1800," *Journal of Social History* 18 (1985): 541–566; and Edward Tebbenhoff, "Tacit Rules and Hidden Structures: Naming Practices and Godparentage in Schenectady, New York, 1680-1800," *Journal of Social History* 18 (1985): 567–585.

100. Wills, 13:534 (1713).

101. Wills, 2:343 (1704).

102. Wills, 12.1:142 (1706).

103. Wills, 12.1:240 (1708).

104. Wills, 12.2:90 (1709).

105. Wills, 11:225 (1702).

106. Wills, 13:617 (1713).

107. Erickson, *Women and Property,* 48.

108. Wills, 1:364 (1669).

109. Wills, 6:170–171 (1698).

110. Wills, 6:225 (1698).

111. Wills, 6:272 (1698).

112. Wills, 2:402 (1675/6).

113. Wills, 4:287 (1687/8).

114. Wills, 12.1:276 (1708).

115. *Calvert Papers,* 1:269.

204   NOTES TO PAGES 66–70

116. Cecilia Haywood, *Records of the Abbey of our Lady of Consolation at Cambrai, 1620–1793*, ed. Joseph Gillow, Publications of the Catholic Record Society 13 (London: Ballantyne, Hanson, 1913), 10–12.

117. Ortner and Whitehead also suggest that "Catholic cultures . . . emphasize mother's nurturance and merciful protection, whereas Protestant-dominated American culture tends to emphasize mother's controlling and manipulative nature" (Sherry B. Ortner and Harriet Whitehead, "Introduction: Accounting for Sexual Meanings," in *Sexual Meanings: The Cultural Construction of Gender and Sexuality* [Cambridge: Cambridge University Press, 1981], 23).

118. Wills, 7:89 (1694).

119. Wills, 4:133 (1685).

120. Wills, 5:185 (1676, Barrot), 5:181 (1676, Cary), 5:184 (1676, Dunn).

121. Jer[emy] Taylor, *A Discourse of the Nature, Offices and Measures of Friendship. With Rules of conducting it* (London, 1671), 5, 62–63, and 69.

122. Neill, *The Founders of Maryland*, 139.

123. Wills, 2:71 (1674).

124. Wills, 1:488 (1672).

125. Wills, 11:219 (1701).

126. Wills, 1:82 (1659).

127. Wills, 1:46 (1653). Edward Cotton was bound to Walter Beane, though he himself owned a servant named David Thomas.

128. Wills, 12.1:350–352 (1708). In a letter to her brother, Constance Fowler described her feelings for her sister-in-law: "there was never any more passionate affectionate lovers than she and I, and that you never knew two creatures more truly and deadly in love with one another than we are." For a few examples of intense love and friendship between two sisters in England, see Crawford and Gowing, *Women's Worlds in Seventeenth-Century England*, 229–232, 237.

129. Wills, 13:315 (1711).

130. For a thorough study of this phenomenon, see Lorena S. Walsh and Russell R. Menard, "Death in the Chesapeake: Two Life Tables for Men in Early Colonial Maryland," *Maryland Historical Magazine* 69 (1974): 211–227. For English patterns see Miranda Chaytor, "Household and Kinship: Ryton in the Late 16th and Early 17th centuries," *History Workshop Journal* 10 (1980): 25–60.

131. By 1700 nearly half of the landowners on the Eastern Shore were related to one another (Robert J. Brugger, *Maryland, A Middle Temperament, 1634–1980* [Baltimore: Johns Hopkins University Press in association with the Maryland Historical Society, 1988], 60).

132. Wills, 6:399 (1693). Edmond Gibbon owned land in Carolina, Barbados, Kent County in Maryland, New Jersey on the Rariton River, Smith Valley in New York, Pennsylvania, and other areas as well (Wills, 4:214 [1685]).

133. Never having met his cousin, Richard had inquired about Abraham's family. Abraham's mention of war referred to France's attempt to restore James II to his throne in England (Harrison Tilghman, ed., "Letters between the English and Ameri-

can Branches of the Tilghman Family, 1697–1764," *Maryland Historical Magazine* 33 [1938]: 152).

3. Religion in the New World

1. Mike Salter, *The Old Parish Churches of Staffordshire* (England: Folly, 1996), 10.

2. Eamon Duffy, *The Stripping of the Altars: Traditional Religion in England, c. 1400–c. 1580* (New Haven, Conn.: Yale University Press, 1992).

3. For additional information see Peter Benes and Philip D. Zimmerman, *New England Meeting House and Church, 1630–1850: A Loan Exhibition at the Currier Gallery of Art, Manchester, New Hampshire* (Boston: Boston University for the Dublin Seminar for New England Folklife, 1979); Marian Donnelly, *The New England Meeting Houses of the Seventeenth Century* (Middletown, Conn.: Wesleyan University Press, 1968); Peter T. Mallary, with photographs by Tim Imrie, *New England Churches and Meetinghouses, 1680–1830* (Secaucus, N.J.: Chartwell, 1985); Edmund Sinnott, *Meetinghouse and Church in Early New England* (New York: McGraw-Hill, 1963); Peter Williams, *Houses of God: Region, Religion, and Architecture in the United States* (Urbana: University of Illinois Press, 1997); and Ola Winslow, *Meetinghouse Hill, 1630–1783* (New York: Macmillan, 1952).

4. John L. Brooke, "'For Honour and Civil Worship to Any Worthy Person': Burial, Baptism, and Community on the Massachusetts Near Frontier, 1730–1790," in *Material Life in America, 1600–1860*, ed. Robert Blair St. George (Boston: Northeastern University Press, 1988), 463–486.

5. Stephen Foster, "Not What But How: Thomas Minor and the Ligatures of Puritanism," in *Puritanism: Transatlantic Perspectives on a Seventeenth-Century Anglo-American Faith*, ed. Francis J. Bremer (Boston: Massachusetts Historical Society, distributed by Northeastern University Press, 1993), 40–43 and 48.

6. Helen West Ridgely, *The Old Brick Churches of Maryland* (New York: Anson D. F. Randolph, 1894), 68.

7. Brooke, "For Honour and Civil Worship to Any Worthy Person," 467.

8. Brooke, "For Honour and Civil Worship to Any Worthy Person," 463.

9. Henry Chandlee Forman, *Jamestown and St. Mary's: Buried Cities of Romance* (Baltimore: Johns Hopkins University Press, 1938), 204, 252. For an account of the brick chapel relics see James Walter Thomas, *Chronicles of Colonial Maryland* (1900; reprint, Baltimore: Clearfield, 1999), 38.

10. Philip Baxter, *Sarum Use: The Development of a Medieval Code of Liturgy and Customs* (Oxford: Oxford University Press, 1994), 14.

11. A rood screen was a metal or wooden screen with a crucifix mounted on it that separated the nave (the part of the church used by the congregation) and the chancel (the part used by the clergy).

12. Catholic fasting required parishioners to skip some meals and observe dietary restrictions when they were allowed to eat or drink. They were also required to abstain from sexual intercourse during Lent. Since Catholics traditionally avoided

taking communion, the Council of Trent mandated that they take the sacrament once a year (John Randall, *Three and Twentie Sermons: or, Catechisticall Lectures upon the Sacrament of the Lords Supper* [London, 1630; STC 20682]; Jeremiah Dyke, *A Worthy Communicant: or, A Treatise, Shewing the Due Order of Receiving the Lords Supper* [London, 1636; STC 7429]; and Richard Leake, *Foure Sermons* [London, 1599; STC 15342]).

13. William P. Treacy, *Old Catholic Maryland and Its Early Jesuit Missionaries* (Baltimore, 1889), 20.

14. Salter, *The Old Parish Churches of Staffordshire*, 11.

15. Treacy, *Old Catholic Maryland*, 21.

16. Thomas, *Chronicles of Colonial Maryland*, appendix.

17. Henry Miller, "Mystery of the Lead Coffins," *American History* 20, no. 4 (September/October 1995): 46–48, 62–65.

18. Typically, colonists bequeathed priests between twenty shillings and three pounds sterling—sometimes left in tobacco rather than hard money—for prayers to be said for their souls. See, for instance, Wills, 6:82, 138, 208 (1697/8), 12:252 (1702), 3.2:470 (1703).

19. Baxter, *Sarum Use*, 51.

20. Oswald Tilghman, *History of Talbot County, Maryland, 1661–1861*, vol. 2 (1915; reprint, Baltimore: Regional Publishing, 1967), 313.

21. An Arminian Anglican church was established on this site, just six miles south of St. Mary's Chapel, as early as 1642 (Ethan Allen, *Who Were the Early Settlers of Maryland: A Paper Read before the Maryland Historical Society at Its Meeting Held Thursday Evening, October 5, 1865*, Maryland Historical Society Pre-fund Publications 2, no. 24 [Baltimore: Printed at the Office of the Am. Quar. Church Review, New Haven, Conn., 1866], 6).

22. In England, additions to the chancel—meant to draw attention to the sacred altar space—tended to be polygonal configurations at the east end of a church, like the sixteenth-century apse at Barton-Under-Needwood St. James church in Staffordshire. The semi-circular apse, like the one at St. John the Baptist church at Burslem, became more common in England in the eighteenth century (Salter, *The Old Parish Churches of Staffordshire*, 20, 29).

23. Ridgely, *The Old Brick Churches of Maryland*, 6. The Arminian Anglican churches in Maryland were sometimes made of imported English stone or brick—as was White Marsh Church (c. 1658)—indicating the importance of using "holy" or "sacred" materials from older churches as the Catholics did (J. H. K. Shannahan, Jr., *Tales of Old Maryland: History and Romance on the Eastern Shore of Maryland* [Baltimore: Meyer and Thalheimer, 1907], 32).

24. Randall, *Three and Twentie Sermons*. See also Dyke, *A Worthy Communicant*, and Leake, *Foure Sermons*.

25. Quoted in Thomas, *Chronicles of Colonial Maryland*, 194. Helen Ridgely, however, insisted that this gravestone was found at St. George's Anglican Church (Ridgely, *The Old Brick Churches of Maryland*, 52).

26. Wills, 1:322 (1668).

27. P. H. R. Mackay, "The Reception of the Five Articles of Perth," *Scottish Church History Society Records* 19 (1975–77): 185.

28. G. W. O. Addleshaw and F. Etchells, *The Architectural Setting of Anglican Worship* (London: Faber and Faber, 1956), 15–22; and George Yule, "James VI and I: Furnishing the Churches in His Two Kingdoms," in *Religion, Culture, and Society in Early Modern Britain: Essays in Honour of Patrick Collinson,* ed. Anthony Fletcher and Peter Roberts (Cambridge: Cambridge University Press, 1994), 182–209.

29. Charles I, *His Majesties Declaration in Defence of the true Protestant Religion: It was maintained by his Royall Father King James [I] of blessed memorie* (London, 1643), n.p.

30. John Nickalls, ed., *The Journal of George Fox* (Cambridge: Cambridge University Press, 1952), 655.

31. Lord and Lady Baltimore (both Roman Catholics) are said to have listened to William Penn speak here in 1700 (Tilghman, *History of Talbot County,* 2:529).

32. Around 1711, the Merion Society of Friends (just outside of Philadelphia) added onto their meetinghouse so that the structure took on a Roman Catholic cruciform shape (Williams, *Houses of God,* 50).

33. J. Reaney Kelly, *Quakers in the Founding of Anne Arundel County, Maryland* (Baltimore: Maryland Historical Society, 1963), 44.

34. Wills, 4:18 (1683).

35. Wills, 4:114 (1684), 7:151 (1695), and 7:271 (1696).

36. Duffy, *The Stripping of the Altars,* chapter 15; and "Thomas Barbur's Last Will and Testament," August 3, 1529, Folger Shakespeare Library, call number X.d. 428 (item # 202), in the Cavendish-Talbot manuscripts.

37. Wills, 1:430 (1670).

38. I used Frederick Warren's 1911 English translation of the 1526 Latin Sarum Missal (*The Sarum Missal in English,* 2 vols. [London: De La More, 1911]). The Roman Catholics may have used the Sarum rite or the newer Trent Missal at this time. Both the Roman Catholic 1572 rite and the 1549 Anglican Mass removed late-medieval accretions from their services; both texts are clearly indebted to their Gregorian and Sarum ancestors; and their Maryland adherents used a mixed selection of available texts. For the purposes of this chapter I used the easily available reprint of the 1675 Book of Common Prayer (London: Ebury, 1992).

39. Patrick Malloy suggests that English Roman Catholic recusant devotional books referred to their Anglican brethren as "fallen" Catholics (Malloy, "A Manual of Prayers, 1583–1850: A Study of Recusant Devotions" [Ph.D. diss., University of Notre Dame, 1991]). Other Roman Catholic texts refer to Anglicans as fallen Catholics while ostracizing Predestinarians. See, for instance, "A disputation with a precise Puritaine" and "The discriptione of a Puritaine" in a Catholic manuscript housed at the Folger Shakespeare Library ("Collection of Poems," call number V.a.137, Catholic Liturgy/Mass, c. 1630).

40. Wills, 7:103 (1694).

41. Wills, 1:310 (c. 1668).

42. Wills, 4:59 (1679), 4:1–2 (1682), and 12:159 (1707). Maryland clergy frequently sent to England for Bibles as well. For example, Jesuit Peter Attwood asked James Carroll to buy a Rheims Bible and "The Catholick Scriptures" for the Widow Jones in 1716 ("Maryland Province Archives," box 1, Special Collections, Georgetown University Library). And the colonial library of the Roman Catholic Neale family contained a copy of the Rheims Bible. Because the 1582 Rheims translation of the New Testament into English influenced King James's 1611 version, we find common Arminian Anglican and Catholic usages—and these may be contrasted with the 1560 English text of the Geneva Bible.

43. Wills, 11:231 (1702).

44. Wills, 12.2:151 (1709). The Book of Common Prayer contains similar expressions of humility and uncertainty. For instance, compare Lyne's sentiments with the language used in "The order for morning Praier," in which Arminian Anglicans confessed their sins "with an humble, lowly, penitent, and obedient heart, to the end that we may obtain forgiveness of the same by his infinite goodness, and mercy."

45. Edward D. Neill, *The Founders of Maryland as Portrayed in Manuscripts, Provincial Records, and Early Documents* (Albany: Joel Munsell, 1876), 148–149.

46. After the Act of Establishment was passed in 1692—mandating state support of Anglican churches—Herring Creeke Parish became St. James' Parish. Fortunately, the earliest church records have been published in Edith Stansbury Dallam's *St. James' Parish: Old Herring Creeke Parish, A History, 1663–1799, Including Copies of the Original Records of the Parish Vestry Minutes and Register of Births, Baptisms, Marriages, and Burials* (Maryland: Port City Press for the Vestry and Library Committee, 1976).

47. Wills, 11:212 (1702).

48. Kenneth Carroll, *Quakerism on the Eastern Shore* (Baltimore: Maryland Historical Society, 1970), 9. For a reprint of Robert Clarkson's letter to Elizabeth Harris thanking her for "the inward truth" she brought to Maryland, see Neill, *The Founders of Maryland*, 141–143.

49. For example, Matthew 3:11 and 16, 4:1, 10:20, 12:31–32, Mark 1:8 and 10, John 14:26, and 1 Corinthians 6:19 contain references to the Holy Spirit or Holy Ghost.

50. Wills, 4:92 (1684/5).

51. Wills, 4:100 (1685). The testator paraphrased Mark 8 and Matthew 10–11.

52. Matthew 10:32–33.

53. Wills, 7:187 (1695).

54. Carroll, *Quakerism on the Eastern Shore*, 3–4.

55. Carroll, *Quakerism on the Eastern Shore*, 3–4, 5, 60–61, 71, and 145. Friends also asked that everyone in the community "Buy convenient Burying Places."

56. Douglas Gwyn, *Apocalypse of the Word: The Life and Message of George Fox* (Richmond, Ind.: Friends United, 1986), 30.

57. Gwyn, *Apocalypse of the Word: The Life and Message of George Fox*, 59–60.

58. Gwyn tells us that Fox found the Puritan ministers to be " 'miserable com-

forters' precisely because they sought to comfort him in and help him adjust to a sinful condition he could not accept" (Gwyn, *Apocalypse of the Word: The Life and Message of George Fox,* 63). Once "convinced," Quakers considered an individual a minister of the faith.

59. The most important work for the Quakers seems to have been charity to the poor (Gwyn, *Apocalypse of the Word: The Life and Message of George Fox,* 139).

60. "Thomas Barbur's Last Will and Testament." For additional examples of pre-Reformation wills see R. N. Swanson, *Catholic England: Faith, Religion, and Observance before the Reformation* (Manchester: Manchester University Press, 1993), chapter 10.

61. Wills, 4:58 (1684).

62. "The order for morning Praier," Book of Common Prayer.

63. Repentance is emphasized in Matthew 4:17 and 9:13. See Wills, 6.2:1 (1692).

64. Wills, 4:163 (1685). The Sarum Missal (1:35) contains repeated references to these intermediaries. These additional intercessors and a desire "to be remembered at the holy altar" helped identify 205 Roman Catholics.

65. "Maryland Province Archives," Special Collections, Georgetown University Library.

66. Elise Greenup Jourdan, *Early Families of Southern Maryland* (Westminster, Md.: Family Line Publications, 1992), 1:315–326 and 2:128–162.

67. Wills, 4:190 (1685).

68. Wills, 11:344 (1703).

69. "American Catholic Sermons Collection," Special Collections, Georgetown University Library.

70. English Catholics had difficulty with some of the ideas espoused by the Jesuits. See E. Duffy, " 'A Rubb-up for Old Soares': Jesuits, Jansenists, and the English Secular Clergy, 1705–1715," *Journal of Ecclesiastical History* 28 (1977): 291–317.

71. Jesuits, members of the Counter-Reformation order of the Society of Jesus, were ranked like military officers and armed themselves with encyclopedic knowledge of church doctrine in order to attack the Protestants.

72. George Gage, archdeacon of London and Middlesex, wrote a letter to Fr. Richard Smith, bishop of Chalcedon and the Superior of the Catholic clergy in England, July 21, 1642. Gage pleaded on behalf of Lord Baltimore, asking for secular priests to be sent to Maryland. A copy of this letter can be found in *Maryland Historical Magazine* 4 (1909): 262–265.

73. Father Pulton dedicated himself to converting the local Native Americans. See Robert Emmett Curran, *American Jesuit Spirituality: The Maryland Tradition, 1634–1900* (New York: Paulist Press, 1988), 66.

74. Luis de Granada, *A Memorial of a Christian Life: Compendiously containing all, that a Soul, Newly Converted to GOD, Ought to do, That it may Attain to the Perfection, After which it ought to aspire,* translated from Spanish (London, 1688), preface.

75. *Journal of Meditations for everyday of the year* (London, 1687). This book, a

third edition, was a new translation from the original Latin version of 1657. (Also available on microfilm: MHR, Carmelite Monastery Records, microfilm M9547, box 58, folder 1.)

76. *Journal of Meditations,* 460. About half of the religious medals found at Historic St. Mary's City depict the Virgin Mary, St. Teresa, or Jesus.

77. A letter written by Charles Calvert (Lord Baltimore) reminds us how important the medieval calendar—with many female saints included—was to Catholics. He wrote, in reference to dates in the calendar, "the feast of the Annunciation of the Blessed Virgin Mary and at the feast of St. Michael the Arch Angel" (Letter to William Osborn, November 15, 1678, Michael Papers, MS 1368, box 1, Manuscripts Division, Maryland Historical Society Library [hereafter MHS]).

78. A. F. the least of Friar Minours, ed., *Liturgical Discourse of the Holy Sacrifice of the Masse By way of Dialogue* (1669).

79. Marc Egnal points out the work of several historians who have examined the gender equality of the Catholic gentry of "New France" (Egnal, "Forum," *William and Mary Quarterly,* 3d ser., 51 [1994]: 725).

80. Marvin O'Connell, *Thomas Stapleton and the Counter Reformation* (New Haven, Conn.: Yale University Press, 1964), 27.

81. Stapleton found refuge in the Low Countries. In 1569 he began studying at the College in Douai for English Catholic resistors to the Elizabethan Settlement, and went on to teach there.

82. O'Connell, *Thomas Stapleton,* 72.

83. O'Connell, *Thomas Stapleton,* 87 and 54.

84. In 1897, Sydney Fisher described Maryland's seventeenth-century society using a similar distinction (Fisher, *Men, Women, and Manners in Colonial Times* [1897; reprint, Philadelphia: J. B. Lippincott, 1902], volume 2, chapter 9: "Puritan and Catholic on the Chesapeake").

85. Malloy, "A Manual of Prayers."

86. John Bossy, "English Catholics after 1688," in *From Persecution to Toleration: The Glorious Revolution and Religion in England,* ed. Peter Grell, Jonathan Israel, and Nicholas Tyacke (Oxford: Clarendon, 1991), 370, 385–386.

87. Wills, 10:75 (1679).

88. Wills, 6:56 (1688).

89. Wills, 12.1:223–224 (1707). In his version of the New Testament, Martin Luther omitted four books, including James, that insisted on good works rather than justification by faith alone. The Arminian Anglicans, Roman Catholics, and Quakers highlighted the book of James, particularly 2:1–7, 3:13–18, and 5:7–18.

90. The Maryland Puritans' connection to New England and the political reasons for Lord Baltimore's extending an invitation to Virginia Puritans to settle in Maryland are outlined in Daniel Randall, "A Puritan Colony in Maryland," in *Johns Hopkins University Studies,* vol. 4, ed. Herbert Adams (Baltimore: N. Murray, 1886), 210–257.

91. Richard Godbeer discusses the ramifications of this theology in his book *The Devil's Dominion: Magic and Religion in Early New England* (New York: Cambridge University Press, 1992).

92. George Davis, *The Day-Star of American Freedom; or, The Birth and Early Growth of Toleration, in the Province of Maryland* (New York: Scribner, 1855), 271.

93. Gerard Croese, *A Brief History of the Rise, Growth, and Progress of Quakerism; Setting Forth, That the Principles and Practices of the Quakers are Antichristian, Antiscriptural, Antimagistratical, Blasphemous, and Idolatrous from plain matter of Fact, out of their most approved Authors, &c. Containing Also, A modest Correction of the General History of the Quakers* (London: Francis Bugg, Senior, 1697), 44 and 77.

4. Women and Religion

1. *The Policy of the Jesuits, Their Insinuation into the Courts of Princes, And most of the noble Families of Europe; discovered* (London, 1658), preface. We know this text was republished many times, for it appeared as a relatively inexpensive pocket-sized book.

2. Abbot Gualdi [Gregorio Leti], *The Life of Donna Olimpia Maldachini, Who Governed the Church, during the time of Innocent the X, which was from the Year 1644–1655* (London: 1666), preface and 7.

3. *A Discoverie of Six women preachers, in Middlesex, Kent, Cambridgshire, and Salisbury* (London, 1641), 2–4.

4. Susannah Hopton, *Daily Devotions, Consisting of Thanksgivings, Confessions, and Prayers. In Two Parts. For the Benefit of the more Devout, and the assistance of weaker Christians* (London: A. Maxwell, 1673).

5. Patricia Crawford, *Women and Religion in England, 1500–1720* (London: Routledge, 1993), 210 and 211.

6. Francis McGrath, *Pillars of Maryland* (Richmond, Va.: Dietz, 1950), 88. Some of the following paragraphs, dealing specifically with Henrietta Maria Neale, are from my essay "Gender and Religion in England's Catholic Province," in *Women and Religion in Old and New Worlds*, ed. Susan Dinan and Debra Meyers (New York: Routledge, 2001), 214–215.

7. Colonel Lloyd served the province in several military expeditions, including one against the Indians on the Eastern Shore. He also served Talbot County as a burgess from 1671 until he died (Christopher Johnston, "Lloyd Family," *Maryland Historical Magazine* 7 [1912]: 423–424).

8. Wills, 4:187.

9. Wills, 2:260 (1693).

10. Quoted in McHenry Howard, "Lloyd Graveyard at Wye House, Talbot County, Maryland," *Maryland Historical Magazine* 15 (1920): 24.

11. See Genesis 29–35, 1 Samuel 25, Acts 16, Luke 10, and John 11–12. Leah and Rachel are also referred to in John Hammond's 1656 promotional tract—meant to entice prospective emigrants—entitled *Leah and Rachel, or, The Two Fruitfull Sisters,*

Virginia and Mary-Land. A reprint of the tract may be found in Clayton Hall, ed., *Narratives of Early Maryland, 1633–1684* (New York: Charles Scribner's Sons, 1910), 277–308.

12. Patricia Crawford notes that English variations in female agency were closely associated with class and social status. See Crawford, "Piety and Spirituality," in *Women and Religion in Old and New Worlds,* ed. Dinan and Meyers. The other essays in this collection suggest that this was true in most regions in the early modern Atlantic world.

13. Wills, 4:317 (1688).

14. Wills, 1:432 (1671).

15. Wills, 13:528 (1713).

16. There were paid female teachers in England as well. See Patricia Crawford and Laura Gowing, eds., *Women's Worlds in Seventeenth-Century England: A Sourcebook* (London: Routledge, 2000), 93–94.

17. Calvinists in New England and England generally agreed that the family patriarch taught children and servants "conscientious Principles" and "reading the sacred Scriptures" in the home. Fathers had a duty to instruct members of their households in prayer as well. See Samuel Clarke, *The Lives of Thirty-Two English Divines, Famous in their Generations for Learning and Piety, And most of them Sufferers in the Cause of Christ* (London, 1677), 237.

18. Edward C. Papenfuse et al., *A Biographical Dictionary of the Maryland Legislature, 1635–1789,* vol. 2 (Baltimore: Johns Hopkins University Press, 1985), 751.

19. Wills, 13:245 (1711).

20. Henry Peden, Jr., ed., *Quaker Records of Southern Maryland: Births, Deaths, Marriages, and Abstracts from the Minutes, 1658–1800* (Westminster, Md.: Family Line Publications, 1992), 13.

21. William Hand Browne, ed., *Archives of Maryland,* 72 vols. (Baltimore: Maryland Historical Society, 1883–1972), 41:146.

22. Phebe Jacobsen, *Quaker Records in Maryland,* Publication no. 14 (Annapolis: The Hall of Records Commission, State of Maryland, 1966), 4. To circumvent the law restricting the amount of land that could be donated to religious groups, women sold property to their churches for a nominal charge.

23. James Walter Thomas, *Chronicles of Colonial Maryland* (1900; reprint, Baltimore: Clearfield, 1999), 198.

24. Thomas, *Chronicles of Colonial Maryland,* 194.

25. In England during Mary Tudor's reign Roman Catholic women such as the widow Jone Morsse and Luce Scely served their communities as church wardens. See J. E. Binney, ed., *Devon and Cornwall Notes and Queries* (London, 1904 supplement), 181 and 200.

26. Wills, 6:380 (1699). Jane Green's sister Mary became Maryland's first native-born nun.

27. George Johnston, *History of Cecil County, Maryland, and the Early Settle-*

ments around the Head of Chesapeake Bay and on the Delaware River, with Sketches of Some of the Old Families of Cecil County (1881; reprint, Baltimore: Regional Publishing, 1967), 195–196.

28. Quoted in Anna Sioussat, "Colonial Women of Maryland," *Maryland Historical Magazine* 2 (1907): 225.

29. Wealthy Roman Catholic women in England often were involved in settling disputes among clerics and gentlemen. See, for instance, the many letters left by the countess of Arundel, the duchess of Norfolk, and Lady Catherine Howard. Letters from men have survived describing the need to persuade female relatives to join them on particular issues. See *Dominicana: Cardinal Howard's Letters, English Dominican Friars, Nuns, Students, Papers and Mission Registers,* Publications of the Catholic Record Society 25 (London: Catholic Record Society, 1925), 7, 19, 71–73, and 76–78.

30. "Miscellaneous Colonial Collection," MS 2018, Manuscripts Division, MHS.

31. Debra Meyers, "The Civic Lives of White Women in Seventeenth-Century Maryland," *Maryland Historical Magazine* 94 (1999): 316.

32. "Maryland Province Archives," box 27, folder 2 (1668), Special Collections, Georgetown University Library.

33. For instance, Suzanne Lebsock in *The Free Women of Petersburg* suggests that white women between 1784 and 1860 were more likely than men to free their slaves and leave money to orphans, because of their divergent value systems (Lebsock, *The Free Women of Petersburg: Status and Culture in a Southern Town, 1784–1860* [New York: Norton, 1984], 137 and 241).

34. *Dominicana,* part 4, page 201.

35. Forty percent of the men leaving charitable bequests were Roman Catholics.

36. Holding land in freehold meant that the owner could sell, mortgage, or otherwise alienate the land as he or she saw fit.

37. Wills, 13:96 (1705), 6:380 (1699), 5:342 (1676), 7:252 (1697), and 7:378 (1697). Elizabeth Darnell Diggs's epitaph can be found in Helen Ridgeley, *Historic Graves of Maryland* (1908; reprint, Baltimore: Genealogical Publishing, 1967), 63. Widow Frances Sayer of Talbot County gave five priests each ten pounds sterling. Already having a chapel on her property, she ordered her executor to build an additional thirty-foot brick one over her and her husband's joint grave (Wills, 6:166 [1698]).

38. Wills, 2:217 (1687) and 11:10 (1700).

39. Patrick Malloy, "A Manual of Prayers, 1583–1850" (Ph.D. diss., University of Notre Dame, 1991), 132.

40. Jo Ann McNamara, in "Wives and Widows in Early Christian Thought," looks at the effect of Christianity on women and finds that it brought a positive change, a victory for women over Roman paganism. She argues that women had increased rights and freedom of choice after the emergence of Christianity in late antiquity. Under Roman law a widow could only remain unmarried if past childbearing age, but Christianity actually frowned on remarriage, thus freeing women from

the inherent risks of childbearing (McNamara, "Wives and Widows in Early Christian Thought," *International Journal of Women's Studies* 2 [1979]: 575–592). Rodney Stark concurs with McNamara's provocative thesis, arguing that most of the early Christians were women who found the social implications of the new religion liberating (Stark, *The Rise of Christianity: A Sociologist Reconsiders History* [Princeton, N.J.: Princeton University Press, 1996]). However, many feminists see Christianity as an oppressive force, particularly Catholicism and its hierarchical structure, presumably because it produces a family structure based on the subordination of women. See, for instance, Margaret Miles, *Desire and Delight: A New Reading of Augustine's Confessions* (New York: Crossroad, 1992), and *Carnal Knowing: Female Nakedness and Religious Meaning in the Christian West* (New York: Vintage, 1991); Robert Orsi, *The Madonna of 115th Street: Faith and Community in Italian Harlem, 1880–1950* (New Haven, Conn.: Yale University Press, 1985); and Elaine Pagels, *Adam, Eve, and the Serpent* (New York: Vintage, 1989).

41. Elizabeth Reis, "The Devil, the Body, and the Feminine Soul in Puritan New England," *Journal of American History* 82 (June 1995): 16, 23, 35–36.

42. See, for instance, the frequently reprinted book by Thomas Grantham, *A Marriage Sermon: A Sermon Called a Wife mistaken, or a Wife and no Wife—or, Leah in stead of Rachel* (London, 1641), 2–5.

43. John Bossy, *The English Catholic Community, 1570–1850* (New York: Oxford University Press, 1976).

44. Alexandra Walsham, *Church Papists: Catholicism, Conformity, and Confessional Polemic in Early Modern England*, The Royal Historical Society (Woodbridge, U.K.: Boydell, 1993), 80–81. See also Colleen Marie Seguin, "'Addicted unto Piety': Catholic Women in England, 1590–1690" (Ph.D. diss., Duke University, 1997).

45. *The Reflections of the Reverend and Learned Montieur Jurieu, Upon the strange and Miraculous Exstasies of Isabel Vincent, the Shepherdess of Savoy in Dauphine; who Ever since February last hath Sung Psalms, Prayed, Preached, and Prophesied about the Present Times, in Her Trances. As also Upon the Wonderful and Portentous Trumpetings and Singing of Psalms, that were heard by Thousands in the Air (in many Parts of France) in the Year 1686 . . . All Faithfully Translated out of the French Copies, for Publick Informacion* (London, 1689).

46. *An Account of the Seducing of Ann, the Daughter of Edward Ketelbey, of Ludlow, Gent. to the Popish Religion, With some very Extraordinary Passages relating thereto, Particularly, Of the gross Prevarications, and insolent Boldness of the two Popish Bishops Leyborn and Gifford in the Management of it* (London, 1700), 1–2.

47. Katherine C. Dorsey, *The Life of Father Thomas Copley: A Founder of Maryland* (Washington, D.C.: Georgetown University Press, 1885), 35.

48. *Dominicana*, part 4, page 228.

49. My correspondence with Sister Elaine Wheeler of the Daughters of Charity of St. Vincent De Paul reveals a long tradition of English Catholics' sending their daughters to convents. Her own family traces its roots to Maryland in 1636, with an

extensive list of women in each generation joining nunneries (Letter from Elaine Wheeler, provincial archivist, De Paul Provincial House, Albany, New York, July 6, 1994).

50. This is important to note, because Catholicism, despite its name ("catholic" means "universal"), has never been either a ubiquitous monolith or a homogeneous group of individuals who adhered to a standard theology. Historically, the Catholic Church has made adjustments according to political, economic, and ethnic and regional diversities in order to remain a viable and relevant institution. A Jesuit at Georgetown in 1792 wrote a book that recognized the existence of many divisions in American Catholicism: *The Pious Guide to Prayer and Devotion: Containing Various Practices of Piety Calculated to Answer the Various Demands of the Different Devout Members of the Roman Catholic Church* (Georgetown: James Doyle, 1792). For a cogent depiction of the diversity of the early "Catholic" experience (a term that was not used until the church had to differentiate itself from the Protestants during the Reformation), see Elaine Pagels, *Adam, Eve, and the Serpent* (New York: Vintage Books, 1988), and her *The Gnostic Gospels* (New York: Random House, 1979); and Peter Brown, *The Body and Society: Men, Women, and Sexual Renunciation in Early Christianity* (New York: Columbia University Press, 1988). For modern ethnic diversity within American Catholicism, see Jay P. Dolan's classic *The American Catholic Experience: A History from Colonial Times to the Present* (New York: Doubleday, 1985); Hasia Diner, *Erin's Daughters in America: Irish Immigrant Women in the Nineteenth Century* (Baltimore: Johns Hopkins University Press, 1983); Orsi, *The Madonna of 115th Street*; Ann Taves, *The Household of Faith: Roman Catholic Devotions in Mid-nineteenth-century America* (Notre Dame, Ind.: University of Notre Dame Press, 1986); and Richard Linkh, *American Catholicism and European Immigrants, 1900–1924* (New York: Center for Migration Studies, 1975). For the diversity of worldwide Catholicism, see Joseph Kenny, *The Catholic Church in Tropical Africa, 1445–1850* (Ibadan, Nigeria: Ibadan University Press, 1983); and Brenda Meehan, *Holy Women of Russia* (San Francisco: Harper, 1993).

51. While French and Irish Catholics immigrated to the province in the seventeenth century, their ethnic names are conspicuously absent from the Carmelite monastery's rolls until the middle of the nineteenth century.

52. The Catholic Enlightenment was a philosophical school that sought to reconcile Isaac Newton's findings with a Christian attitude toward nature.

53. MHR, Carmelite Monastery Records, microfilm M9537, box 48, folder 1, "Correspondence: John Carroll."

54. Gertrude More, *The Holy Practices of a Devine Lover* (Paris, 1657), 25–26, 34–36, 219–220.

55. Jacobus de Voragine, *The Golden Legend: Readings on the Saints*, vol. 1 (Princeton, N.J.: Princeton University Press, 1993), 324–325.

56. "Digby Family Spiritual Exercises," (c. 1650), unpublished manuscript, Folger Shakespeare Library call number V.a.473. For a discussion of Catherine of

Siena's and Catherine of Genoa's excessive fasting and eucharistic devotion, see Caroline Walker Bynum, *Holy Feast and Holy Fast: The Religious Significance of Food to Medieval Women* (Berkeley: University of California Press, 1987), 165–186.

57. G. Needham, *An Abridgment of the Prerogatives of St. Ann, Mother of the Mother of God* (London, 1687), preface, 19–20.

58. Malloy, "A Manual of Prayers," 132.

59. Alexis de Salo, *An Admirable Method to Love, Serve, and Honour the B. Virgin Mary*, translated from Italian (1639), English Recusant Literature, 1558–1640, edited and selected by D. M. Rogers, vol. 178 (Ilkley: Scolar Press, 1974), 284–285.

60. Justus Lipsius, *Miracles of the B. Virgin. Or, an Historical Account of the Original, and Stupendious Performances of the Image, entituled Our Blessed Lady of Halle. Viz. Restoring the Dead to Life, Healing the Sick, Delivering of Captives, &c.* (London, 1688), 1–3, 8–9. The book was published in Latin in 1604, and translated into French, Dutch, and English. See also George Hickes, *Speculum Beatæ Virginis: A Discourse of the Due Praise and Honour of the Virgin Mary* (London: Randal Taylor, 1686).

61. "American Catholic Sermons Collection," Special Collections, Georgetown University Library.

62. Letter from Charles Calvert (Lord Baltimore) to William Osborn, November 15, 1678, Michael Papers, MS 1368, box 1, Manuscripts Division, MHS.

63. "American Catholic Sermons Collection."

64. Charles I, *His Majesties Declaration in Defence of the true Protestant Religion: It was maintained by his Royall Father King James [I] of blessed memorie* (London, 1643), n.p.

65. Adam Widenfeldt, *Wolsome advices from the Blessed Virgin, to her Indescreet Worshippers* (London, 1687), 6–11, 17.

66. Crawford, *Women and Religion in England*, 188.

67. *The Arminian Nunnery; or, A Briefe Description and Relation of the late erected Monasticall Place, called the Arminian Nunnery at little Gidding in Huntington-Shire* (London: printed for Thomas Underhill, 1641).

68. *The Arminian Nunnery*, 2–4, 6, 9.

69. Bridget Hill, "A Refuge from Men: The Idea of a Protestant Nunnery," *Past and Present* 117 (1987): 107–108, 112–114.

70. Paul Parrish, "Richard Crashaw, Mary Collet, and the 'Arminian Nunnery' of Little Gidding," in *Representing Women in Renaissance England*, ed. Claude Summers and Ted-Larry Pebworth (Columbia: University of Missouri Press, 1997), 187–200.

71. *A Letter Touching a Colledge of Maids; or, A Virgin-Society* (London, 1675), n.p.

72. William Blake, *The Ladies Charity School-house Roll of Highgate; or, A Subscription of many Noble, well disposed Ladies for the easie carrying of it on* (London, 1670), 2, 50, 59, 74–75, 81, 177, 199, 224.

73. Barry Reay, *The Quakers and the English Revolution* (London: Temple Smith, 1985), 9.

74. Kenneth Carroll, *Quakerism on the Eastern Shore* (Baltimore: Maryland Historical Society, 1970), 9 and 22. For a reprint of Robert Clarkson's letter to Elizabeth Harris thanking her for "the inward truth" she brought to Maryland, see Edward D. Neill, *The Founders of Maryland as Portrayed in Manuscripts, Provincial Records, and Early Documents* (Albany: Joel Munsell, 1876), 141–143. For a portion of Fox's journal that referred to his Maryland trip, see Hall, *Narratives of Early Maryland*, 389–406.

75. Phyllis Mack, "Gender and Spirituality in Early English Quakerism, 1650–1665," in *Witnesses for Change: Quaker Women over Three Centuries*, ed. Elizabeth P. Brown and Susan M. Stuard (New Brunswick, N.J.: Rutgers University Press, 1989), 31–64.

76. Gerard Croese, *A Brief History of the Rise, Growth, and Progress of Quakerism; Setting Forth, That the Principles and Practices of the Quakers are Antichristian, Antiscriptural, Antimagistratical, Blasphemous, and Idolatrous from plain matter of Fact, out of their most approved Authors, &c. Containing Also, A modest Correction of the General History of the Quakers* (London: Francis Bugg, Senior, 1697), 74, 86.

77. Richard Richardson, *Testimony To The Fulfilling the Promise of God, relating to such Women who Through the pouring out of Gods Spirit upon them, are become Prophetesses* (London: Thomas Camm, 1689), n.p.

78. "Miscellaneous Colonial Collection," MS 2018, Manuscripts Division, MHS. Doctor Peter Sharpe's 1672 will also mentions several women in the Quaker ministry, such as Alice Gary and Sarah Mash (Wills, 1:496 [1671]).

79. J. Reaney Kelly, *Quakers in the Founding of Anne Arundel County, Maryland* (Baltimore: Maryland Historical Society, 1963), 44 (Chew) and 59 (Galloway).

80. Katharine Whitton, *Epistle from the Women's Yearly Meeting at York, 1688, and An Epistle from Mary Waite* (London, 1689), 8.

81. Whitton, *Epistle from the Women's Yearly Meeting at York*, 6–8, 14, 16.

82. Crawford, *Women and Religion in England*, 210 and 211.

5. Religion, Property, and the Family

1. Amy Louise Erickson, *Women and Property in Early Modern England* (London: Routledge, 1997). Christine Churches's recent case study of the area surrounding Whitehaven in the seventeenth and eighteenth centuries tends to support Erickson's assertions (Christine Churches, "Women and Property in Early Modern England: A Case Study," *Social History* 23 [1998]: 165–180).

2. Erickson, *Women and Property*, 5.

3. Erickson, *Women and Property*, 19, 225, and 226.

4. James Walter Thomas, *Chronicles of Colonial Maryland* (1900; reprint, Baltimore: Clearfield, 1999), 136 n.

5. Lois G. Carr, "Inheritance in the Colonial Chesapeake," in *Women in the Age of the American Revolution*, ed. Ronald Hoffman and Peter J. Albert (Charlottesville: Published for the United States Capitol Historical Society by the University Press of Virginia, 1989), 155–208. Additionally, there are two crucial demographic studies of Maryland family life: Lois Carr and Lorena Walsh, "The Planter's Wife:

The Experience of White Women in Seventeenth-Century Maryland," *William and Mary Quarterly,* 3d ser., 34 (1977): 542–571; and Lorena Walsh, "'Till Death Us Do Part': Marriage and Family in Seventeenth-Century Maryland," in *The Chesapeake in the Seventeenth Century: Essays on Anglo-American Society,* ed. Thad W. Tate and David L. Ammerman (New York: W. W. Norton, 1979).

6. John J. Waters, "Family, Inheritance, and Migration in Colonial New England: The Evidence from Guilford, Connecticut," *William and Mary Quarterly,* 3d ser., 39 (1982): 64–86. See also his *The Otis Family in Provincial and Revolutionary Massachusetts* (Chapel Hill: Published for the Institute of Early American History and Culture at Williamsburg, Va., by the University of North Carolina Press, 1968), 41.

7. Kim Lacy Rogers, "Relicts of the New World: Conditions of Widowhood in Seventeenth-Century New England," in *Woman's Being, Woman's Place: Female Identity and Vocation in American History,* ed. Mary Kelley (Boston: G. K. Hall, 1979), 36.

8. William Ricketson, "To Be Young, Poor and Alone: The Experience of Widowhood in the Massachusetts Bay Colony, 1675–1676," *New England Quarterly* 64, no. 1 (1991): 113–127.

9. By analyzing the soteriological language of the preambles to these wills (see chapter 3), I was able to identify almost 28 percent of the testators as either humble and penitent Free Will Christians [N = 733] or confident Predestinarians [N = 145]. The first group includes Arminian Anglicans, Catholics, and Quakers; the second, Particular Baptists, Presbyterians, and Puritans. I also used the extensive Anglican, Jesuit, and Quaker records to identify the religious affiliations of another 532 testators (Edward C. Papenfuse et al., *A Biographical Dictionary of the Maryland Legislature, 1635–1789,* 2 vols. [Baltimore: Johns Hopkins University Press, 1979–85]; Clayton Torrence, *Old Somerset on the Eastern Shore of Maryland: A Study in Foundations and Founders* [1935; reprint, Baltimore: Clearfield, 1993]; and the Provincial Court records, Thomas Bray's letters, and other documents at the Maryland Historical Society). All the surviving wills between 1634 and 1713 [N = 3190]—including those of married, single, and widowed women and men—were systematically analyzed using the SAS Institute's JMP program.

10. Eamon Duffy discusses the historiography of the use of preambles to classify individuals according to religious affiliation in his book *The Stripping of the Altars: Traditional Religion in England, c. 1400–c. 1580* (New Haven, Conn.: Yale University Press, 1992), chapter 15. For arguments concerning categorization and labeling denominations, see Patrick Collinson, *English Puritanism* (London: Historical Association, 1989), and *The Puritan Character: Polemics and Polarities in Early Seventeenth-Century English Culture* (Los Angeles: University of California Press, 1989); Stephen Foster, *The Long Argument: English Puritanism and the Shaping of New England Culture, 1570–1700* (Chapel Hill: University of North Carolina Press, 1991); Peter Lake, *Anglicans and Puritans? Presbyterianism and English Conformist Thought from Whitgift to Hooker* (London: Unwin Hyman, 1988); Geoffrey F. Nut-

tall, *The Holy Spirit in Puritan Faith and Experience* (Chicago: University of Chicago Press, 1992); and Tom Webster, *Godly Clergy in Early Stuart England: The Caroline Puritan Movement, c. 1620–1643* (Cambridge: Cambridge University Press, 1997).

11. Several studies using samples of the aggregate probated colonial Maryland population have been done. Carole Shammas summarized Marylynn Salmon's suggestion that Maryland, unlike many other colonies, opposed the shrinkage of dower rights, adding that Maryland "specifically granted widows dower rights in personalty as well as realty" prior to 1690. Yet historians have failed to fully explain what actually took place due to the differences in gender construction between the Predestinarians and Free Will Christians. The larger number of Free Will Christians may have dictated the intestate laws' effort to ensure that women received their rightful shares of both land and property if a husband died without a will. See Carole Shammas, "Early American Women and Control over Capital," in *Women in the Age of the American Revolution*, ed. Hoffman and Albert, 158. For English practices see Lloyd Bonfield, *Marriage Settlements, 1601–1740: The Adoption of the Strict Settlement* (Cambridge: Cambridge University Press, 1983); John Brewer and Susan Staves, eds., *Early Modern Conceptions of Property* (New York: Routledge, 1995); and R. M. Smith, "Women's Property Rights under Customary Law: Some Developments in the Thirteenth and Fourteenth Centuries," *Transactions of the Royal Historical Society*, 5th ser., 36 (1986): 165–194.

12. Erickson, *Women and Property*, 232.

13. A 1699 Maryland law specified the widow's dower right to one-third of the property held jointly. The Predestinarians tended to ignore the rights of their wives by merely leaving them personal property in their wills. For more information on inheritance law in Maryland see Carr, "Inheritance in the Colonial Chesapeake," 155–208.

14. Wills, 12.1:4 (c. 1706). This was a nuncupative (verbal) will.

15. Wills, 12.1:184–187 (1707). The 1642 Assembly passed the "Act Touching Succession to Land" to deal with property distribution when a man died intestate. The act stipulates that in the absence of a will "the next heire shall suceed as hath right by the Law of England In defect of such heire the neerest heire living within the Province may enter upon the Land and hold it for the use of such next heire And if none neerer enter or clayme in 7 years he shall hold it till the same right & estate as if he had been next heire." The widow "shall succeed to the thirds of the Lands & to the mansion house to hold it dureing her widdow hood as her husband was seized of at any time dureing the Coverture in such manner as she may by the Law of England. This Act to endure till the end of the next Assembly." Following ecclesiastic law, the widow was entitled to all the personal goods if the couple had no living children, half if they had one child, and one-third if more than one child was living (William Hand Browne, ed., *Archives of Maryland*, 72 vols. [Baltimore: Maryland Historical Society, 1883–1972], 1:156–157). I have argued elsewhere that women regularly controlled their own property during marriage, and therefore this statute would apply, not to a widow's separate estate, but only to the land that "her hus-

band was seized of at any time dureing the Coverture" (Debra Meyers, "The Civic Lives of White Women in Seventeenth-Century Maryland," *Maryland Historical Magazine* 94 [1999]: 321–324). Moreover, the governor and his council exercised jurisdiction in equity cases until the High Court of Chancery was organized in 1661. Whether or not they adhered to the Assembly's Act of 1642 is unclear. In 1673, Lord Baltimore created the office of Commissary General, "for the probate of wills and granting of letters of administration within the whole Province . . . [and to act] according to the laws of England, where no law of the Province prevailed" (Thomas, *Chronicles of Colonial Maryland*, 136–137 and 139).

16. The personal estate, or personalty, included items that might be left to both females and males: livestock, books, cookware, dishes, servants, slaves, featherbeds, furniture, clothing, rugs, Indian corn, tobacco, fabric and trim, prized horses, saddles, mirrors, sloops, nails, and silver plate—mostly in spoons and tankards, but items such as buttons, shoe buckles, watches, tobacco boxes, and the amusing "tooth picker and eare picker" (Wills, 5:55) also appear. Gender differentiation was reserved for the tools of such crafts as carpentry, cooperage, wheelmaking, and gun repair.

17. Wills, 6.2:2 (1692).

18. Wills, 6:163 (1698). One of the Hanslap daughters married Captain Thomas Gassaway and they share a grave at All Hallow's Church.

19. Wills, 12.1:279–283 (1708). Contee probably died of amoebic dysentery.

20. Wills, 5:20 (1676). Anglican Arminian William Chandler also referred to his wife as his "dear wife and yoakefellow" (Wills, 4:113 [1685]). This yoke metaphor is found in Matthew 11:29–30 and the *Oxford English Dictionary* notes that as early as 1382 people used the term to indicate a cooperative union in holy matrimony.

21. Wills, 1:387 (1670). Testators commonly sheltered bequests to children from probate in this way. See, for instance, Robert Burle's will, in which he wrote, "It is my Will that he [his son Stephen] shall possess as his owne [a certain chest] after my decease without being brought into the Inventory & appraisement of my estate, because the said Chest was my Grandfathers the said bason was his mothers grandfathers as forfeit to him being Sealmaster of Goldsmith Hall in London" (Wills, 5:151 [1676]).

22. Many historians have viewed Roman Catholicism as a beneficial influence on gender roles. Thus Lawrence Stone contrasts the Catholic view of marriage, with its implication of a binding contract of mutual obligation, to the Calvinist nuclear family, with its strong head of household (Stone, *The Family, Sex, and Marriage in England, 1500–1800* [New York: Harper and Row, 1977], 135–141). John Bossy argues that the Elizabethan era marked a decidedly matriarchal period in English Catholicism (Bossy, *The English Catholic Community, 1570–1850* [New York: Oxford University Press, 1976]). And Jo Ann McNamara suggests that early Christianity had a positive effect on women's status and life choices (McNamara, "Wives and Widows in Early Christian Thought," *International Journal of Women's Studies* 2 [1979]: 575–592). However, others have posited the idea that Catholicism, in general, led to the

construction of negative female gender roles. See Ramon A. Gutiérrez, *When Jesus Came the Corn Mothers Went Away: Marriage, Sexuality, and Power in New Mexico, 1500–1846* (Stanford, Calif.: Stanford University Press, 1991); and Margaret Miles, *Desire and Delight: A New Reading of Augustine's Confessions* (New York: Crossroad, 1992). The solution to this paradox may lie in the divergent ethnic and class backgrounds of the groups studied, since Catholic piety was never a universal norm.

    23. Wills, 4:313–315 (1688).

    24. Liber S.: folio 219, Manuscripts Division, MHS.

    25. Wills, 13:265 (1711).

    26. Wills, 4:302 (1688).

    27. Wills, 4:276–278 (1687).

    28. Wills, 2:371 (1670).

    29. Wills, 2:396 (1675).

    30. Evidence suggests that some women owned estates separately from their husbands in Maryland, just as they had in England. See Erickson, *Women and Property*, 103–113, 122–124, 131, 136–137, 183–184, 200–201, 214, and 231. Suzanne Lebsock argues that, on this side of the Atlantic, marriage partners entered into this type of arrangement in order to protect parts of their estate in case of financial failure (Lebsock, *The Free Women of Petersburg: Status and Culture in a Southern Town, 1784–1860* (New York: Norton, 1984), 60–61, 72–77.

    31. Wills, 6:209 (1698).

    32. My reference to "the family will" here is intentional. The structuring of these wills permitted testators, after consulting with their wives, to allocate the resources equitably amongst the family members for a generation, thus freeing their widows from writing a will. For instance, if a testator left his wife the entire estate during her life and stipulated that it was to pass equally to their children when she died, his wife would not have to draw up a will to protect her heirs. I would argue that the key to the small number of female wills left during this time period [N = 211] rests with a wife's power to negotiate with her husband.

    33. Egerton Papers, MS 331, Manuscripts Division, MHS.

    34. Wills, 10:1 (1679/80).

    35. Letter from John Playton to Robert Brent, April 28, 1717, University of Notre Dame Archives, "Archdiocese of Baltimore Collection" (CABA), box 1, folder 1.

    36. Wills, 2:143–146 (1681).

    37. Wills, 2:144 (1681).

    38. Wills, 2:144 (1681).

    39. Wills, 4:161 (1685).

    40. Wills, 6:327 (1699).

    41. Wills, 1:495–496 (1672). On the other hand, Quakers tended to concede their wives' right to one-third of the entire estate even when a marriage proved disappointing (Wills, 2:149–150 [1681]).

    42. Wills, 4:165 (1685).

43. Mother of at least nine children, Anne maintained her prominence in the community after her husband's death and the Society of Friends met at her home on Herring Bay for many years (Francis Culver, "Chew Family," *Maryland Historical Magazine* 30 [1935]: 159–160).

44. Wills, 5:246 (1677). J. William Frost cites George Fox's emphasis on joint parental authority based on scripture (e.g., Deut. 27:16), in *The Quaker Family in Colonial America: A Portrait of the Society of Friends* (New York: St. Martin's, 1973), 84.

45. Frost argues that the Quakers were very different from the Catholics, and that at least by the eighteenth century a woman held an "inferior social position" outside the meetinghouse. However, he suggests that Quakers believed that marriage partners "contributed to each other's happiness and comfort and served as spiritual helpmates" (Frost, *The Quaker Family,* 177, 151, and 183).

46. Wills, 2:72 (1675). Erickson found that lone English women often headed their own households and controlled their children (Erickson, *Women and Property,* chapter 11).

47. Wills, 9:33 (1677).

48. Wills, 13:261 (1711).

49. Wills, 4:104 (1685).

50. Wills, 4:111 (1685).

51. Wills, 11:243 (1702).

52. Wills, 4:234 (1686).

53. Wills, 12.2:182 (1708/9).

54. Wills, 2:307 (1693).

55. Wills, 2:308 (1693).

56. Wills, 5:73 (1678).

57. Wills, 5:325 (1677). Erickson found that testamentary patterns were more egalitarian in England than in New England (Erickson, *Women and Property,* 165–166).

58. Wills, 12.2:33 (1709). From the evidence, it seems that his daughter had been given her share of the estate when she married.

59. Wills, 13:381 (1709). The married daughter, Frances Erving, and her husband received more than seven hundred acres.

60. Wills, 7:163 (1695).

61. Wills, 1:383 (1670).

62. For example, Presbyterian Ninian Beale left his dwelling plantation and one-third of the personal estate to his "deare & loving wife" for life (Wills, 13:157 [1710]).

63. This was not the case for all women in Maryland. See Meyers, "The Civic Lives of White Women," 322–325.

64. Wills, 6:29 (1688, Smith), and 4:37 (1683, Eareckson).

65. Wills, 7:377 (1697, Browne) and 6:239 (1697, Aldry).

66. Meyers, "The Civic Lives of White Women," 322–325. Some of the following paragraphs that deal specifically with women's wills are taken from my essay "Gender and Religion in England's Catholic Province," in *Women and Religion in*

Old and New Worlds, ed. Susan Dinan and Debra Meyers (New York: Routledge, 2001), 221–223.

67. Wills, 4:157 (1681).

68. For more biographical information see Debra Meyers, "Verlinda Stone," in *Chronology of Women Worldwide: People, Places, and Events That Shaped Women's History,* ed. Lynne Brakeman (Detroit: Gale, 1996), 113.

69. William Stevenson, "The Economic and Social Status of Protestant Sectarians in Huntingdonshire, Cambridgeshire, and Bedfordshire (1650–1725)" (Ph.D. diss., University of Cambridge, 1990), 343.

70. Stevenson, "The Economic and Social Status of Protestant Sectarians," 83, 87, 88.

71. Wills of the Archdeaconry of Sudbury held by the Suffolk Records Society in England, R2/57/210 (1637).

72. Wills of the Archdeaconry of Sudbury held by the Suffolk Records Society in England, R2/57/374 (1638).

73. J. Jackson Howard and H. Farnham Burke, eds., *Genealogical Collections Illustrating the History of Roman Catholic Families of England: Based on the Lawson Manuscript,* vol. 1, *Fermor and Petre Families* (Printed for private circulation, 1887), 27, 73, 78.

74. J. Jackson Howard and H. Seymour Hughes, eds., *Genealogical Collections Illustrating the History of Roman Catholic Families of England: Based on the Lawson Manuscript,* vol. 3, *Arundell Family* (Printed for private circulation, n.d.), 198.

75. Stevenson, "The Economic and Social Status of Protestant Sectarians," 111–112.

76. Allan Brockett, *Nonconformity in Exeter, 1650–1875* (Manchester: Manchester University Press, 1962), 58–59 and 72.

77. E. A. Fry, ed., *Calendars of Wills and Administrations Relating to the Counties of Devon and Cornwall Proved in the Court of the Principal Registry of the Bishop of Exeter, 1599–1799* (Plymouth: Devonshire Association for the Advancement of Science and Literature, 1908), 618.

78. Devon Record Office, Exeter, England.

79. Whitelocke's last will appears in Ruth Spalding's biography, *The Improbable Puritan: A Life of Bulstrode Whitelocke, 1605–1675* (London: Faber and Faber, 1975), 254.

80. J. Harvey Bloom, *Wayman Wills and Administrations Preserved in the Prerogative Court of Canterbury, 1383–1821* (London: Wallace Gandy, 1922), 23.

81. David Fischer's *Albion's Seed* suggests that the place of origin is the primary determinant of behavior patterns in the New World. I agree that regional factors, prior social status, and religion produced American colonies with divergent characteristics. If new documents are found that allow this, regional variations in Maryland should be compared (Fischer, *Albion's Seed: Four British Folkways in America* [New York: Oxford University Press, 1989]).

82. Single male testators of this period followed similar patterns.

83. Erickson, *Women and Property,* chapter 11.

6. Free Will Christian Women's Public Authority

1. George Davis, *The Day-Star of American Freedom; or, The Birth and Early Growth of Toleration, in the Province of Maryland* (New York: Scribner, 1855), 73–74.

2. Widow Mary Harmer successfully petitioned the court in St. Mary's City to allow her to prove her husband's will in Baltimore County, where she lived, due to the expense of the trip and her inability to "take security here" because she had "no acquaintance at St Mary's to give in Security" (Wills, 1:613 [1674]).

3. MHR, Prerogative Court Testamentary Proceedings, 1:33.

4. William Hand Browne, ed., *Archives of Maryland*, 72 vols. (Baltimore: Maryland Historical Society, 1883–1972), 4:72 and 96.

5. Amy Louise Erickson, *Women and Property in Early Modern England* (London: Routledge, 1997), 157–158.

6. Wills, 2:156 (1681).

7. Wills, 13:507 (1711).

8. Documents referring to Margaret Prior—also spelled Pryer and Pryor—and several other women are located in the "Miscellaneous Colonial Collection," MS 2018, Manuscripts Division, MHS.

9. The receipt for this transaction—dated January 12, 1696/7—can be found in the "Miscellaneous Colonial Collection," MS 2018, Manuscripts Division, MHS. Tobacco remained the primary means of exchange in Maryland well into the eighteenth century despite Queen Anne's attempt to establish a coinage.

10. Wills, 6:349 (1698). Peter Coldham lists him as purchasing one hundred acres in 1689 (Coldham, *Settlers of Maryland, 1679–1700* [Baltimore: Genealogical Publishing, 1995], 28.

11. Browne, *Archives of Maryland*, 4:48–49; Egerton Papers, MS 331, Manuscripts Division, MHS; and Francis Culver, "Egerton Family," *Maryland Historical Magazine* 35 (1940): 296.

12. Browne, *Archives of Maryland*, 4:288 (Basha) and 4:145, 154 and 226 (Cockshott).

13. "Land Notes," *Maryland Historical Magazine* 8 (1913): 258.

14. MHR, Prerogative Court Testamentary Proceedings, 1:1–3.

15. Browne, *Archives of Maryland*, 41:277.

16. Browne, *Archives of Maryland*, 4:224.

17. Browne, *Archives of Maryland*, 54:157.

18. Browne, *Archives of Maryland*, 54:224–226 and 228.

19. Browne, *Archives of Maryland*, 54:194, 222, 223, 236 (Barnes), 41:332–333 (Gillford), 54:230 (Sprye).

20. Browne, *Archives of Maryland*, 49:33.

21. Browne, *Archives of Maryland*, 66:342 and 4:421.

22. Browne, *Archives of Maryland*, 41:474.

23. For a more thorough discussion of women in the public sphere, see Debra Meyers, "The Civic Lives of White Women in Seventeenth-Century Maryland," *Maryland Historical Magazine* 94 (1999): 309–327.

24. Lady Peregrina Chaytor, for example, wrote to her husband as she prepared for the birth of her child in 1697 expressing both her trepidation and her desire to provide an inheritance to each of her living children. The "most truly affectionate wife" opened her letter with "I being to pass the great peril of child bearing and not knowing how God may please to dispose of me could not but write you down my desires in this paper which I hope you will so far take notice of as to take care they be observed" (Patricia Crawford and Laura Gowing, eds., *Women's Worlds in Seventeenth-Century England: A Sourcebook* [London: Routledge, 2000], 135).

25. Marylynn Salmon discusses the use of prenuptial contracts in colonial South Carolina in her article "Women and Property in South Carolina: The Evidence from Marriage Settlements, 1730–1830," *William and Mary Quarterly*, 3d ser., 39 (1982): 655–685. While few powers of attorney or prenuptial contracts other than the wills themselves have survived in Maryland, Daniel Clarke did grant his wife Katherine power of attorney in Dorchester County ("Miscellaneous Colonial Collection," MS 2018, Manuscripts Division, MHS).

26. Wills, 6:26 (1688).

27. Robert Barnes mentions the 1649 antenuptial contract between Cuthbert Fenwick and Mrs. Jane Moryson, widow of Virginian Robert Moryson (Barnes, *Maryland Marriages, 1634–1777* [Baltimore: Genealogical Publishing, 1975], 206; see also Browne, *Archives of Maryland*, 41:262).

28. Joseph H. Smith and Philip A. Crowl, eds., *Court Records of Prince Georges County, Maryland 1696–99* (Washington, D.C.: American Historical Association, 1964), 164.

29. Browne, *Archives of Maryland*, 65:684.

30. Wills, 13:389 (1711/12).

31. Wills, 12.1:338–339 (1708).

32. Women repudiated undesirable alliances with joint executors as often as they rejected their husbands' wills altogether. George Willson appointed his wife executrix; but, finding the distribution of property in the will not to her liking, she demanded her third of the real and personal estate. When she went to prove her husband's will, the clerk observed, she "would not accept of the bequests in the S[ai]d Will Menconed but Expected the third part of the dec[ease]d['s] Estate." Of course, the court granted her request (Wills, 12.2:176 [1709]).

33. MHR, Prerogative Court Testamentary Proceedings, 8:350–351.

34. Wills, 7:69 (1695). Widows were not the only ones to avoid sharing executorships. James Sedgwick left his estate to his cousin Mary Wrightson and made her joint executor with James Murphy. Murphy declined his right and relinquished it to "Mary Wrightson his Kinswoman" (Wills, 7:78 [1694]).

35. Wills, 12.1:150 (1707).

36. Wills, 13:623 (1710).

37. Wills, 1:147 (c. 1662). Thomas Garrett resided in England.

38. MHR, Prerogative Court Testamentary Proceedings, 8:49–50.

39. Browne, *Archives of Maryland*, 4:5–6.

40. In addition to wives, female friends, daughters, and other relatives also served as executors. For example, Richard Jenkins left some livestock to the three orphans he took care of, and the bulk of his estate went to his executrix and "beloved friend" Rebecca Duphex, who lived with him. Also, Richard Tillyard named his sister his executrix and Catholic John Londey named his friend Widow Henrietta Marie Lloyd to the position (Wills, 13:586 [1713, Jenkins], 12.2:212 [1709, Tillyard], and 2:260 [1693, Londey]).

41. Edward D. Neill, *The Founders of Maryland as Portrayed in Manuscripts, Provincial Records, and Early Documents* (Albany: Joel Munsell, 1876), 67.

42. Browne, *Archives of Maryland,* 17:129, 7:195–201.

43. Wills, 13:467 (1711).

44. Wills, 12.2:77 (1704).

45. *The Calvert Papers,* 3 vols., Maryland Historical Society Fund Publications 28 (Baltimore: J. Murphy, 1889–99), 1:48–50.

46. Browne, *Archives of Maryland,* 55:192–193.

47. Wills, 11:59 (1698).

48. Wills, 4:283 (1687).

49. Pictures of Ann's jewelry are included in Hester Dorsey Richardson's *Sidelights on Maryland History: With Sketches of Early Maryland Families* (Baltimore: Williams and Wilkins, 1913; reprint, Cambridge, Md.: Tidewater, 1967), 186. Legend has it that Queen Henrietta Maria attempted to flee to Ann's side in Maryland after her husband's execution, but Cromwell sent a naval force to bring her back to England. For more detailed information about the Queen's attempt to flee England, see Paul Wilstach, *Tidewater Maryland* (New York: Tudor, 1931), 316–317.

50. Edward C. Papenfuse et al., *A Biographical Dictionary of the Maryland Legislature, 1635–1789,* vol. 2 (Baltimore: Johns Hopkins University Press, 1985), 609.

51. MHR, Prerogative Court Testamentary Proceedings, 13:131, 152, 168, 169, 171.

52. Wills, 13:616 (1713).

53. Wills, 12.1:335–336 (1708).

54. Wills, 7:147–148 (1696).

55. Wills, 1:530–531 (1673).

56. Wills, 12.1:54 (1705).

57. Wills, 2:406 (1675).

58. Kim Lacy Rogers, "Relicts of the New World: Conditions of Widowhood in Seventeenth-Century New England," in *Woman's Being, Woman's Place: Female Identity and Vocation in American History,* ed. Mary Kelley (Boston: G. K. Hall, 1979), 36.

59. Mary Beth Norton, *Founding Mothers and Fathers: Gendered Power and the Forming of American Society* (New York: Alfred A. Knopf, 1996), 148.

60. Wills, 13:432 (1712).

61. Wills, 2:363 (1661).

62. Wills, 2:152–153 (1681).

63. Wills, 9:46 (1684).

64. *The Calvert Papers*, 3 vols., Maryland Historical Society Fund Publications 28, 34–35 (Baltimore: J. Murphy, 1889–99), 1:263.

65. John T. Scharf, *History of Maryland: From the Earliest Period to the Present Day* (Baltimore: John B. Piet, 1879), 377.

66. In a sample of sixty-three letters written by Maryland colonists and the Lords Baltimore, I counted 134 references to women involved in commerce or litigation. Marylanders' general acceptance of such female activity also shows up in the gender-inclusive phrases (e.g., "to any p[er]son or p[er]sons whatsoever") frequently used in legal documents, including legislation and personal records. Of course, women's participation in the public realm did not extend to holding political office. For a discussion of women's office-holding as it is related to the early modern period in Europe, see Martha Howell, "Citizenship and Gender: Women's Political Status in Northern European Cities," in *Women and Power in the Middle Ages*, ed. Mary Erler and Maryanne Kowaleski (Athens: University of Georgia Press, 1988), 37–60.

67. British Library call number ADD 61424, in the Blenheim Papers, pages 13, 46–47, and 86.

68. A. Marsh, *The Confession of the New Married Couple, Being the Second Part of the Ten Pleasures of Marriage* (London, 1683), 12–13, 15, 31–33, and 50.

69. *An Impartial Account of the Tryal of Francis Smith Upon an Information Brought against him for Printing and Publishing a late Book commonly known by the Name of Tom Ticklefoot, &c. As Also Of the Tryal of Jane Curtis, Upon an Information brought against her for Publishing and putting to Sale a Scandalous Libel, called A Satyr upon Injustice: or Scroggs upon Scroggs* (London, 1680), 6.

70. Wilstach, *Tidewater Maryland*, 158 and 198.

71. Anne Norton, "Liminality: Identity and Difference," in *Reflections on Political Identity* (Baltimore: Johns Hopkins University Press, 1988), 79.

72. Wills, 6:339 (1699).

73. Wills, 11:145 (1701/2). See also Wills, 7:90 (1694).

74. Wills, 13:544 (1712).

75. Wills, 2:348 (1674, Foster), 6.2:7 (1692, Lowe).

76. Wills, 6.2:8 (1692).

77. MHR, Prerogative Court Testamentary Proceedings, 12B: 245 and 247. For England, see Erickson, *Women and Property*, 19 and 225–226.

78. These letters are in the British Library, call number ADD 61427, pages 167–170 and 181, and call number ADD 61424, page 13, both in the Blenheim Papers.

79. Henrietta Maria to Charles I, from York, March 30, 1644, in *The King's Cabinet Opened* (1645), reprinted in *The Harleian Miscellany*, vol. 5 (London, 1808–11), 536–537.

80. George Johnston, *History of Cecil County, Maryland, and the Early Settlements around the Head of Chesapeake Bay and on the Delaware River, with Sketches of Some of the Old Families of Cecil County* (1881; reprint, Baltimore: Regional Publishing, 1967), 126–127.

81. Oswald Tilghman, *History of Talbot County, Maryland, 1661–1861*, vol. 2 (1915; reprint, Baltimore: Regional Publishing, 1967), 65.

82. Scharf, *History of Maryland*, 322–323.

83. *The Faithful and Diligent Christian described and exemplified. Or, A Sermon (with some Additions,) Preached at the Funeral of the Lady Elizabeth Brooke, the Relict of Sir Robert Brooke Kt. of Cockfield-Hall* (London, 1683), 67, 70, 77, 76 and 81.

Conclusion

1. The ability of a woman to maintain control over the land she brought to a marriage is discussed in Debra Meyers, "The Civic Lives of White Women in Seventeenth-Century Maryland," *Maryland Historical Magazine* 94 (1999): 309–327.

2. Lois Carr and Lorena Walsh, "The Planter's Wife: The Experience of White Women in Seventeenth-Century Maryland," *William and Mary Quarterly*, 3d ser., 34 (1977): 542–571.

3. Lois Carr also alludes to factors such as religion and ethnicity (Carr, "Inheritance in the Colonial Chesapeake," in *Women in the Age of the American Revolution*, ed. Ronald Hoffman and Peter J. Albert [Charlottesville: Published for the United States Capital Historical Society by the University Press of Virginia, 1989], 52–54).

4. Robert Emmett Curran, "'The Finger of God Is Here': The Advent of the Miraculous in the Nineteenth-Century American Catholic Community," *Catholic Historical Review* 73 (1978): 41–61; and Jay P. Dolan's classic work *The American Catholic Experience: A History from Colonial Times to the Present* (New York: Doubleday, 1985).

5. Wills, 7:183.

6. Garrett Power, *Parceling Out Land in Baltimore, 1632–1796* (Baltimore: Maryland Historical Society, 1993), 165.

7. See Carr, "Inheritance in the Colonial Chesapeake." For information on the Welsh migration see Mildred Campbells, "Social Origins of Some Early Americans," in *Seventeenth-Century America: Essays in Colonial History*, ed. James Smith (Chapel Hill: Institute of Early American History and Culture, 1959), and Elizabeth French, *List of Emigrants to America from Liverpool, 1697–1707* (Baltimore: Genealogical Publishing, 1962). See Margaret Kellow, "Indentured Servitude in Eighteenth-Century Maryland," *Histoire Sociale/Social History* 42 (1984): 236–237, for the increase in Irish servant immigration. Beatriz Hardy has suggested that analyzing the influence of the Germans and Scots-Irish Presbyterians on the communities they settled in will tell us more about the possibility of acculturation (personal communication).

8. The importation of convicts began before 1720. See Robert J. Brugger, *Maryland, A Middle Temperament, 1634–1980* (Baltimore: Johns Hopkins University Press in association with the Maryland Historical Society, 1988), 86.

9. Sydney Fisher, *Men, Women, and Manners in Colonial Times*, vol. 2 (1897; reprint, Philadelphia: J. B. Lippincott, 1902), 232–233.

Selected Bibliography

Unpublished documents cited in this book are located at the Maryland Hall of Records in Annapolis, the Manuscripts Division at the Maryland Historical Society in Baltimore, the Special Collections Division of the Georgetown University Library, the Carmelite Monastery Library in Baltimore, the University of Notre Dame's Archives, the Folger Institute Library in Washington, D.C., the Public Record Office in Kew, and the British Library.

Maryland

Bozman, John L. *The History of Maryland*. Baltimore: Lucas and Deaver, 1837.

Brown, George William. *The Origin and Growth of Civil Liberty in Maryland: A Discourse Delivered before the Maryland Historical Society, Baltimore, April 12, 1850*. Baltimore: John Toy, 1850.

Browne, William Hand. *Maryland: The History of a Palatinate*. Boston: Houghton Mifflin, 1899.

Brugger, Robert J. *Maryland, A Middle Temperament, 1634–1980*. Baltimore: Johns Hopkins University Press in association with the Maryland Historical Society, 1988.

Carr, Lois. "The Development of the Maryland Orphan's Court, 1654–1715." In *Law, Society, and Politics in Early Maryland*, ed. Aubrey C. Land, Lois Green Carr, and Edward C. Papenfuse. Baltimore: Johns Hopkins University Press, 1977.

————. "Sources of Political Stability and Upheaval in Seventeenth-Century Maryland." *Maryland Historical Magazine* 79 (1984): 44–69.

Carr, Lois, and David Jordan. *Maryland's Revolution of Government, 1689–1692*. Ithaca, N.Y.: Cornell University Press, 1974.

Carr, Lois, Russell Menard, and Lorena S. Walsh. *Robert Cole's World: Agriculture and Society in Early Maryland*. Chapel Hill: University of North Carolina Press, 1991.

Carr, Lois Green, Philip D. Morgan, and Jean B. Russo, eds. *Colonial Chesapeake Society*. Chapel Hill: Published for the Institute of Early American History and Culture, Williamsburg, Virginia, by the University of North Carolina Press, 1988.

Carr, Lois, and Lorena Walsh. "The Planter's Wife: The Experience of White Women in Seventeenth-Century Maryland." *William and Mary Quarterly*, 3d ser.,

34 (1977): 542–571. Reprinted in *In Search of Early America: The William and Mary Quarterly, 1943–1993* (Richmond: Institute of Early American History, 1993).

Cushing, John D. *The Laws of the Province of Maryland.* Wilmington, Del.: Michael Glazier, 1978.

Davis, George. *The Day-Star of American Freedom; or, The Birth and Early Growth of Toleration, in the Province of Maryland.* New York: Scribner, 1855.

Douglass, John. "Between Pettifoggers and Professionals: Pleaders and Practitioners and the Beginnings of the Legal Profession in Colonial Maryland, 1634–1731." *American Journal of Legal History* 39 (July 1995): 359–384.

Doyle, J. A. *English Colonies in America: Virginia, Maryland, and the Carolinas.* New York: Henry Holt, 1882.

Everstine, Carl. *The General Assembly of Maryland, 1634–1776.* Charlottesville, Va.: Michie, 1980.

———. "Maryland's Toleration Act: An Appraisal." *Maryland Historical Magazine* 79 (1984): 99–115.

Footner, Hulbert. *Maryland Main and the Eastern Shore.* 1942. Reprint, Hatboro, Pa.: Tradition, 1967.

Gambrall, Theodore. *Studies in the Civil, Social, and Ecclesiastical History of Early Maryland.* New York: Thomas Whittaker, 1893.

Hall, Clayton, ed. *Narratives of Early Maryland, 1633–1684.* New York: Charles Scribner's Sons, 1910.

Hammett, Regina C. *History of St. Mary's County, Maryland.* Ridge, Md.: R. Hammett, 1977.

Hoffman, Ronald. "'Marylando-Hibernus': Charles Carroll the Settler, 1660–1720." *William and Mary Quarterly,* 3d ser., 45 (1988): 207–236.

Jordan, David. *Foundations of Representative Government in Maryland, 1632–1715.* Cambridge: Cambridge University Press, 1987.

———. "'Gods Candle' within Government: Quakers and Politics in Early Maryland." *William and Mary Quarterly,* 3d ser., 39 (1982): 628–654.

Kellow, Margaret. "Indentured Servitude in Eighteenth-Century Maryland." *Histoire Sociale/Social History* 17 (1984): 229–255.

Land, Aubrey C. *Colonial Maryland: A History.* Millwood, N.Y.: KTO Press, 1981.

Lippincott, Constance. *Maryland as a Palatinate.* Philadelphia: J. B. Lippincott, 1902.

Main, Gloria. *Tobacco Colony: Life in Early Maryland, 1650–1720.* Princeton, N.J.: Princeton University Press, 1982.

McSherry, James. *History of Maryland: From Its First Settlement in 1634, to the Year 1848.* Baltimore: John Murphy, 1849.

Menard, Russell R. "British Migration to the Chesapeake Colonies in the Seventeenth Century." In *Colonial Chesapeake Society,* ed. Lois Green Carr, Philip D. Morgan, and Jean B. Russo. Chapel Hill: Published for the Institute of Early American History and Culture, Williamsburg, Virginia, by the University of North Carolina Press, 1988.

——. "Population, Economy, and Society in Seventeenth-Century Maryland." *Maryland Historical Magazine* 79 (1984): 71–91.

Meyers, Debra. "The Civic Lives of White Women in Seventeenth-Century Maryland." *Maryland Historical Magazine* 94 (1999): 309–327.

Morris, John G. *The Lords Baltimore.* Baltimore: John Murphy for the Maryland Historical Society, 1874.

Neill, Edward D. *The Founders of Maryland as Portrayed in Manuscripts, Provincial Records, and Early Documents.* Albany: Joel Munsell, 1876.

——. *Maryland in the Beginning: A Brief Submitted to the Historical & Political Science Association of Johns Hopkins University.* Baltimore: Cushings and Bailey, 1884.

Norton, Mary Beth. *Founding Mothers and Fathers: Gendered Power and the Forming of American Society.* New York: Alfred A. Knopf, 1996.

Ramey, Mary. *Chronicles of Mistress Margaret Brent.* Privately published, 1915.

Sioussat, Anna. "Colonial Women of Maryland." *Maryland Historical Magazine* 2 (1907): 214–226.

Tate, Thad W., and David L. Ammerman, eds. *The Chesapeake in the Seventeenth Century: Essays on Anglo-American Society.* New York: W. W. Norton, 1979.

Thomas, James Walter. *Chronicles of Colonial Maryland.* 1900. Reprint, Baltimore: Clearfield, 1999.

Walsh, Lorena S. "'Till Death Us Do Part': Marriage and Family in Seventeenth-Century Maryland." In *The Chesapeake in the Seventeenth Century: Essays on Anglo-American Society,* ed. Thad W. Tate and David L. Ammerman. New York: W. W. Norton, 1979.

Wilstach, Paul. *Tidewater Maryland.* New York: Tudor, 1931.

Yentsch, Anne. *A Chesapeake Family and Their Slaves: A Study in Historical Archaeology.* New York: Cambridge University Press, 1994.

——. "An Interpretive Study of the Use of Land and Space on Lot 83, Annapolis, Md." *New Perspectives on Maryland Historical Archaeology* 26 (1990): 21–53.

Religion

Beitzell, Edwin W. *The Jesuit Missions of St. Mary's County.* Abell, Md.: E. Beitzell, 1959.

Bossy, John. *The English Catholic Community, 1570–1850.* New York: Oxford University Press, 1976.

——. "English Catholics after 1688." In *From Persecution to Toleration: The Glorious Revolution and Religion in England,* ed. Peter Grell, Jonathan Israel, and Nicholas Tyacke. Oxford: Clarendon, 1991.

Bremer, Francis J., ed. *Puritanism: Transatlantic Perspectives on a Seventeenth-Century Anglo-American Faith.* Boston: Massachusetts Historical Society, distributed by Northeastern University Press, 1993.

Carroll, Kenneth. *Quakerism on the Eastern Shore.* Baltimore: Maryland Historical Society, 1970.

————. *Three Hundred Years and More of Third Haven Quakerism*. Baltimore: The Queen Anne Press, 1984.

Collinson, Patrick. *English Puritanism*. London: Historical Association, 1989.

Crawford, Patricia. *Women and Religion in England, 1500–1720*. London: Routledge, 1993.

Cressy, David. *Birth, Marriage, and Death: Ritual, Religion, and the Life-cycle in Tudor and Stuart England*. New York: Oxford University Press, 1997.

Curran, Robert Emmett. *American Jesuit Spirituality: The Maryland Tradition, 1634–1900*. New York: Paulist Press, 1988.

Dallam, Edith Stansbury. *St. James' Parish, Old Herring Creeke Parish: A History, 1663–1799, Including Copies of the Original Records of the Parish Vestry Minutes and Register of Births, Baptisms, Marriages, and Burials*. Maryland: Vestry and Library Committee, 1976.

Davies, Julian. *Caroline Captivity of the Church: Charles I and the Remoulding of Anglicanism, 1625–1641*. Oxford: Oxford University Press, 1992.

Fogarty, Gerald. "The Origins of the Mission, 1634–1773." In *The Maryland Jesuits, 1634–1833*, ed. R. E. Curran, J. T. Durkin, and G. P. Fogarty. Baltimore: Corporation of the Roman Catholic Clergymen, 1976.

Gambrall, Theodore C. *Studies in the Civil, Social, and Ecclesiastical History of Early Maryland: Lectures Delivered to the Young Men of the Agricultural College of Maryland*. New York: Thomas Whittaker, 1893.

Gleissner, Richard. "Religious Causes of the Glorious Revolution in Maryland." *Maryland Historical Magazine* 64 (1969): 327–341.

Graham, Michael. "The Collapse of Equality: Catholic and Quaker Dissenters in Maryland, 1692–1720." *Maryland Historical Magazine* 88 (1993): 5–25.

————. "Meetinghouse and Chapel: Religion and Community in Seventeenth-Century Maryland." In *Colonial Chesapeake Society*, ed. Lois Green Carr, Philip D. Morgan, and Jean B. Russo. Chapel Hill: Published for the Institute of Early American History and Culture, Williamsburg, Virginia, by the University of North Carolina Press, 1988.

Hanley, Thomas O'Brien. *Their Rights and Liberties: The Beginnings of Religious and Political Freedom in Maryland*. Chicago: Loyola University Press, 1984.

Hartdagen, Gerald. "The Vestries and Morals in Colonial Maryland." *Maryland Historical Magazine* 63 (1968): 360–378.

Hill, Bridget. "A Refuge from Men: The Idea of a Protestant Nunnery." *Past and Present* 117 (1987): 107–130.

Kelly, J. Reaney. *Quakers in the Founding of Anne Arundel County, Maryland*. Baltimore: Maryland Historical Society, 1963.

Krugler, John. " 'With promise of Liberty in Religion': The Catholic Lords Baltimore and Toleration in Seventeenth-Century Maryland, 1634–1692." *Maryland Historical Magazine* 79 (1984): 21–43.

Krugler, John D., and Timothy B. Riordan. " 'Scandalous and Offensive to the Government': The 'Popish Chappel' at St. Mary's City, Maryland, and the Society of Jesus, 1634 to 1705." *Mid-America* 73 (1991): 187–208.

Lahey, R. J. "The Role of Religion in Lord Baltimore's Colonial Enterprise." *Maryland Historical Magazine* 72 (1977): 492–511.

Lake, Peter. *Anglicans and Puritans? Presbyterianism and English Conformist Thought from Whitgift to Hooker.* London: Unwin Hyman, 1988.

Lurie, Maxine. "Theory and Practice of Religious Toleration in the Seventeenth Century: The Proprietary Colonies as a Case Study." *Maryland Historical Magazine* 79 (1984): 117–125.

McNamara, Robert F. "John Carroll and Interfaith Marriages: The Case of the Belle Vue Carrolls." In *Studies in Catholic History in Honor of John Tracy Ellis,* ed. Nelson Minnich, Robert Eno, and Robert Trisco. Wilmington, Del.: Michael Glazier, 1985.

Meyers, Debra. "Gender and Religion in England's Catholic Province." In *Women and Religion in Old and New Worlds,* ed. Susan Dinan and Debra Meyers. New York: Routledge, 2001.

Morgan, Edmund S. *Visible Saints: The History of a Puritan Idea.* 1963. Reprint, Ithaca, N.Y.: Cornell University Press, 1994.

Randall, Daniel. "A Puritan Colony in Maryland." In *Johns Hopkins University Studies,* vol. 4, ed. Herbert Adams. Baltimore: N. Murray, 1886.

Smith, David L. "Catholic, Anglican, or Puritan? Edward Sackville, Fourth Earl of Dorset, and the Ambiguities of Religion in Early Stuart England." *Transactions of the Royal Historical Society* 2 (1992): 105–124.

Sommerville, C. John. "Anglican, Puritan, and Sectarian in Empirical Perspective." *Social Science History* 13 (1989): 109–135.

Torrence, Clayton. *Old Somerset on the Eastern Shore of Maryland: A Study in Foundations and Founders.* 1935. Reprint, Baltimore: Clearfield, 1993.

Treacy, William P. *Old Catholic Maryland and Its Early Jesuit Missionaries.* Swedesboro, N.J.: St. Joseph's Rectory, 1889.

Tyacke, Nicholas. *Anti-Calvinists: The Rise of English Arminianism, c. 1590–1640.* Oxford: Clarendon, 1987.

Inheritance Practices

Alston, Lee J., and Morton Owen Schapiro. "Inheritance Laws across Colonies: Causes and Consequences." *Journal of Economic History* 44 (1984): 277–287.

Bonfield, Lloyd. *Marriage Settlements, 1601–1740: The Adoption of the Strict Settlement.* Cambridge: Cambridge University Press, 1983.

Churches, Christine. "Women and Property in Early Modern England: A Case Study." *Social History* 23 (1998): 165–180.

Erickson, Amy Louise. *Women and Property in Early Modern England.* London: Routledge, 1997.

Goody, Jack. "Inheritance, Property, and Women: Some Comparative Considerations." In *Family and Inheritance: Rural Society in Western Europe, 1200–1800,* ed. Jack Goody, Joan Thirsk, and E. P. Thompson. Cambridge: Cambridge University Press, 1976.

Grigg, Susan. "Women and Family Property: A Review of U.S. Inheritance Studies." *Historical Methods* 22 (1989): 116–122.

Haskins, George L. "The Beginnings of Partible Inheritance in the American Colonies." *Yale Law Journal* 51 (1941–42): 1280–1315.

Keim, C. Ray. "Primogeniture and Entail in Colonial Virginia." *William and Mary Quarterly*, 3d ser., 25 (1968): 545–586.

Lee, Jean Butenhoff. "Land and Labor: Parental Bequest Practices in Charles County, Maryland, 1732–1783." In *Colonial Chesapeake Society*, ed. Lois Green Carr, Philip D. Morgan, and Jean B. Russo. Chapel Hill: Published for the Institute of Early American History and Culture, Williamsburg, Virginia, by the University of North Carolina Press, 1988.

Narrett, David. *Inheritance and Family Life in Colonial New York City.* Ithaca, N.Y.: Cornell University Press, 1992.

Rogers, Kim Lacy. "Relicts of the New World: Conditions of Widowhood in Seventeenth-Century New England." In *Woman's Being, Woman's Place: Female Identity and Vocation in American History*, ed. Mary Kelley. Boston: G. K. Hall, 1979.

Salmon, Marylynn. "The Legal Status of Women in Early America: A Reappraisal." *Law and History Review* 1 (1983): 128–151.

———. *Women and the Law of Property in Early America.* Chapel Hill: University of North Carolina Press, 1986.

Shammas, Carole. "Early American Women and Control over Capital." In *Women in the Age of the American Revolution: Perspectives on the American Revolution*, ed. Ronald Hoffman and Peter J. Albert. Charlottesville: Published for the United States Capital Historical Society by the University of Virginia Press, 1989.

———. "English Inheritance Law and Its Transfer to the Colonies." *American Journal of Legal History* 31 (1987): 145–163.

Shammas, Carole, Marylynn Salmon, and Michel Dahlin. *Inheritance in America from Colonial Times to the Present.* New Brunswick, N.J.: Rutgers University Press, 1987.

Smith, R. M. "Women's Property Rights under Customary Law: Some Developments in the Thirteenth and Fourteenth Centuries." *Transactions of the Royal Historical Society*, 5th ser., 36 (1986): 165–194.

Speth, Linda E. "More Than Her 'Thirds': Wives and Widows in Colonial Virginia." *Women and History* 4 (1982): 5–41.

Waters, John J. "Family, Inheritance, and Migration in Colonial New England: The Evidence from Guilford, Connecticut." *William and Mary Quarterly*, 3d ser., 39 (1982): 64–86.

———. "Patrimony, Succession, and Social Stability." *Perspectives on American History* 10 (1976): 131–160.

Source Names Index

Croese, Gerard, 100, 123
Crosse, William, 142
Crouch, Ralph, 160
Curtis, Jane, 174
Curtis, Langley, 174

Darby, Elizabeth, 64
Darcy family, 114
Darnall, Ann, 51
Darnall, John, 31–32
Darnell, Elizabeth, 161
Darnell, Henry, 50–51
Darnell, John, 168
Darrington, Theophilus, 34
Dashiell, George, 169
Dashiell, Isabel, 169
Dashiell, James, 169
Dashiell, Robert, 169
Dashiell, Thomas, 169
Davis, Deborah, 106–107
Dawbeney, Robert, 150
Dayefeild, Thomas, 83, 88
Delany, Thomas, 32
Dent, John, 34
Dent, Rebecca, 134
Dent, Thomas, 134
Dent, William, 51, 68
Devall, Marreen, 162
Dickinson, Clare Joseph, 114
Digby, Katherine, 49, 116–17
Digby, Sir Kenelm, 26
Digges, Mary, 189n15
Digges, William, 6, 43, 189n15
Diggs, Elizabeth, 111
Diniard, Thomas, 68
Dormer, Anne, 58
Doyne, Jane, Jr., 64
Doyne, Joshua, 64
Dulany, Daniel, 192n21
Dundasse, George, 31
Dunn, Susanna, 67
Duphex, Rebecca, 226n40
Durand, William, 28
Duvall, Mareen, 47

Eareckson, Elizabeth, 147
Edlow, Joseph, 44
Edmondson, John, 81
Edwards, Hannah, 35
Egerton, Charles, 137
Ellet, John, 88–89

Emerson, Thomas, 150
Ennalls, Bartholomew, 97
Erbery, Edward, 19
Evans, John, 135
Evelin, George, 22
Everendon, Thomas, 58

Fendel (governor). *See* Fendel, Josias
Fendel, Josias, 28, 29
Fenwick, Cuthbert, 135
Fenwick, Jane, 135, 160
Fermor, Henry, 150
Finch, Francis, 141
Fisher (Father). *See* Fisher, Philip
Fisher, Philip, 24, 193n33
Fletcher, Anne, 160
Fossee, John, 63
Foster, Seth, 176
Fowke, Anne, 51
Fowke, Elizabeth, 51
Fowke, Gerard, 51
Fowke, Mary, 51
Fowler, Constance, 204n128
Fowler, Rebecca, 35
Franklin, Robert, Jr., 63
Fraser, John, 133–34
Freasorer, L., 176
Fuller, Thomas, 122
Fuller, William, 28

Gage, George, 209n72
Galloway, Ann, 124–25
Galloway family, 114
Gardiner, Elizabeth, 136
Gardiner, Richard, 135–36
Garey, John, 139
Garrett, Nathaniell, 169
Garrett, Thomas, 165
Gary, Alice, 158
Gary, Elizabeth, 48
Gary, John, 158
Gerard, Thomas, 6, 27
Gerrard (captain), 28–29
Gerrard, Susannah, 107
Gerrard, Thomas, 22
Gibbon, Edmond, 204n132
Gibson, Thomas, 92
Gilbert, Rose, 165
Gill, Ann, 103, 111, 167–68
Goddard, Sarah, 64
Goodhand, Christopher, 149

General Index

DEBRA MEYERS is Assistant Professor of History at Northern Kentucky University and co-editor of *Women and Religion in Old and New Worlds*.